INTERNATIONAL

INTERIOR DESIGN

INTERNATIONAL
INTERIOR DESIGN

LUCY BULLIVANT

Coordinating Researcher
JENNIFER HUDSON

Abbeville Press · Publishers

New York · London · Paris

Library of Congress Catalog Card Number
91–16794

ISBN 1–55859–235–0

This book was produced by John Calmann
and King Ltd, London.

Designed by Cara Gallardo
and Richard Smith, Area, London.
Printed and bound in Singapore.

First edition

Acknowledgements. The author and the
publishers would like to thank Mayumi Hosokawa
and Annett Francis for their invaluable assistance
with the research of Japanese and American
projects; all the designers and architects involved
for their enthusiastic cooperation; and the
photographers whose work is reproduced. The
following photographic credits are given, with page
numbers in brackets: Farshid Assassi (144 right;
170–1; 174–7); Ashley Barber: photos by courtesy
of *Interior Architecture Magazine* (102–5); Gabriele
Basilico (150–1); Luc Boegly/ARCHIPRESS (64–5);
Nicolas Borel (200; 201 bottom left); Richard Bryant/
ARCAID (14; 144 left, middle; 166–7; 196; 198–9;
218–21); Lluís Casals (192–3); Robert César/
ARCHIPRESS (111; 180–1); Martin Charles (41; 66
left; 88–91); Jeremy Cockayne/ARCAID (55–6); Peter
Cook (8 left and right; 16–17; 22–5; 40; 43; 54; 57;
63 left; 98–9; 108–110; 146; 148–9; 154–161;
163; 178–9; 208; 209, all except top left; 240–1);
Stéphane Couturier/ARCHIPRESS (26–7; 140–3;
164–5; 236–9); Grey Crawford (97); Richard Davies
(60; 62; 63 right); Thomas Delbeck/Ambiente (212;
214 bottom; 215); Mitsumasa Fujitsuka (168);
Hiroshi Fujiwara (107–7); Katsuaki Furudate (234);
Dennis Gilbert (8 middle; 36–7; 76–7; 79); John
Gollings (44–5); Alain Goustard/ARCHIPRESS (186
right; 202 right; 201 top and bottom right); Paul
Hester (58–9); Timothy Hursley (48; 50–1; 242–5);
Yasuhiro Ishibashi (224–7); Christian Kandzia/
Behnisch & Partners (213; 214 top); Toshiharu
Kitajima (38 top); Wilmar Koenig (188; 190–1); Ian
Lambot/ARCAID (80–1); © Richard Mandelkorn
(172–3); Mitsuo Matsuoka/*The Japan Architect*
(210–11; 222–3); © Peter Mauss/ESTO (204);
Brigitte Meuwissen (46–7); Fujitsuka Mitsumasa
(186 left; 232–3; 235); Jean-Marie Monthiers (202
left; 205); Grant Mudford (72–3); Nacasa & Partners
Inc. (120; 66 right; 82; 84–7; 92; 94–5; 120; 122;
124–5); Taisuke Ogawa/*The Japan Architect* (38
bottom; 39); Takayuki Osumi (118); Richard Payne
(209 top left); Julie Phipps (28–31; 78); Ronald
Pollard (66 middle; 96); Stephen Robson (52–3);
Jordi Sarra (128; 130–1; 136–9); Wolfgang
Schwager (132; 134; 135 top, bottom right); Peter
Seidel (228; 231); Yoshio Shiratori /ZOOM (title
page; 32; 32–5; 100–1; 112–3); Tim Street-Porter
(194–5); Hisao Suzuki (74–5); Y. Takase (185;
182–5); Edward Valentine-Hames (68; 70–1);
Rafael Vargas (121; 123); Deidi von Schaewen (133;
135 bottom left); © Paul Warchol (10–13; 114–7;
206); Alan Williams (152–3); Miro Zagnoli (126);
Gerald Zugmann (18–21).

Contents

Introduction

This is an anthology of public interior design projects completed during the last two years. The selection has a strong international bias, without claiming to be comprehensively global in breadth. For ease of reference, the projects have been divided into four convenient categories of case study: workspaces; restaurants, bars, hotels and clubs; retail spaces; and cultural buildings.

The 76 projects chosen cannot be said to embrace an orthodoxy of style, but in the methods used by many of the architects and designers featured there is a common theme: their work embodies a broad vision of the relationship between aesthetics and function. Shallow decorative gestures and narrow functionalism have tended to give way to a maturer understanding of the importance of context, the flexibility of form, and the role of metaphor, light, colour — 'soft' design features — within modern interiors. Intelligent designers consider context in its various manifestations — the site, the brief, usage, and historical, socio-economic and geographical conditions — for inherent possibilities to be exploited as well as problems to be confronted. They employ a rich language of aesthetics to express function and impart meaning to interior spaces.

Design can be a potent communication tool, and will inevitably continue to be used as a cosmetic product applied to create a flattering image for the client. However, the effects of recession in some areas of the world have forced many to abandon such superficial, short-term strategies. The projects chosen demonstrate that there can be a greater richness in interior design solutions, a more direct response to context. Adopting a holistic approach involves using a wider range of conceptual skills. In the wake of a growing fascination with the connections between art, architecture and design, there are signs of a considered expansion and refinement of the role aesthetics can play in the creation of all kinds of public interiors.

Interior design is free of many of architecture's restrictions (and, unfortunately, all too frequently some of its aspirations); it nonetheless has the potential to wrap together aesthetics and function in a more profoundly interactive resolution. Its very nature as a discipline means that the finishes can be smoother, the tolerances higher; the language of its forms is more sophisticated. As environmental design it should support our physical and mental well-being: its very intimacy influences our behaviour, for better or worse. Sadly, many new interiors fail to meet even basic requirements of comfort or practicality, providing solutions afflicted by a severe poverty of resources. A short-term mentality and inability to gauge the benefits of a more rewarding investment dictate a project's built-in obsolescence, and perpetuate interior design's identity as a marketing toy.

As a necessary corrective to this pervasive use of interior design as image-building alone — a creature without a backbone — this volume brings together projects which demonstrate a lively response to history, to the site, to the needs and desires of users, to technological change. Interior design can negotiate the flux and the noise of contemporary life, not by mute acceptance of the present, but by its ability to research and offer up new ways of ordering our existence. The designers featured here fuse disciplines and use the tactics of art, but are focused in their method of approach. They demonstrate what can be achieved with a wide variety of budgets; ultimately, cost is not the determining factor in ensuring quality of result.

The commissions involved are eclectic, and often multi-layered. Cross-cultural collaborations such as Hotel Il Palazzo or Barna Crossing test and stretch designers' skills and assumptions about context. Other projects can extend the language of form by using local materials in an innovative fashion (for instance, the use of clay pipes and galvanized sheet steel at Paramount Laundry). Conversions or insertions in the inner city (Imagination's headquarters) are often also site-sensitive (Studios at Camden Town, Polideportivo de Gracia, or Spaarkrediet Bank). Redundant buildings — particularly those built to serve a specific industrial function, such as the water tower now housing the Wasserturm Hotel, or the turbine hall of the power station converted into the Metropolis recording studios — offer sites rich for transformation without the need to resort to lame revivalism.

We live in a post-industrial age with few moral or aesthetic imperatives. One dilemma the designer faces is that it is almost impossible to make projections of the future, such is the speed of modern communications. Today, it is more important for those commissioned to design interior spaces for public use to have a dynamic sense of the present, providing a detached commentary.

Speculative projects provide opportunities to develop a programme that goes beyond the constraints of commercial reality, advancing valuable research. There are clients and patrons — exceptionally the state, but more often the property developer, the industrialist or the retailer — who seek an unusual and resonant architectural solution to an aim, like the private art collector who decided to build a museum on the site of his former home (the Gotoh Museum). It is their financial speculation, and willingness to see more than a short-term trade-off, that enables innovative projects to be realised. Their ability to take risks is also generally tempered with a keen sense of asset-building, but the return in commercial terms is often a far less than rock-solid proposition at the outset. Competitions are standard practice for many large-scale projects, but even with small-scale complexes such as Metropolis, the process of appraisal can help clarify the issues, and give architects and designers the opportunity to size up a wider range of commissions.

The restraints of the brief, and of the prevailing financial, political and geographical conditions, are all factors that impinge on the final form of an interior design project. Over a longer period, changing patterns of use drastically affect what might appear to be clear-cut building types. For instance, in the 1980s, the museum's cultural role took on a particularly commercial twist to boost attendances. The addition of retail, catering and media facilities to exhibition spaces threatened to crowd out the museum's more enduring assets. The museums selected here show that one challenge now is to reconcile a museum's raison d'être — to show selected artefacts of civilization in an illuminating way — with modern communication techniques, without the latter overpowering the former. Cultural buildings have been used to affirm the status of a society since pre-history, so France's programme of *grands projets* is not a new phenomenon; but its diversity, encompassing regional developments, has offered designers many challenges. Quick-footed developers also recognise that buildings embodying cultural values can function as catalysts, luring the affluent, and signalling the imminent contraction of down-at-heel urban spaces.

In the retail sector, the selling 'cycle' has in some countries turned to less glamorous forms of marketing as a response to recession. Here, the improvement of the more fundamental elements of a company's activities — its merchandise, circulation and service — has kept the momentum going, and brought consideration of customers' needs to the forefront. The focus of creative innovation in general lies in smaller-scale boutiques offering highly specialized and finely wrought goods to 'niche' markets of customers demanding quality, not quantity.

The rapid growth of the service and leisure industries has created a plethora of possibilities — ostensibly within the reach of a wider community. At the same time, global communications have led the more affluent among us to demand a variety of stimulating environments, but also to expect a secure sense of place. Global travellers want to enjoy the superficial thrill of cultural differentiation between cities, regions and countries; they expect public spaces to possess varying and charged atmospheres, a mix of new and old. New responses to such demands represented in this volume include sensory adventure playgrounds activated by computer-generated optic fibre lighting, as well as soothing enclaves of almost monastic calm created by the interpenetration of sculptural volumes and diffused natural light. We are simultaneously highly demanding and easily satiated by the forms of public interior space: building types, although slow to change dramatically, are now evolving in response to expressed needs — for comfort, flexibility, security, stimulation, differentiation. There are now signs that architectural theory is catching up, and getting to grips with human inconsistency and irrationality. Such a process of re-evaluation should in the long run entail a greater flexibility in the more overtly commercial sectors of interior design.

Architects and designers now need to design buildings which are both flexible and responsive inside and out because of the constantly changing nature of the institutions which occupy them, and evolving patterns of use. Workspaces in particular must allow the user a greater control over his or her life — if only to open the window or avoid the noxious excesses of air-conditioning. The notion of flexible design also implies the ability to cope with the ephemerality of interior spaces: to respond to demographic changes, or new patterns of work. A flexible approach can address the challenge of projects which age gracefully, providing enduring qualities which defy the relentless progression of fashion. The adaptability of a kit of parts, such as Morphosis has created for Leon Max, or the individualized nature of the customized fittings found in Belfort's town hall chambers, the Hotel Otaru Marittimo and the Grand Louvre, provide a refreshing contrast to the static friction between materials and form experienced in many interiors.

New technology can provide the necessary lightness that adds adaptability and aids efficiency without impeding movement or enforcing an aesthetically impoverished identity. Imagination's courtyard bridges, Tepia's walls, the mobile ceiling at Isometrix, Joseph's creatively engineered staircase and, on a smaller scale, the compact network of power 'totems' within Foster Associates' Riverside offices — all these help to equip their environments with modern work tools and resources without lessening other spatial options. Technology can 'tune' an environment: acoustics can be applied as a flexible science, and adapted to dovetail with aesthetic requirements in order to provide rich compositions of form and layout (as at Metropolis, Cité de la Musique or, in a large-scale, public context, the Morton H. Meyerson Symphony Center). Once certain environmental requirements are fulfilled, the quality of sound is as much a subjective area as aesthetics, and can be adapted to precise needs.

In looking at how aesthetics and function might be more profoundly interwoven in interior design, the nature of the language used is crucial. Expressive design often uses 'soft' elements for psychological impact. The impact of light, water and other sensory effects is now being rediscovered, and fused with new technology. These can be computer-generated (Torres de Avila, Maelstrom/Ac on ca gua, or Bar Zsa Zsa) or based on age-old techniques (the nymphaeum at Arizona University's Fine Arts Center). Natural light can be manipulated by subtle diffusion (Riverside, Vitra Museum and many others) or dramatic control (California Museum of Photography). Ambient light can be restricted to glowing, incandescent surfaces (Wasserturm Hotel, or Epsylon); its fittings can be given a miniaturized versatility, using low-voltage halogen fittings, often no bigger than ears of wheat (Angeli Mare, Jasper Conran). Webs of optic fibre skeins are atmospheric devices providing sensory diversions (Hotel Otaru Marittimo, Torres de Avila). Colour, applied in undiluted form, or juxtaposed with contrasting materials (as at Dry Bar, Factory Communications, or Vivid Productions) establishes an immediate character, but its handling must be deft so that the results are not overloaded and draining.

Some interiors — especially hotels — have protective overtones, expressed in terms of the fortress, prison, subterranean cave, or womb-like

retreat (Wasserturm, D-Hotel, La Villa, Hotel-Restaurant Saint James). Others — nightclubs in particular — are souped-up containers of visual and aural tricks (Epsylon, Torres de Avila, Barna Crossing). Sensuous materials such as velvet, suede or leather applied in a range of contexts provide 'touchy-feely' surfaces which respond to basic psychological needs — to relax, to be oneself, even to try another persona. Designers now seem to want to bring the tactile nature of form to our attention. Perhaps a greater intimacy with external artefacts and forms can be attained, or at least suggested, and one day the standard of comfort, expressiveness and pliability we expect from clothing will be applied to our interior environments.

With entire building commissions, the external appearance of a project is often designed to convey enigmatic power, turning the façade into a decoy which belies the nature of its interior, perhaps only discovered by degree (Teatriz, Arizona University's Fine Arts Center). Provocative forms, tantamount to sculpture (such as the rusty metal grids of Hotel-Restaurant Saint James) can also announce or introduce the character of an interior presence (La Flamme d'Or, the Grand Louvre, Morton H. Meyerson Symphony Center). Those given a brief for an interior alone often ignore the monolithic exterior of its container (as with Angeli Mare), and create a softer, more responsive contrast (at Belfort's town hall, this was part of the brief).

The impact of crafted forms within an interior embellishes its architectonic nature. Individually made or small batch produced lighting, furniture, textiles and accessories set up a dialogue, evoke a range of origins, and offer a customized, multi-layered statement which can work in a number of ways, depending upon how brash or intimate a result is required. The skills applied to architectural materials (used for wall and floor surfaces, such as at the Architects and Designers Building, Angeli Mare or Ecru) make references to methods of construction, past and present. The input of commissioned artists, creative engineers, and their methods of treating materials, give an interior a contemporaneous edge not possible on a larger scale. It has to be remembered that such forms of imaginative application cannot be defined in terms of a set of rules (who needs another orthodoxy?), but as an entire approach to the creation of an environment.

There is a discernible move in many areas of innovative design practice towards greater austerity in the use of materials. This is clearly a matter of expediency, particularly in developed countries suffering from recession, and undoubtedly a more responsible use of the world's resources. But it is also an aesthetic choice, representing a gradual sloughing off of the rich veneer and ostentatious ornamentalism of the 1980s. Viewed cynically, under-designed effects using *arte povera* can, after a surfeit of post-modernism, undoubtedly 'cleanse' a client's image. However, the fundamental qualities — and possibilities — of wood, stone, metal and glass are being rediscovered on a wide scale, and often juxtaposed or recycled with newer materials, not for a pristine aura of novelty, but to give greater authenticity to an interior. This is not a new movement by purist kill-joys. Designers may be side-stepping overloaded materials or decorative effects, but many are also moving towards a knowing design with a healthy sense of irony, which knows it is not there purely to support our foibles. As Teatriz demonstrates, drama is not necessarily the same thing as banal opulence. An interior can convey playful accessibility as well as

exclusivity (La Flamme d'Or's beer hall is one example).

Many of the projects featured here actively extend the scope of interior design by blurring the margins which separate it from architecture, or art, but without changing its entire identity as a design discipline, and losing its particular strengths in the process. A hybrid language can be articulated which draws on literary, theatrical, musical, archaeological and biomorphic references in order to focus a specific method of working. The relative degree of freedom to dictate method, form and language also offers the opportunity to play various roles, to apply visual and spatial trickery of one sort or another — extended metaphor, *trompe l'oeil*, or an abstractly defined compositional language. An interior environment can evoke other, more historically rooted architectural types — a palazzo, a church, a theatre, a meeting place — redefining the identity of a tired context by reference to earlier forms. All such tactics rely on the abilities of the designer to carry them out imaginatively.

There are pockets of activity around the world where the energies and skills of designers being invested in commercial public interiors are also being energetically channelled into projects which serve the basic needs of a whole community: state housing, schools, hospitals, public transport facilities. However, the reining-in of public spending in response to financial difficulties has meant that in many countries modern architecture and interior design play a restricted role. Many of the designers featured are actively involved in these areas. Sensitively planned, thoughtful interiors intended for the local community, such as the Polideportivo de Gracia in Barcelona, or the Shonandai Cultural Center in Japan, offer expressive qualities of design more commonly found in privately funded projects for smaller audiences. Within the private sector, clever industrial conversions such as the Paramount Laundry, Wasserturm Hotel and Metropolis studios, or workspaces such as the Imagination headquarters, Factory Communications, or Gallimard Jeunesse, demonstrate what can be done to transform old urban fabric, reinventing its interior spaces to provide flexible solutions without the need for the wholesale demolition of structures. Such projects could be carried out on a wider scale through the patronage of the state, of developers and corporate bodies, if only civic pride could be meshed with a greater sense of social responsibility and imagination.

Innovation is an age-old cultural problem that is constantly with us. To apply its benefits to our interior environments in a way that has a chance of enduring involves an enrichment of the impoverished agenda set by so much of the design world in recent years. The projects which follow show that interior design has the potential to become a broader discipline, encompassing a wide range of complementary skills, but also healthy measures of idealism, independence of mind, and a more responsive sensibility.

Paramount Laundry
(see pages 22–25).

Vivid Productions
(see pages 36–37).

Isometrix
(see pages 16–17).

1
Workspaces, Offices & Studios

An exquisite blend of tones and forms: across an expanse of concrete, inlaid with stainless steel lines which add movement, is a wall-relief custom-made by the architect in burnished stainless steel and bronze, cold rolled steel, with various patinated metal finishes.

1.1

Architects & Designers Building Lobby

P. MICHAEL MARINO ARCHITECTS
New York, USA

Traditionally, lobbies to commercial buildings in New York — such as the Rockefeller Center and the Chrysler and Fuller Buildings, all designed earlier this century — asserted an elegant richness of surface and crafted ornamental detail, sadly lacking in many of today's public workspaces. These decorative elements expressed a positive corporate image of the diverse commercial activities being carried out within, and undoubtedly raised the morale of both employees and visitors.

Marino and his project team aimed to bring a similar spirit of liveliness and warmth to their conversion of the lobby of the hitherto dull, haphazard and careworn Architects & Designers Building, so named because of its wealth of showrooms 'catering to the trade'. A multi-storey block dating from the 1960s with two entrances on separate streets that visitors found difficult to distinguish from adjoining storefronts, its internal route was to be revived as a bright and animated

pedestrian street. This would still incorporate the retail spaces compulsory in New York's commercial buildings, but place them within a rationalized context, with clear signage. They could then be located more easily, but were to be scaled down, and set in proportion with the other functions of the lobby.

Marino's task was to renovate the extended lobby and the façades at both entrances, on 150 East 58th Street and 964 Third Avenue. Each area of the lobby presented a number of design challenges: the vestibules on both sides; lifts; tenant display areas; public corridors; security desks; signage, including the building directories, and a newsstand. Very few alterations to the linear plan configuration were possible because of the existing retail, tenant and showroom spaces on the ground floor, although ceiling heights could be modified.

Marino hoped to give a narrative or scenographic quality to the visitor's passage from the street to the interior. To do this he has applied a range of materials and finishes to walls, floors and coloured wall-reliefs which owe their layering of burnished and patinated metal to Cubist works. None of the materials employed

A glimpse at the time gives a view of another, spatial, orientation device in the form of a sign set into an illuminated decorative glass screen.

was precious or rare, in order to keep within a strict budget laid down by the otherwise relatively open-minded owners of the building. Because of the small scale of the spaces it was vital at key points to integrate these decorative elements with the structural forms to give a sense of purpose to what are essentially public areas. Marino maintains a policy of involving artists and craftsmen in his projects, to inject the additional interactive qualities that visual and decorative arts can bring to architecture. For this project, a colour consultant, Donald Kaufmann, worked with the various manufacturers of stucco, cement and other materials, experimenting with various pigments to find perfectly modulated tones.

Close to the stunning metal wall-reliefs are rows of horizontal, stainless steel bands, placed at handrail height. Above are back-lit transparency display cases set between flat metal columns, providing a consistent context for the building's tenants to present their work. Telephone kiosks of sandblasted glass and steel extend from the wall with the jauntiness of sailboards. A rhythmic structure of elements recurs throughout the space, overlaid on walls and set in the stone floor grid, ceiling vaults and soffits. A combination of custom-designed and manufactured lighting fixtures accentuates contrasting areas, providing a lively change of scenery.

Most of the existing floor surface had to be retained, and fortunately the designers rather liked the brown and buff 'crab orchard' sandstone floor. To enhance the overall sense of rhythm and proportion, they inserted green-tinged rough-hewn slate in certain places, as well as pilaster figures and areas of poured concrete with a stainless steel inlay.

The creation of a vibrant and interesting walkway that people are happy to use within a formerly 'atrocious' space fulfils only part of the brief. A key element of the architectural renovation has been to improve the physical comfort of the building's users and the overall efficiency of the space. A reconfigured air-conditioning system, new porch and insulated glazing all contribute to greater energy efficiency. New and improved signage, doors and hardware mean increased ease of operation and access.

Close-up of the glass screen. Sandblasted glass is mixed with burnished bronze, oxidized copper and burnished stainless steel, to create a versatile, multi-functional element which is also decorative, an ambient light source and a directional sign.

Asymmetrical elements in semi-relief on the wall surface: the curved reception desk is in stainless steel, positioned in front of an elegant series of metal-framed directories designed as 'a graphic text within a larger wall canvas', made of warm cherry wood panelling with a subtle grid pattern.

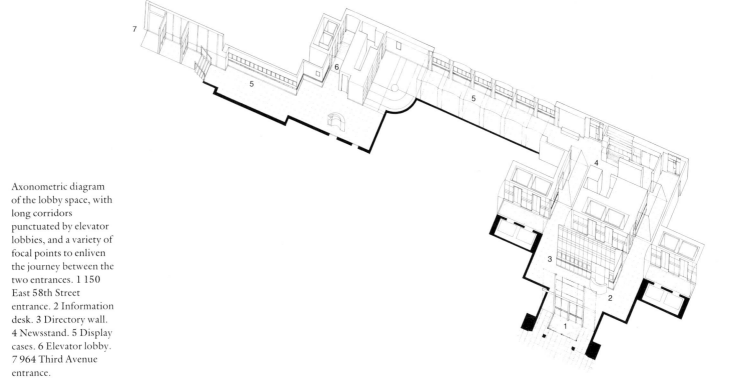

Axonometric diagram of the lobby space, with long corridors punctuated by elevator lobbies, and a variety of focal points to enliven the journey between the two entrances. 1 150 East 58th Street entrance. 2 Information desk. 3 Directory wall. 4 Newsstand. 5 Display cases. 6 Elevator lobby. 7 964 Third Avenue entrance.

Site plan. 1 Main entrance. 2 Spiral staircase. 3 Entrance staircase to offices. 4 Café/bar. 5 Reception desk. 6 Computer terminals. 7 Worktables. 8 Stairs to mezzanine floor. 9 Model-making workshop. 10 Computer rooms. 11 Kitchen. 12 Washrooms. 13 Library shelving.

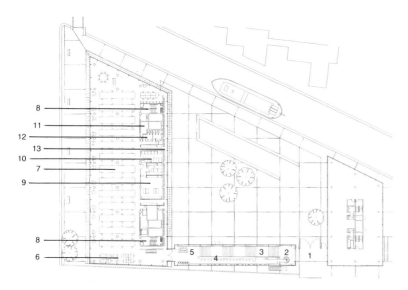

The main entrance
stairs to the new offices
and studio, overlooked
by a narrow staff café
bar area. Finished in
Kuru granite with a
non-slip surface, the
stairs were divided into
four small flights with a
shallow gradient.

1.2
Riverside

FOSTER ASSOCIATES
London, UK

Foster Associates' design for their new offices by the River Thames at Battersea involved a thorough analysis and reorganisation of the various office systems used by the staff. It also required a rethinking of the life style the practice had adopted in their former Great Portland Street premises. By the late 1980s a growing number of international commissions meant that they were fast outgrowing the open-plan, but cramped, spaces in central London; lack of privacy was a continual complaint by the staff. The new headquarters provided the opportunity to recreate and rationalize the practice's workspaces, with expanded floor areas and handsome vistas of the north bank of the river.

Riverside is a simple, elegant building at Chelsea Reach, a low-key site between Battersea Bridge and Albert Bridge, and is set back from the river behind a public walkway. Developed on a commercial basis, it incorporates five floors of apartments above the offices, topped by Sir Norman Foster's penthouse and studio, all designed by the practice.

The offices are reached from Hester Road, the main access road set away from the river. A long glazed entrance lobby leads up to a reception area via a wide staircase of shallow gradient, made in Kuru granite. This is divided into four small flights with 3.6 metre landings, flanked by high white walls, providing an extended and airy point of entry. Towards the reception, a melamine bar-top runs

the remaining length of the staircase on the left-hand side, providing a café area with stainless steel stools.

A glass-topped Tecno desk is positioned in the reception area, facing a small display area, with Eames furniture for guests. A raised access floor of calcium silicate tiles and steel-framed wire-glass doors leads to the main working area, a double-height studio with white columns around the perimeter, which runs the length of the room. The studio's height and the generous expanse of river-facing windows present a scene of striking spaciousness, into which natural light floods.

After experimenting with new designs for semi-screened work desks, the practice decided that it was best to retain the open-plan solution, but this time on a much more generous scale and with much improved lighting. Although everything is now on a larger scale, the project teams maintain a sense of community around each of the thirteen work tables, 11 × 2 metres in size, which are ranged in rows along the studio. Made to a Foster Associates design, they sit on sturdy, four-legged metal frames. On the long sides are aluminium cylinders for storing drawings. Acid-etched glass desk-dividers house files and work materials, and under each table are wide storage units. On each table are two Ackermann 'totem pole' power points designed by Foster, into which all electrical equipment plugs neatly, an essential coordinating element in increasingly computerized offices.

The work-tables are set back from the glass wall facing the river, allowing space for a row of circular tables, with Eames wire chairs for more informal meetings, interspersed with display cases of models. Much of the furniture has been designed by the practice — some for previous projects — or custom-designed for very specific functions; the rest has been obtained from Vitra International.

Above the mezzanine are meeting rooms, an audio-visual room, slide library, technical library and drawing office. Below, in an equally pragmatic example of space planning, the mail room, model-making shop (fitted with a dust extraction system) and computer room are housed behind double-glazed partitions to keep excessive noise out of the studio.

Air-conditioning ducts with floor outlets run around the studio's perimeter, below the carpet tiles. The majority of services — fluorescent downlighters, sprinkler system, fire alarm, smoke detectors, fan coil units (along the perimeter) — are based in the ceiling, concealed by panels of white candrell fabric stretched rigid.

A grandly scaled library shelving system covers the entire back wall space, constructed from aluminium and steel extrusions. It houses paperwork, including the frighteningly huge quantity of technical documents which architects need at their disposal. Anything above arm's reach can be accessed via adjustable aluminium ladders and a raised platform.

The office is designed to the highest of efficiency specifications: every item of equipment or support service is within reach, and adequately stored or housed. The design language is unerringly consistent throughout, and the studio a grandly scaled and beautifully located room open to the riverside. The ever-changing weather conditions are an unpredictable, and evocative, element which infuses the workspaces with light in its infinite variety.

View from the
mezzanine of the main
studio, with thirteen
long 11 × 2 metre
worktables fitted with
storage units and
'totem poles' into
which electrical
equipment neatly plugs.
On the ceiling,
tensioned panels of
white candrell fabric
conceal the services.

Floor plan. 1 Entrance.
2 Administration/
reception. 3 Meeting
room. 4 Fish tank.
5 Kitchen. 6 Toilet.
7 Designers' studio.
8 Office. 9 Workshop.

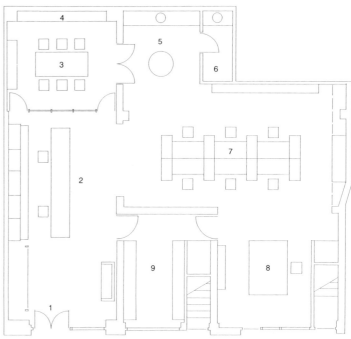

Etched mirror-glass
doors to the kitchen
cupboards match the
rimless acid-etched
glass door to the toilet,
where the terrazzo
worktop surface
continues. Danny
Lane's irregularly
shaped glass-topped
table with its
decorative, etched
metal base, gives the
kitchen a dramatic
quality.

A smooth laminated
oak top dominates the
reception area, which is
separated from the
meeting room by a glass
screen. Doors open on
either side, with strands
of the metal reed
sculpture attached to
their frames. Matthew
Wells' adjustable ceiling
is visible in the meeting
room.

Isometrix

SPENCER FUNG
London, UK

Designing a suite of new offices for the internationally acclaimed lighting designers Isometrix which would also function as a showroom proved to be a salutary experience for architect Spencer Fung in one of his first solo projects. A very limited budget and an eight-month schedule provided restricted means to realise a project involving individual fixtures and fittings. His elegant solution uses a small range of high-quality materials in a flexible backdrop intended for the demonstration of sophisticated lighting effects and as a working atelier: showpiece and work space overlap in a calming environment.

Isometrix director Arnold Chan designs lighting for well-known architects and designers such as Eva Jiricna and Philippe Starck. In the ground floor of a quiet mews building in Knightsbridge he aimed to accommodate both clients and co-workers in an environment which would complement and demonstrate the versatility of his specialist design work. He and Fung were agreed that lighting and furniture should be set within a white backdrop, in which there would be a minimum of dark tones. Furniture, partitions and doors are made of either unadorned oak or various treatments of glass, which provide both solidity and reflective surfaces without crowding the spaces.

From the entrance, the reception table forms a long dramatic sweep of laminated oak, leading to a spectacular, small-scale *mise-en-scène* in the meeting room beyond: four long stainless-steel framed fish tanks are encased within a continuous array of textured steel reeds, bowing and swaying as if blown by a soft wind. Strands of this metal sculpture, by Antony Donaldson, are laid across the pristine, acid-etched glass doors of the meeting room. Its attenuated lines are given a more stylized form at the tank's base and above it, where they thin out to the ceiling. Such a potent combination of rough-cut steel and green-tinged water provides an ideal backdrop for subtle lighting displays.

The open-plan layout provides a comfortable working space, with easy access between rooms. Here, sophisticated effects can work for the benefit of all who use the space, not just visitors. The reception room has a lighting pelmet along its top perimeter, which provides a concealed uplighting effect that washes and reflects from the ceiling. In the meeting room a tripartite ceiling, designed by Matthew Wells, can be

lowered to display a variety of lighting effects. Others can be seen on remote control-operated video monitors. Cantilevered beams hold a host of uplighters – fluorescent, incandescent and low voltage – which can be effectively demonstrated in this atmospheric setting.

It was important that this wealth of technology did not have a soulless context. Fung has designed a calm kitchen space adjoining the meeting room, with terrazzo work surfaces and acid-etched glass doors with oak frames. An elaborate table in jagged glass and metal by Danny Lane is given pride of place; like the sculpture-adorned fish tank, it adds a personal, almost domestic, aura.

In the large open workspace, oak workstations provide privacy as well as concealing computer monitors. Along the wall there are long workbenches close to the window, so that mock-ups and lighting fixtures can be prepared in daylight.

The company had to move in and make some of the space operational while building and installation work was still taking place. The final stage of a close collaboration between architect and designers, this was done by screening off half the office, and moving around gradually until the metamorphosis was complete.

The meeting room table, with a solid white Carrara marble base and 25mm thick glass top, is accompanied by black Philippe Starck chairs, their dark presence dramatized further by Antony Donaldson's textured steel sculpture behind.

The extended roof trusses of the production hall's far left corner defies the logic of the rectangular volume of which it is a part, as an expressive, skeletal structure breaking the boundaries between wall and ceiling, exterior and interior.

Section through the production hall and office of Funder Factory 3 with its 'disintegrated' south-facing glass corner.

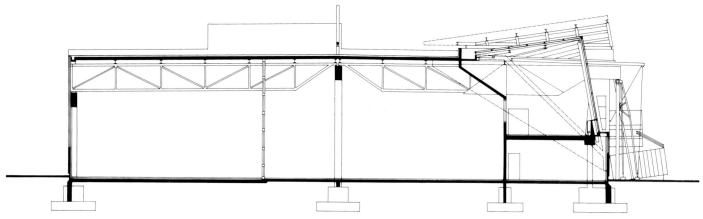

1.4

Funder Factory 1 & 3

COOP HIMMELBLAU
St. Veit/Glan, Carinthia, Austria

The commission for Funder Factory involved tackling, in two separate phases, one entire building and one 'insertion'. Although it represents a larger-scale project than any of Coop Himmelblau's inventive interiors of the 1980s, many of which were also work spaces (such as Iso-Holding and Rooftop Remodelling), the challenge has evidently not dulled the practice's appetite for creating experimental 'performance' architecture. The two phases comprise Funder Factory 3, a new industrial building for a wood and paper company, sited within a landscape and monument protection zone on the edge of the town of St. Veit/Glan; and its counterpart, Funder Factory 1, an executive office suite within an old building in the town.

Wolf Prix and Helmut Swiczinsky's strategy was to exploit and overcome economic and functional constraints in order to create dynamic, 'multi-dimensional design' at both sites. With Funder Factory 3 they have questioned bland industrial 'box' forms by twisting and tilting various architectural elements to create a strong and unique visual identity. Working through hundreds of conceptual sketches, the architects dismantled an orthodox, rectangular form into sculpturally designed elements which, when combined, endow the total complex with an unmistakable head and a body. Starting with a low, white steel-framed rectangular volume (intended to be a ventilation centre/production hall), they sliced off an end portion (the energy centre, to be sited 46 metres away), and broke into the edges of the remaining form, disintegrating the southern corner and replacing it with a protruding glass window. To the energy centre they added tall, slanting, 'dancing' chimneys which, towering above a sculptural metal 'cascade' with trellis framework, endow it with a medley of soaring vertical features.

A flying roof structure supported by trusses (echoing an aeroplane hangar) extends over to the independent energy centre. Below, a 'mediating' bridge covered with metal and acrylic panels cuts across the huge flying roof to connect the two sites of power and production. Their relationship as well as their distinctive qualities are highlighted by these dynamic and formal elements.

This extraordinary structure is given a neutral white and grey exterior; however, lodged at its side is a bright red coxcomb of zigzagged planes, intended 'to heighten the dynamics of the production process', which acts as an entrance at the side of the production hall. This creates a powerful white and red façade, designed to be visible from the elevated main road.

Inside, the production hall is kept deliberately sparse. The lower part of the walls is reinforced concrete; above lie sheet steel panels. Light streams through vertical bands of windows, but on the south-west façade this pattern is forcefully interrupted, creating an unusual space. Its tilted corner of steel-framed glass, bombarded by roof trusses and a diagonal beam, breaks up the rectilinearity of the hall and creates a network of light patterns in the production office.

The glass corner of the production hall opens up its box-like form. At the side, a brilliant red coxcomb-shaped porch signals entry to a multi-dimensional industrial building.

At Funder Factory 1, the designers have unleashed their energies on one large executive office and entrance hall within a nineteenth-century Viennese building, reinterpreting its traditional spaces with new materials and lighting. Here, the architects' conceptual dissolution process, worked out with drawings, takes each of the wall, ceiling and floor planes in turn and replaces them with a realigned substitute.

A huge sliding wall of frosted safety glass in a steel frame slices through the arched entrance to the offices (a traditional blend of louvred wood and decorative curling ironwork) and, inside the hall, meets a slanting, chrome-plated radiator almost its own height. When fully open, it reveals the adjoining conference space. With its end portion extending outside, over a red-painted strip across the top step, this huge glass wall at right angles to the building seems not unlike a piece of furniture too big to get through the door, or a permanently planted blade cutting into the building's old fabric. But appearances are deceptive: when a meeting is in session, the automated glass door contracts into the building, through the narrow gap carved out for it, out of sight from the exterior.

This astonishing sculptural intervention creates a new, irregular opening into the main office – a bare, grey-green carpeted space, divided diagonally into two by a textured wall of polished concrete. At the other end of this office, another smaller sliding door, this time in plywood, runs parallel with the first, concealing a bar and a built-in cabinet.

Between these mobile elements, the lighting fixtures illuminate the new spatial relationships. Halogen downlights set behind the glass wall create a white glow along its top perimeter, dramatizing its presence in the marble tiled hall. In the office, the architects have suspended a sculptural sheet rock ceiling diagonally across the room, following the concrete wall partition. Integrated halogen downlights point up its long, hovering structure. Alongside, two narrow horizontal light beams set in the ceiling dart between the pinpoint of a single recessed downlight – these are Coop Himmelblau's energy lines, which metaphorically 'dissolve' the power of the room's rectilinear volume.

By paring down the design to the three elements of movement, lighting and sculpture, Coop Himmelblau have brought a language of mobile form to Funder Factory 1. At the out-of-town factory building, Funder Factory 3, they have reinterpreted the industrial shed, giving it a highly wrought, even eccentric, expression which is highly appropriate to its creative, transforming function.

A view from the foyer into the conference room through the sliding glass door which forms both an entrance and a new, opaque wall. At the end of its track, a tall metal radiator adds another sculptural object to this dramatic intervention.

At Funder Factory 1, the administrative offices, a 5.5-metre long automated sliding glass door to the inner conference room slices through the existing fabric of the building. Here it is shown fully extended.

WORKSPACES, OFFICES & STUDIOS

1.5

Paramount Laundry

ERIC OWEN MOSS
Culver City, California, USA

The entry canopy of Paramount Laundry is supported by detailed steel braces. Moss's row of distinctive clay pipe columns ends with one breaking the mould, lurching out on to the street with a double elbow bend.

A wooden bench provides a resting point close to the black steel suspension devices attached to the roof trusses, which were cut back to create a connecting bridge on the third floor.

Paramount Laundry on Ince Boulevard is a 20,000-square-foot structure built in 1940, and last used as a warehouse. It has been converted by Moss into office/studio space currently occupied by the graphic design firm Sussmann/Prejza. Together with the smaller Lindblade Tower, situated on the other side of the building's side driveway, the project is one of many local industrial conversions gradually regenerating this area where Moss's own office is located.

The original building had a concrete structure with a wood truss supported roof. It also had 'two essential organizational elements' which provided the key to further expansion: it is built on two floors, and has an open, double-height volume, centrally positioned in plan with clerestory windows, and spanned by wooden trusses. Moss added 6,000 square feet to the building – the maximum allowed under parking regulations – by extending the existing second floor to the south, and by creating a new, two-part, third floor.

After the initial gutting, concrete walls and steel sash windows were replastered, repaired or replaced, leaving the exterior of much of the building with an efficient aspect. A commanding view of its façade can be had from the Santa Monica freeway: for this view Moss devised new exterior elements which would grab the attention, and give the building its own distinct and revitalized quality. He has added a new canopy and central lobby, capped with a vault covered in galvanized sheet steel – a material which features prominently throughout the building. The vault is adjusted in plan towards the traffic flow on the freeway, and is supported by clay pipe columns filled with reinforced concrete, one of which is splayed, giving the building a witty, surreal 'peg-leg'.

The transformation, however, is much more than skin deep. The most dynamic aspect of Moss's imaginative and careful conversion is the modified vault positioned over the entrance lobby, above a bridge connecting the two sections of the new third floor, and over a new rear exit stair. Where the vault is inserted, the existing roof sheathing is removed and both vault and supporting walls extend vertically above the original roof, visible from the floors below.

This new vaulted roof brings natural light through the clerestory windows to the bridge from the north. The segmented arched windows are one of many strong elements of the front façade; set back from the wall, they incorporate a steel door leading to a small balcony overlooking the street. The windows allow light to penetrate the front hall and surrounding staircase, set in a spectacular, three-storey, oval light well with a curved plaster wall dramatically cut away on the ground floor to provide access to offices and studios.

The new second floor projects into the central space and is supported by sturdy columns made of vitrified clay drainpipes (providing shuttering for reinforced concrete), which also support the laminated wood girders of the bridge. Moss has introduced ordinary building materials, such as sheet metal, concrete pipe, etc. – which are also used in the exterior – to house the services; they also contribute to the structure. The squatness and colour of the pipes is not as overwhelming as it might be, and the general air of lofty grandeur of this high-ceilinged warehouse is not diminished. A mix of contrasting tough materials and structural elements has room to breathe without excessively imposing its strong character on the users. The workspaces have been fitted out to allow for varying work patterns.

The entirely new third floor consists of separate working areas positioned at opposite ends of the building's conspicuous structure. They are linked by a bridge aligned with the new vault roof, which cuts a circulation path on this floor from one end of the building to another. In order to allow an unimpeded journey, Moss removed 4-foot portions of the wooden roof trusses' bottom chords in three places, and then restructured them using black steel tube suspension devices clamped over the white chords. The effect dramatically emphasises the structure of the building, and the addition of two wooden benches to this area implies that it should become the venue for informal meetings or gatherings away from the offices below.

A complex and daring conversion, which rejects more traditional notions of how to revive dilapidated, redundant space, Paramount Laundry combines the rough with the smooth – a highly individual vision.

A wide, segmented arched window, set into the new vaulted roof (made of painted sheets of steel) above the third floor. A galvanized steel door seen from across the light, double-height entrance hall leads through the steel-framed window to the exterior balcony.

Linked workspaces combine original stonework, exposed wood roof trusses, girders and sheet metal partitioning.

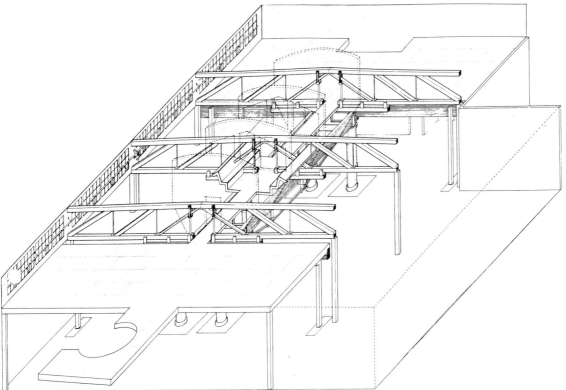

Flexible workspaces, in which Moss's exposed wood trusses and vitrified clay pipes have a dominant, but not overpowering, presence.

Axonometric diagram showing the new two-part third floor of the office building behind the front stair and hall. Vitrified clay columns carry wood girders which in turn carry a connecting bridge. Reconstructed truss chords allow access across the central volume.

Mezzanine floor plan.
7 Glass-roofed
courtyards. 8 Director's
office. 9 Void over
studio. 10 Workspaces
for writers and readers.
11 Offices.

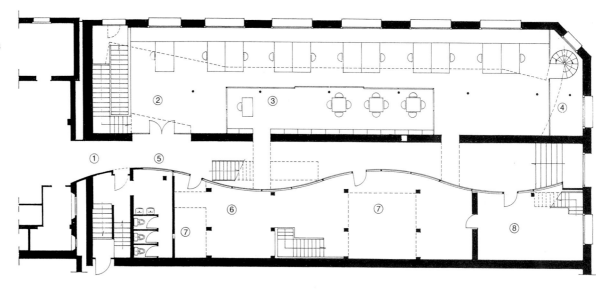

The mezzanine's angled base, wrapped in riveted steel sheets, suggests an aeroplane wing. Its curved front tilts up over the library, presenting another reflective surface. To this are bonded clear glass sheets enclosing the library. The mezzanine above is reached by a spiral staircase; its row of frameless glass windows can be tilted open on a pivot, or kept shut for quieter work.

Gallimard Jeunesse

**JEAN LÉONARD AND
XAVIER GONZALEZ
Paris, France**

Gallimard's headquarters in the rue Sebastien Bottin were originally built in 1875 as offices for Bottin, the creator of the Almanac. Since the respected family firm of publishers moved in, it has expanded rapidly both in terms of numbers of staff and its sphere of operations.

In the mid-1980s Managing Director Claude Gallimard involved young architects Jean Léonard and Xavier Gonzalez in an independent office conversion for associates Denoël. When the job was completed Denoël left the rather cramped main building, and space became available for the much-longed-for centralization of Gallimard's children's books department. At last the editorial and production offices could become part of a self-contained unit on the ground floor, and the architects were again commissioned to devise a design scheme to suit both users and clients.

The rectangular ground floor space to be transformed was 4.2 metres high, and divided by a thick structural wall: one half benefited from large openings to the street, the other received light only from two narrow courtyards. The courtyard side was insufficiently lit, and the whole space did not provide enough room for the fifty staff members to be accommodated. One immediate solution was to insert a mezzanine, providing 800 square metres of floor space. Intentionally conspicuous, the mezzanine's angled metallic form now provides an intermediate floor for the editors of individual booths in natural wood which overlook the floor below and face high windows set in the double-height wall. Because of the low (2.03 metres) ceiling height on this upper floor, the partitions stop well short to give a sense of space.

The Gallimard Jeunesse team of editors, writers and production staff work together in close consultation, but also need separate working areas and access to an on-site library in order to develop projects further. Léonard and Gonzalez have therefore given high priority to open space, and the result is a sense of transparency between working areas. After some thought about how actual surface textures could be treated, they decided that the play of light should become the governing aesthetic. Natural light is encouraged throughout the split-level offices, penetrating the editors' workspaces through the frosted glass of the corridor from the courtyard.

The high-ceilinged corridor running through the centre of the ground floor is walled on one side, with a sensuous curve of translucent, frosted glass on the other. Light penetrates this semi-opaque surface, and moving shapes behind become intriguingly distorted projections. Once again, the aim is to bring in light, and to manipulate its interaction with glazed surfaces to create a range of subtle effects.

The most striking feature of the new mezzanine is the row of clear glass windows, which shut off the editors' desks into an acoustically self-contained area, but which can also tilt open, reflecting light from the windows opposite and piercing the barrier between upper and lower spaces.

Under the metal-clad mezzanine floor, supported by black steel columns, the library walls are clear panels of glass, held in a metal frame. Highly reflective panels without a discernible structure could be potentially dangerous to users, so venetian blinds can be rolled down inside for a semi-shuttered effect.

The architects' insertion of modern, informal but efficient spaces into an old industrial building is precisely ordered and resourceful, using various types of glass panels to bring a sense of animated transparency to a compact, double-height area. The budget was 4,380,000 francs.

The high-ceilinged corridor has a curved wall in opaque glass held in place by a metal frame, which transmits light and moving shapes across the parquet floor below. The walkway leads to the editors' desks on the mezzanine.

What looks like a burrowing creature or a segment of an industrial boiler turns out to be a zinc-clad bulkhead protecting the staircase up to the open-plan, maple-floored conference space on the top floor. Below a new slate roof (with provision for rooflights), the steel roof structure adds a rhythmic geometry.

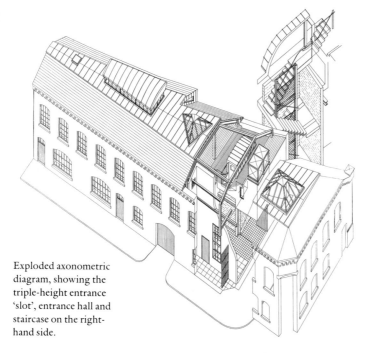

Exploded axonometric diagram, showing the triple-height entrance 'slot', entrance hall and staircase on the right-hand side.

The Factory logo is punched on to steel entrance gates, flanked by blue-glazed brick facings.

WORKSPACES, OFFICES & STUDIOS

Factory Communications Headquarters

BEN KELLY DESIGN (BKD)
Manchester, UK

Factory Communications promotes popular culture by layering it with innovative art and design. This culturally enlightened approach to the leisure industries could represent economic suicide in other hands, but its application to record covers, posters and key clubs and bars such as the Haçienda and Dry 201 (see pages 76–9), has undeniably helped the company carve out a unique identity as a catalyst of pop culture. Now their recently completed headquarters has provided Factory staff with a centralized working space in which these ideals can be applied closer to home.

Previously, Factory's administrative premises operated from low-key private accommodation. The takeover of a large, dilapidated, three-storey warehouse on Princess Street in the mid-eighties created an enviable three-dimensional site for posters, but still no central working base. Eventually, they got contractors to clean away the layers of grime and reveal the original brickwork. Since they were still not convinced of the need for full-scale occupation, the company's initial plan was to make good a basement and upper floor principally for warehouse space. A new licensing deal, however, reduced their need for space to store product and, more importantly, the involvement of longstanding collaborators Ben Kelly Design (BKD) put them in a position to give their staff stimulating and salubrious surroundings. Factory's

activities operate for 24 hours a day, but they did not want a high-profile building proclaiming their status constantly to the street, nor interiors which might suggest the sort of hierarchy the company tries to avoid in its operations.

Kelly and his team have applied newly constituted elements to an existing context with considerable conviction, establishing a dynamic interaction between new and old forms, which respects the logic of open-plan working space. In keeping with Factory's cultural policies, the interior of the building is treated to a heady series of material combinations which pull together in a relaxed atmosphere. The mixing is audacious in both work and landing areas: red wood stairs with galvanized steel handrails lead to marble-tiled landings with walls of recycled floorboards; in the main office area the sandblasted brick structure is flanked with walls painted with bright red and blue pigment squeezed straight out of the tube; in the ground-floor reception, a floor trough of seawashed pebbles is juxtaposed with an oak door

and metallic rendered beams.

BKD have retained the original structure of the building, apart from one corner, the entrance. Here, they have created a tall opening by raising the stone lintel and facing the wall with blue-glazed bricks which refer to the pillar outside the Dry 201 Bar. A visual play on scale and perspective, the mammoth aperture stands astride a narrow, recessed, galvanized steel gateway – the new Factory fortress. Below, two enigmatic blue glass windows set in the sandblasted brick wall suggest an abstract composition, pointing out the elevation of aesthetic values.

Once inside the double-height ground-floor reception, the aesthetic composition of carefully selected architectural elements continues, with another play on scale. A tall, steel-framed window set in a soft blue plaster wall reveals nothing through its grid of white flashed opal glazing; it is a larger, neutral version of the blue window over the entrance. Flanking the dwarfed door is a wall of 'Yves Klein blue' pigmented render. This goes right up to the first floor where, topped by a metal balustrade, its vivid colour wraps around the balcony. An expanse of block flooring in textured, fumed, end-grain oak leads to a stark area of bleached Portland stone and up a wooden ramp (a door mat on a slant) to an

The stairways mix dark red Lauan wood treads and risers, stainless steel handrails with galvanized steel fixings and gloss black epoxy stairwell channels. Deep blue marble floors add a polished surface.

It is a spacious, open-plan meeting area, designed to suit the informal communality of Factory staff meetings. Originally it was an unusable upper level, but by raising the roof with structural steel beams BKD created an entirely new floor which they have devised as a sculptural landscape. Kelly is particularly fond of the articulated stair enclosure, a mighty bulkhead clad in zinc. Eventually, three geometrically shaped roof-lights will be incorporated into the building's new slate roof, to open up this atmospheric space and add natural light to the proceedings and yet another layer to the imaginative design.

oak door. These graduated sequences of materials continue throughout the whole building, using contrasting permutations of materials and colour — hard and smooth, solid and tonal, new and recycled — to provide a strong sense of place.

After such a swift succession of contrasting forms, the spacious upper floor is a wide expanse of timber floorboards and sandblasted brickwork punctuated by windows. Although the project is illustrated here before occupation (the company has added its own furniture which has inevitably muted the drama of the space), its details convey the deeply rooted effect that designer and client agreed was crucial: Factory wanted an interior which, in spite of its obvious novelty, also had a lived-in character that would pre-date the new design. Kelly has not achieved this by adding fake distressed elements, but has instead recycled materials, such as timber floorboards which he has reinvigorated by fire-rating and lacquering them before use as wall panels around the side entrance. These old elements help to anchor the new materials, just as rough surfaces ease smooth pigmented ones between them, and offset their change in appearance through ageing. The galvanized exteriors of radiators are left exposed and rough. Industrial light fittings made of Klee-Klamp tubing are suspended from the ceiling, chosen by BKD to supply VDU-friendly, non-reflective illumination.

The entire top floor is devoted to the company's boardroom/conference space.

The ground-floor reception is enigmatic and off-beat. The red oak door with its ramp over a clear expanse of Portland stone recedes into the light blue plaster wall, dwarfed by a high window.

The first-floor work space is a spacious and airy environment, with sandblasted brick walls, timber floors and industrial light fittings and radiators, which absorb the brightness of the end walls.

An airy wooden spiral staircase leads up to the fashion resource centre.

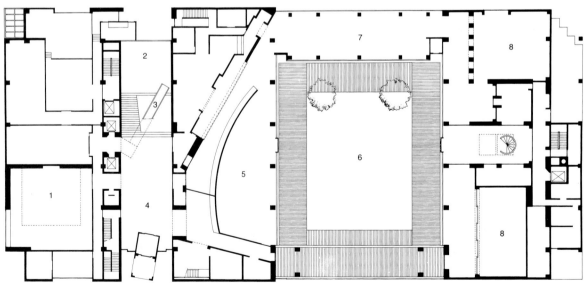

Ground-floor plan.
1 Conference room.
2 Entrance hall.
3 Ramp (access
to showrooms).
4 Hall. 5 Restaurant.
6 Garden. 7 Café.
8 Art gallery.

1.8

World: Creative Fashion Dome

**STUDIO CITTERIO/DWAN
WITH TOSHIYUKI KITA**
Kobe, Japan

World Co.'s Creative Fashion Dome is situated on the man-made Fashion Island in the historic port of Kobe, south of Osaka. World Co. is one of the largest fashion companies in Japan, and its administration headquarters is just one part of a continually expanding community of fashion trading companies. Viewed from the outside, the building assumes an attitude of stylish simplicity, with its serene, mirrored surfaces reflecting the world outside.

Determined to reflect their distinct corporate identity in the architectural forms of the new headquarters, World Co.'s directors travelled to Milan to engage Studio Citterio/Dwan to design the interiors, with Japanese designer Toshiyuki Kita their close associate. The collaboration was a challenge for both design groups. Not surprisingly, the differences between Italian and Japanese architectural regulations became glaringly apparent, but a similarity between those in force in California (where Dwan obtained her qualifications) and in Japan was also a major strength, and arises from similar climatic, seismic and construction conditions. Italian regulations permit more flexibility: in consequence, some of the steel elements such as ramps and stairs included in the original design were either not included or were changed.

One major restraint placed upon the designers was that no structural changes were allowed to the proposed exteriors of the building. It had originally been designed as part of a larger complex of World offices, and foundations were already in place. Although World itself had made some re-evaluation of required work space due to an expanding market before Citterio/Dwan began, the building's structural loading could not be altered without causing considerable delay. In response to the brief requesting a high-profile space, the designers decided to

concentrate on bringing a sense of formal urban order to the interior. This manifests itself in scenographic elements which help to create a strong environment in which bold, white shapes and large expanses of beech flooring interact. This is accentuated by a combination of natural lighting, which penetrates through the atrium's roof canopy, and strategically positioned fluorescent downlighters.

About 80 per cent of the work consisted of organising the optimum layout of the working spaces within a relatively modest budget. The remaining 20 per cent was left for the cultivation of an effective image, and the designers' perfectionist approach was extended to the refinement of interior forms.

The goal was to create a strong but relaxed working environment in which 'work' could be interpreted as designing fashion as well as administration. With this open-ended notion of function, the designers introduced the duality of both western and eastern concepts of working space. A total area of 16,420 square metres allowed them to create an impact with some outstanding features – such as the entrance atrium with stairs and a ramp; a spiral staircase set in a white

Reception desk in the atrium space. Halide lighting hangs from the ceiling; on the walls are incandescent outdoor lights, positioned in twos like small hooded eyes.

mesh cylinder, and a spacious enclosed garden which takes up about one sixth of the total space. The ground floor is mostly public space with a reception area leading directly into the atrium; it includes an auditorium, bars, restaurant, library, gallery, conference and storage rooms. Above are three floors of offices, a showroom, studios for designers, and offices for artistic directors and other administrative personnel.

The main architectural elements of the interior are carefully scaled, in particular the broad windows of the atrium; the wooden ramp crossing the area diagonally; the spiral staircase to the fashion resource centre; the wooden terrace facing the garden; the dynamic curve of the restaurant wall, and the doors of the showroom and studios. Considerable time spent drawing at the scale of 1:1 enabled the designers to create the clearest forms.

Particularly scrupulous attention is paid to details used with materials which could convey the essence of World. Most of the furniture was designed in beech, to

blend in with the floor surfaces; the signage system was also custom designed, to achieve a well-rounded result.

World employs an almost scientific approach to fashion, which is echoed in its careful layout: the library has a substantial 'colour and trend room' for forecasting. Floor upon floor of busy specialists and stylists create designs supported by a blend of rigorously researched data and imaginative predictions, in a building which effectively upholds World's classic principles of harmonized elements.

The atrium looking back at the entrance from one side of the ramp, which crosses the space over wooden steps.

The staff restaurant has
a dramatic curved wall
to give dynamism to a
large, otherwise plain,
open space, lit by
converging lines of
recessed spots.

The library, with
furniture and fittings in
beech.

A curved acquamarine partition faces the entrance in the reception area. Behind this is the open-plan office, easily accessible via openings on either side. The strips of perforated metal lighting track create the illusion of a lower ceiling plane.

Viewing room, with Cassina's Corbusier sofa in red wool, chosen by the designer and the client to coordinate with the many other coloured surfaces at Vivid.

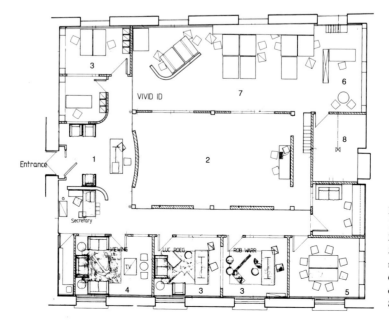

Floor plan.
1 Reception.
2 Open-plan office.
3 Offices. 4 Viewing room. 5 Meeting room.
6 Library. 7 Additional office space.
8 Darkroom.

1.9
Vivid Productions

GARY KNIBBS
London, UK

Vivid is a company of video-makers and graphic designers now based in a newly converted warehouse in Camden Town, North London. Prior to the move, help from young interior designer Gary Knibbs was enlisted to find a space that would accommodate both elements of the company equally well within a new design scheme. The resulting 325-square-metre offices feature three key design elements, specified to high professional standards: colour, space and light. It is a simultaneously vivid and carefully conceived solution.

The clients wished to retain the open warehouse spaces without adding corridors which, they felt, would prevent a relaxed circulation between offices. The number of video production staff often increased three-fold when productions were in operation, and a layout flexible enough to absorb fluctuating numbers was essential. Production schedules are frequently gruelling and the company was keen not to live in monochrome surroundings which might add to tension, but in large, inviting areas of sophisticated colour, carefully lit.

Into the outer areas of one single open space with six centrally positioned steel columns, Knibbs has introduced a number of full-height partitions, many of which are predominantly glazed in sections. These divide and enclose offices and production rooms around part of the periphery, although the glass allows light to penetrate. The rest of the outer area is kept as open as possible, and is connected to the central open-plan office, exposed on three sides behind a curved reception wall so that a flow can be maintained around the space.

The designer deliberately left conduit ducting for electrical and air-conditioning services exposed, but not before ensuring that they were positioned in an aesthetically pleasing manner (one

track forms an arch behind an office desk). To continue the industrial workspace aesthetic he has suspended wide strips of perforated metal lighting track from the ceiling, crossing at right angles along the length of the offices. Hanging from the sides of these are SKK's 'Stickleback' spot lights, backed up by chunkier car headlights attached to fine metal rods, which give stronger ambient light in the reception and between the offices. Large open spaces need adequate heating; as gas was not available, the heating system had to be placed under the floorboards, since any other solution would have been ungainly in appearance.

The colour scheme is consistently bright in each room, but not overwhelming. Citrus shades of lime green coexist beautifully with acquamarine and vermilion, juxtaposed with white walls to provide unadorned and dramatic backdrops to an equally discerning collection of furniture – the meeting room, for example, contains Pallucco's 'Saltamartino' glass table and Philippe Starck's 'Dr Glob' chairs. Decorative rugs cover expanses of polished, red-toned Merbau wood flooring used in the reception and meeting rooms (workspaces are given a durable turquoise vinyl floor instead). Knibbs has exercised great judgement in the metamorphosis of a bare warehouse space: a relatively modest £120,000 has been put to very good use.

Lush African Merbau wooden strip floors have a shiny, textured appearance enhanced by a gloss finish in this highly lit corridor area. Below a glass wall a row of tiny light bulbs adds a starry line reflected on the polished floor.

South-west view of the
pavilion from the street.

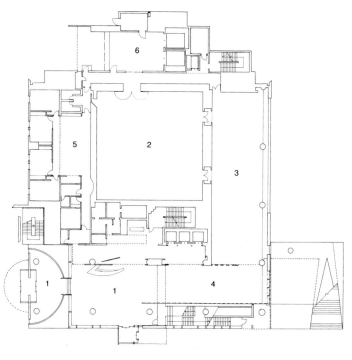

First-floor plan.
1 Entrance hall.
2–4 Plaza (exhibition
space). 5 Office.
6 Service entrance.

A light and
unoppressive foyer on
the ground floor
includes an open bridge
between the second-
floor library, lecture
room and café, and a
streamlined glass
reception desk.

1.10
Tepia

**FUMIHIKO MAKI,
MAKI & ASSOCIATES**
Tokyo, Japan

Tepia is a pavilion for science and high technology in the Meiji Memorial Park near the centre of Tokyo. It is a most privileged position, indicative of the respect and status accorded to advanced technology, which has been Japan's lifeblood during the last few decades. In his design, Maki has been able to take advantage of the relaxed regulations in force within the Park district, which allow a greater volume and height of building above ground than elsewhere in Tokyo. The building's exemplary design owes its quality to the scrupulous standards of technology and craftsmanship widely maintained within the Japanese building industry – skills which Maki feels 'may not endure indefinitely'. As such, Tepia is 'a testimony to Japanese society of today'.

Surrounded by verdant open spaces, Tepia is a modern temple celebrating within its walls advanced scientific research, but one which is open to all comers. Owned by an organisation affiliated to MITI (the Ministry of International Trade and Industry), it offers a place to exhibit some of the fruits of science – robots, computers, computer art and other product design.

Four floors above ground house exhibition space, video library, lecture rooms, café, conference hall, seminar rooms, and membership club rooms around a courtyard on the top floor. Below ground are two floors with a restaurant, sports club and garage.

Tepia's design is based on 'energy points'. Where its planes and lines intersect is a nodal point, 'the third primary element in the composition'. One example of this is on the interior stairway, where panels of aluminium are suspended by cables, leaving lines of light between each one. As with the building's distinctive skyline – a combination of vertical walls and intersecting horizontal overhangs – a narrow gap is evident, representing 'the tension of collision and separation'. This spiritual 'motif' is explored throughout.

As with Maki's earlier projects such as the innovative SPIRAL building in Tokyo, he has chosen metal and glass as the primary materials of his composition of planes, lines and points. However, increasingly sophisticated techniques have allowed a synthesis of ideas and forms not possible six years ago when SPIRAL was built. Exterior aluminium panels 5mm thick, structural glass, solar panels in aluminium extrusions on the roof – all are used with great precision of detailing.

In an attempt to avoid a repetition of the same materials, finishes and details, Maki has introduced variation in their uses. The same principle applies to the colour spectrum which includes white, grey, silver and black, only interrupted on occasion to emphasise the effect – red in the lounge carpet, green in the courtyard. Furniture throughout is designed by Kazuko Fujie in keeping with the spirit of the interiors.

As with the SPIRAL building, light is of prime importance, and the majority of the public spaces within Tepia's 13,810 square metres of floor area above ground gain their ambience from the large glass windows extending from floor to ceiling. High technology, skilfully applied, creates a hard-working building in which a further understanding and appreciation of Japan's driving force can be generated.

The open stairway is lightly screened by structural glass, allowing people to enjoy views of the garden while in transit around the building.

The two blocks in the courtyard are not identically scaled, and no attempt has been made to create a uniform pattern of windows. In Herron's 'background' architecture, the exposed white extract duct becomes an architectural element.

The lofty courtyard plays host to a huge baroque planter salvaged from Paris, and a staircase leading to an open conference area. Overhead, the two main building blocks are linked by ten lightweight steel and aluminium bridges.

The naturally lit top floor gallery space, with access to a roof terrace overlooking Bedford Square.

WORKSPACES, OFFICES & STUDIOS

1.11

Imagination Headquarters

HERRON ASSOCIATES/IMAGINATION
London, UK

The snowy peaks of Herron Associates' tensioned roof, given pride of place above London's streets.

Imagination is a name to conjure with. When this multi-media design company, based in London, decided to move from Covent Garden to new headquarters, Chairman Gary Withers approached Ron Herron of Herron Associates to undertake a spectacular conversion of a forbidding and neglected Edwardian school building in Store Street. Not only did the project coincide with a new phase of activity for Imagination, suddenly serious competition for other design consultancies, but it led to a formal merger with Herron Associates who now have an increased range of potential applications for their own imaginative and ingenious structures.

Herron and his team saw their work as adding new flesh to the building's basic structure, rationalizing it in the process. The curved external façade could not be altered, but now presents a smarter image. It is the building's interior conversion which shows the architects'

commitment to the task of transformation, while 'providing a clear distinction between old and new'.

Their proposition involved demolishing the centre of the building, creating a seven-metre high courtyard between two separate blocks, linked by bridges at each level. The front block consists of load-bearing masonry walls structured around the central curve of the mews. It contains five floors of offices, with larger studio spaces at each end. Gary Withers' office occupies a two-storey space at the top of this block, with a roof garden. The rectangular rear block is a post-and-beam construction, with studios up to fourth-floor level and an airy, south-facing gallery on the fifth floor, with access to a terrace overlooking Bedford Square. Technical and other space-consuming activities (recording studio, video-editing suite and photographic facilities) have been sited in the basement, and a redundant rear courtyard area covered over to create a staff gymnasium and workshops.

The huge space created between the two newly rationalized blocks exerts a considerable impact, attaining a luxurious interior volume rarely found in workspace in London's densely packed centre. In this stunning courtyard Ron Herron's view of architecture as 'a background for things to happen' gains a particular force. The flexibility and generous spirit of the conversion have created an arena of great scenographic impact, ideal for a whole host of activities. As a company, Imagination's wide and ambitious embrace of media activities has a pioneering, no-holds-barred feel about it; the architecture has re-scaled and reworked the original building so that it now reflects and celebrates this optimistic impulse with great panache.

Each end of the courtyard is lined with white enamelled perforated

aluminium tiles, which can be removed to allow the installation of exhibits through lower side doors. Sash windows have been replaced by single panes of glass punctuating the lofty elevations which have been painted white. The windows do not face each other, but this does not matter: instead of striving to achieve synchronization, the architects have concentrated on the elimination of detail in order to emphasise the solidity of the walls. As a result, the courtyard walls act as a robust backdrop to the space itself, which is flooded with natural light. The only fixed lights are positioned towards the top of the courtyard; the rest are flexible fittings which can be moved around to create a variety of effects.

Laced across the void is a series of elegant steel walkways at different levels, beautifully constructed off-site and lifted in. Their light, semi-transparent appearance creates a subtle, layered effect which does not impede the spectacular loftiness of the courtyard.

The major innovation applied to the Imagination building is one of Herron Associates' architectural specialities: a temporary structure, in the form of a tent-like fabric canopy roof which covers the top of the courtyard and the rear block — pinioned to the side walls, it plays the role of a permanent fixture. Light coming into the courtyard is subtly filtered by this gigantic white translucent roof, a tensile membrane structure made of PVC-coated polyester scrim. The architects originally thought the roof might work in clear glass, but eventually chose the much lighter, more flexible and above all more economical option of a tensioned fabric roof (it has an estimated life of 15 years, and cost a quarter of the glazed alternative — approximately £39,000 of the £5.5 million budget). Initially, Herron considered extending the white 'skin' internally down over the end walls of the courtyard to create a swathed effect like one of Christo's wrapped sculptures, but inconclusive fire tests meant that this did not get approval.

The enveloping 'skin' also provides an unusual roof for the top-floor gallery space, a venue for temporary shows, and serves as its most outstanding feature: when viewed from the giddy heights at the top of an access ladder, it stands out as a series of snowy peaks among the grey forms of London's skyline. The delicate appearance of the support structure greatly belies the importance of its task. The lightweight steel-framed grid is supported and stressed at strategic points by aluminium push-ups on stainless steel tie-rods, or 'compression umbrellas', which from below look like feathery studs.

The five floors of offices and studios were planned by company interior designer Shirley Walker to provide light and flexible spaces for around two hundred staff, not all of whom could be seated adjacent to the courtyard windows. She has achieved an efficient and pleasant repertoire of elements on a restricted budget. New fittings and items of furniture — including a few reproductions of Eileen Gray, Le Corbusier and Marcel Breuer — are carefully blended with the company's old favourites, like the many Hille Supporto chairs which have been retained.

A rather more image-conscious aesthetic is applied within the main reception, an upbeat and sheenily white-tiled space with softly curving white walls and a hint of infinite space reinforced by an end wall of mirrors below a bank of television monitors in front of a small display area. A few bold sculptural forms hold their weight here: a diagonally positioned reception desk in stainless steel and beech, and the streamlined curve of a small bench seat, playfully slicing the front wall. The visitor would not suspect the close proximity or the dramatic size of the courtyard beyond. Through the doors, against a white backdrop, and forcefully underlining this change of scale, Gary Withers has placed another favourite object — a huge, decorative planter which commands centre stage with great aplomb.

Withers' enthusiasm for introducing unusual objects of character extends to 'Gary's', Imagination's small staff restaurant adjacent to the courtyard, in which are incorporated eight adapted rococo metal light fittings he retrieved from an old Parisian cinema. Interior designer Shirley Walker was wary of using catering units which might impose an unappealing air of functionality unsuited to the restaurant's use for both daily staff catering and a regular rota of special events. She introduced a servery counter made of mild steel instead of aluminium, incorporating an eye-level lighting unit/shelf. Its curved supports neatly match the rococo light forms, chairs, candlesticks and a menu frame. Extending the imagery even further, she had an acanthus leaf motif acid-etched on to the fascia of the servery counter. Light sources are hidden behind seven ostentatious fibrous plaster wall sculptures by Simon Bradley which boldly hug the walls of this civilised, playful and intimately scaled dining room.

High up in 'the gods', Gary Withers' double-height office is a fetching blend of technological and antique forms, well equipped for work and entertainment. He has gathered in this spacious eyrie an impressive array of *objets trouvés* and personal effects which add resonance to the sleek and efficient layout: a restored wardrobe, a grand piano, decorative mirrors and plant troughs.

The art of the possible has been surpassed at Imagination. The right vehicle and a strong vision have enabled architect and client to imbue the distressed fabric of an urban building with new life, setting the scene for further events of the same calibre.

Cross-section showing the 18-metre-high courtyard between the front and rear blocks, the link bridges and the fabric roof.

The simple rectangular space is organised around a wide central 'street' with conference rooms, library, workrooms and other facilities as freestanding elements on one side, and open workstations along the other.

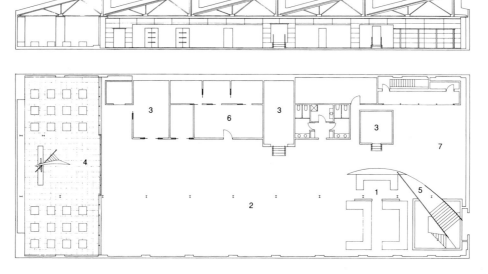

Section (top) and ground plan of the warehouse offices.
1 Reception. 2 Open-plan offices.
3 Conference room and workrooms.
4 Sculpture terrace.
5 Entrance/staircase.
6 Library. 7 Waiting area.

WORKSPACES, OFFICES & STUDIOS

Emery Vincent
& Associates

DENTON CORKER MARSHALL PTY LTD
Melbourne, Australia

The architects of the Denton Corker Marshall practice are masters of cultural space-planning. Their recently completed permanent exhibition spaces for Sydney's Powerhouse Museum of Applied Arts and Sciences have brought world-standard museum design to Australia. Meanwhile, on the city fringes of Melbourne, they have been busy with a project on a much more intimate scale: studios and offices for graphic designers Emery Vincent which explore the increasingly fertile territory in which public and private spaces overlap.

Their long time friends and colleagues Emery Vincent display an equally discerning approach to their craft. Their brief to DCM was to convert a warehouse space into offices and studios, on a limited budget, which would reinforce Emery Vincent's sophisticated image. The design had to draw on the raw character of the original warehouse, and create an efficient, spacious working space. DCM's familiarity with the company bred a superior knowledge of what could be done to meet the clients' satisfaction, but DCM nonetheless conducted a careful audit to ensure that both parties were in agreement with each other.

The building is a two-storey warehouse in a light industrial area on the outskirts of Melbourne. From low-key beginnings, it is now undergoing a gradual shift to more commercial uses, with the arrival of creative firms in need of large, economically priced studio spaces. The architects left the raw brick façade of the building unpainted in a deliberate ploy to downplay its new role. Re-rendered in grey cement, it is articulated by a grid of galvanized zinc plates.

The openings have been treated as double-height galvanized steel panels, set back from the masonry façade. The front door opens into a two-storey, zinc-clad box, containing a dramatic concrete and steel stair with granite inlay, leading to a landing which splits in two directions. One rises above the other, only to come to a dead end like one of Escher's *trompe l'oeil* staircases. The real staircase — a painted mild steel plate tunnel, which reverberates with the visitor's step — continues unabashed, but the deliberately disorientating effect heightens the theatrical impact gained on arrival. Causing only momentary intimidation, this intermediate space, dimly lit and confined, leads to brightly lit, quiet and spacious studios.

An immediate view of the entire space is gained on entering. On one side a

light grey upper level is arranged as an internal 'street', with large open workstations. On the other, a series of elevated conference, storage and display areas enclosed within white walls faces the open-plan studio. To establish the library as the dominant room, it is raised by three steps, projected forward, and clad in galvanized sheet steel panels in a rusticated pattern that refers to older, grander public institutions.

At the beginning of the 'street', clear expanses of studio provide waiting space for visitors and, at the very end, a large open courtyard for staff. The waiting area is generous and open, with a sculptural reception desk in steel plate backing on to two solid forms which surround the point of arrival, shielding visitors from immediate access to the working areas.

At the other end of a strong axis, the roof has been removed from one bay, and large glazed sliding doors open to an outdoor space floored with a deck of galvanized steel planks laid as a foil to three sculptures by Akio Makigawa.

The hard-edged forms and clear surfaces of the space reinforce the building's industrial character, and are unembellished by decoration. The simplicity of detail, materials and colour speaks of a budget where much has been achieved with an economy of means. Its expression signals its occupants' desire to adopt a rational, democratic approach to graphic design.

The front door opens into a two-storey, zinc-clad box, containing a dramatic concrete-and-steel stair to the floor above.

View of the entrance to the public counter room from the central double-height hall, with an overhanging balcony on a mezzanine above.

Longitudinal perspective section showing the raised public counter room on the right (with access ramp) and offices, and first-floor exhibition space at the rear, separated by a central hall.

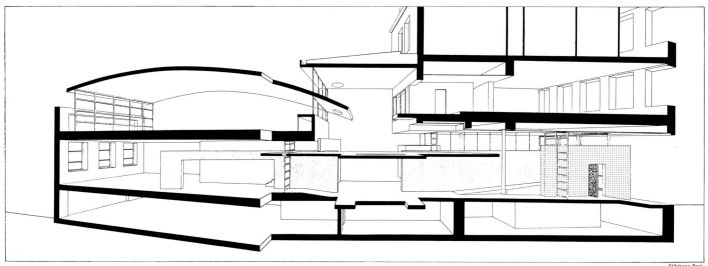

Stéphane Beel

STÉPHANE BEEL
Bruges, Belgium

Historic Bruges is hardly the most likely place to find a bank designed in a confidently modern idiom replacing a traditional shop property. The desire to preserve the city's medieval forms has meant little new architecture, other than innocuous designs that slavishly support its ancient fabric. However, architect Stéphane Beel insists that 'even in a conservative city it is possible to renovate in a contemporary way,' and the sculptural forms and light-filled spaces of the Spaarkrediet Bank are a clear demonstration of this.

Although many banks have smartened up their corporate identities in recent years – both on paper and in their interiors – they are still not generally renowned as pleasant places to wait in line. The desire to promote efficiency in bank operations often goes hand-in-hand with a stuffy, impersonal atmosphere. A parallel trend has also been a marketing-led approach, employing gimmicks which appeal only to one sector of the bank's customers (or which are intended to serve as an enticement to potential customers). The challenge of meeting these dual needs – to attract and maintain a clientèle from a wide socio-economic grouping – has in the past invariably meant safe and dull surroundings, littered with incongruously fashion-conscious literature. Space for employees away from the counters is often cramped and badly planned, although it is the visible 'other half' of the interior, and not situated away from the public gaze.

Beel and his project team were keen to avoid a design which might debase the credibility that a banking organization like the Spaarkrediet must convey at all times. A comfortable and modern working environment that could be enjoyed by both customers and employees was vital.

Within a compact 850-square-metre space occupying a narrow site are two floors and a mezzanine, established on either side of a double-height central hall. The service room is a small but welcoming space set a metre above ground level, with large windows at the front. The service desk, consultation office and entrance to the vaults are combined into one piece of wooden furniture. The room is visible from the street, but activities are screened off. By placing this room on a mezzanine level greater privacy was achieved and, in the process, a better view obtained of the neoclassical theatre opposite. The mezzanine is reached by a slope which leads down to a double-height central

hall. Beel's intention here was to create the feel of a small plaza, by evoking associations with the central glass spaces found in the Art Nouveau buildings of Victor Horta. It is in the bank's clear orientation and functional light sources that this debt makes itself felt most strongly.

The central hall firmly divides the public front area from the rear spaces occupied by the manager, and is overlooked by a curved balcony overhanging the main staircase. Dividing these public and private spaces are two walls of equal height, finish and direction, which act as the 'spine' of the spatial construction. At first floor level they are given glass windows to open up the space. Here, an elevated boardroom offers a view outside over the consultation rooms, and receives light from a cupola via an oval opening in the curved ceiling. The first floor is occupied at the front by offices and at the rear, at a slightly lower level, by a temporary exhibition space with a curved ceiling which extends into the upper area of the central hall.

The key to the success of this project is the way its walls are designed to divide, arrange, connect and create space and direct light within a long, narrow building. This has been achieved on the relatively modest budget of 20,000 Belgian francs.

Inside the public counter area, opaque glass screens aid privacy. A wooden counter, consultation room and stairs to a lower vault give the room a strong character. The upper walls are glass panels, continued over the metal-framed door.

The walls in the Commons are articulated stainless steel. Here, the enamel-panelled elevator core carries a cantilevered glass block landing with steel mesh railing at ground level.

This high-technology centre in the woods of Virginia was part of an ambitious, evolving programme prompted by the state's development of the Center for Innovative Technology, to encourage economic development in this lucrative area. In conjunction with Ward/Hall Associates, Bernard Fort-Brescia and Laurinda Spear of Arquitectonica prepared a master-plan for a 35-acre site, to be constructed in stages, of which the Center is the first. Its aesthetic dramatically symbolizes advances in twentieth-century technology.

The project is located in woodland on the crest of a hill – a high-profile site overlooking Eero Saarinen's famous terminal at Dulles International Airport. A conjunction of irregular shapes, it is arranged on a raised platform of trapezoid shape which slices through the hilltop, hiding all the parking beneath and thus preserving the forest to its edge. Three contrasting buildings create a powerful silhouette which can be seen from a distance, the patterned, metallic surfaces reflecting the changing landscape.

The buildings house various aspects of the research facility for computer

1.14
Center for Innovative Technology

ARQUITECTONICA WITH WARD/HALL ASSOCIATES
Herndon, Virginia, USA

software. The CIT Tower is most symbolic of the Center's aims and resources, and is located at the highest point of the site. Increasing its square footage as it rises, it takes on an eye-catching, reverse-pyramidal effect. To emphasise its verticality, a random gold, green and black glass pattern runs from the ground upwards to the roof, cut off at an angle against the sky, but implying infinity.

On the other side of an elevated forecourt whose circular shape represents the top of the platform lies a building housing CIT's collaborators, the Software Productivity Consortium. Unlike the CIT Tower, which is to be used mostly for administration and to provide space for high-technology firms benefiting from proximity to CIT, the SPC building was designed to house a large computer facility for software research, as well as offices. Consequently, it needs large floor plates to accommodate the equipment, which results in a horizontal building. In contrast with the soaring verticality of the CIT Tower, the SPC's form is a parallelogram 'sliding' off the parking platform. Supporting this horizontal movement is a random pattern of silver, blue and black exterior glass – rich surfaces which belie the building's highly functional, rectangular interior spaces.

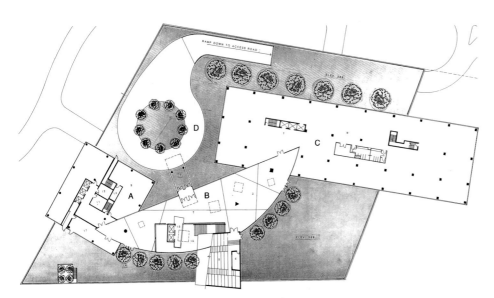

Ground-floor plan showing the layout of the three buildings of the CIT complex.
A CIT Tower.
B Commons/lobby and exhibition space (with auditorium at the rear).
C Software Productivity Consortium. D Entry plaza.

Linking these boldly shaped buildings is a common area, containing services for both: the main lobby, an exhibition gallery, an auditorium, a cafeteria, classrooms and a briefing room. It is segment-shaped, a clear glass prism, to give maximum transparency and allow the beautiful landscape to dominate its light, high spaces. Intersecting this volume is a white, marble-clad auditorium. The materials used in the common area reflect the technological innovation of the tenants: stainless steel ironmongery, a metallic elevator shaft, a 'floating' glass block bridge and cantilevered glass railings — all foregrounds to the lush landscaping outside.

The terraced areas outside CIT, such as its podium forecourt, are landscaped by Martha Schwartz. Her response to the building's irregular angles was to create a directionality which would encourage a clearer perception of their forms from close up, but also give dramatic delineation from above for visitors flying in. Stripes of Virginia stone and gravel and a circle of yellowtwig dogwood deftly punctuate the pattern of the podium forecourt. CIT's glazed cafeteria and dining rooms are given outdoor terraces with views of Schwartz's work, including crisp circles of trees to sharpen the contrast between the site landscape and the wilder woodland around the complex.

CIT represents a new building type. Its aesthetic, while giving a jolt to some of Virginia's more conservative-minded locals, matches the Center's innovative image. Its spacious and well-serviced interiors are housed not in anonymous boxes, but in dynamically shaped forms embellished with richly patterned and transparent surfaces, reflecting its beautiful setting. Bernard Fort-Brescia has called the complex 'the machine in the forest' (*Progressive Architecture*, August 1989), symbolizing Virginia's technological future in harmony with its rural past.

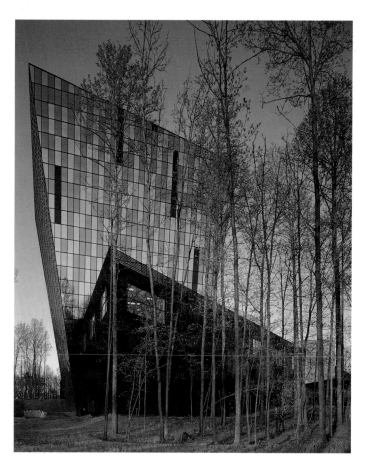

The CIT Tower, seen through the trees from the main approach road, is based on a grey-black metal grid platform containing a cafeteria and a garage.

The interior of the Commons building's clear glass prism, shaped like the segment of a circle to house the main lobby and exhibition space.

The CIT Tower's entrance lobby is framed by reflective glass, which continues from the exterior into its lofty spaces.

The small waiting area of the reception faces the glass wall of the meeting room. Upholstered armchairs and 'Dove' floor lights provide a restful contrast to the sculptural forms of the elliptical screen.

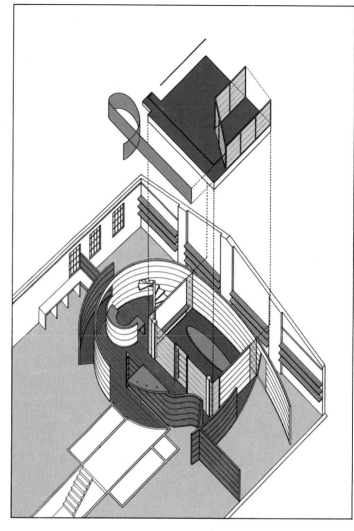

Within an industrial unit, an elliptical free-standing screen creates a semi-enclosed oval space. Inside, the central meeting room is surrounded on three sides by an ash-floored reception area. Above is an additional work space reached by a spiral staircase. In this axonometric diagram, the glass walls of the meeting room are shown in green; outer areas are studios, shown in grey.

A spiral staircase leads from the reception area up to an open mezzanine above the reception room, easily accommodated within the industrial unit's high ceiling.

1.15

Wickens Tutt Southgate

APICELLA ASSOCIATES
London, UK

The sleek ash strip floor of the waiting area meets a curved white reception desk (made of ash and medium density fibreboard), set in front of a cut-away entrance in the large elliptical screen, designed to encompass smaller working areas.

At a certain point in the life of a successful small business capital is often made available to redesign the work environment. Not all businesses, however — even design businesses — perceive the need to create a workspace which is both a promotional asset and a practical resource: often, clients are entertained in splendour while employees are left to graft away in relative squalor. Increasingly, good business managers in certain sectors now understand that an equal appreciation of the differing needs of both client and employee pays off in the end. Even on a low budget such an impulse can make its presence felt.

When young graphic designers Wickens Tutt Southgate commissioned Apicella Associates to design their new offices in Parsons Green, London, they were determined not to relinquish 'the sense of intimacy and team spirit' enjoyed in their first, more modest, studio. They wanted the new offices to allow them to feel at home, but also to serve as grander surroundings, conveying an air of confidence and a sense of their creative spirit to visiting clients — in other words, a public, as well as a private, domain.

Working with the raw material of an 'unremarkable' space within a light industrial shed, Lorenzo Apicella has created an elliptical, free-standing screen (encompassing an area of 345 square metres) as a device which meets the public entrance without an abrupt halt. Instead it draws visitors into the reception area via a trapezium-shaped opening in its curved white wall. The bold, white, semi-circular desk, the neat row of oyster-pink loose-covered armchairs and the bird-like forms of the floor lamps add further curvilinear elements to the space. Soft-toned ash strip flooring running lengthways and around the reception area creates a dappled, relaxed effect.

Inside this compact space are

design studios, offices, a conference room and service areas, all on one floor, with a small mezzanine level. Although the internal spaces carved out by Apicella's screens are modest in size, he has given each a distinct quality by specifying appropriate lighting: functional white light (metal halide uplighters and task lighting) for the studios; fine-tuned low voltage in the reception and conference room.

The conference room at the heart of the space is fronted by a glass wall, with additional strips of glass set into the screens on all four corners. Discreet, fine-slatted venetian blinds divert attention from the activity taking place within, but allow light to filter out. As a result the reception area, which fits around two sides of the room, maintains a purposeful air and a dynamic connection with the rest of the working spaces.

Apicella's design was carried out at an economical £150 per square metre. It included initial space planning to allow for future extensions. 'There are no off-the-shelf solutions,' according to Apicella. 'Every design opportunity is distinctive, and should be regarded as a fresh beginning, to be approached imaginatively with its particular conditions in mind. The goal is an original and appropriate solution.'

The geometry of the studios' façade symbolizes their equally symmetrical interiors. The double-height glass block screens diffuse light; they also maintain privacy and provide controlled views from the top-lit studios.

A ground-floor extension of one of the studios is infused with light from windows partially screened by opaque panels, as well as from circular rooflights.

WORKSPACES, OFFICES & STUDIOS

1.16

Studios, Camden Town

DAVID CHIPPERFIELD ARCHITECTS
London, UK

Developing attractive business premises within the dense residential areas of London's inner city is a delicate task. Derwent Valley Property Developments Ltd, owners of David Chipperfield's studio building in Camden Town, obtained permission to build on the site only after the local council satisfied itself that the studios would not overlook neighbouring properties, and would be occupied for what is considered to be 'creative' business use.

The challenge, therefore, was to keep everyone happy and, crucially, to avoid a construction of claustrophobic boxes which would hamper creativity. Chipperfield is renowned for his concise, beautifully composed, atmospheric interiors. However, he is also gradually moving to larger buildings and has done so without compromising either their intent or his own aesthetic values. Situated on the site of a former scrapyard, the studios represent the replacement of randomness and chaos by the orderly presence of geometrically defined spaces.

The building is in a triangular site enveloped by the back gardens of surrounding houses, and reached by a winding side road: its geometry and position would make a prominent façade absurd. Instead, Chipperfield's strategy involved developing two large, top-lit, loft-like spaces (of 3,500 and 2,400 square feet) with mezzanine upper floors reached by internal side stairs. This versatile treatment of space was commonly employed by nineteenth-century builders in the construction of artists' studios in London, an inspiring historical precedent.

However, the complex of calmly composed loft studios owes its force to more contemporary impulses – and a strict budget of £85 per square foot. The construction and materials demonstrate economical means without revealing any visible lack of resources. The façade is a symmetrical steel-and-glass block frame with a central porch. The double-height glass block screens incorporate smaller rectangles of clear glass, their overall form symbolizing the rational layout of the studios within. Inside, the two studio units are split by an exposed in-situ concrete spine wall, on either side of which staircases run up to the mezzanine spaces above, through wide stairwells which maintain a link between the levels. The concrete dividing wall and stairs are left unadorned, providing an austere introduction to the interior. On the ground floor, the concrete continues on each side until a smooth wooden floor takes over: exterior and interior merge as the hard slabs are brought inside, forming the backbone of the two studios.

Light streams into the workspaces through skylights, small side windows and rear courtyard spaces. The glass block screens and concrete walls help to diffuse excessive light at both levels. The ceilings are of average height, but the effect of the rooflights is to lift and open out the space, so that changing light patterns are always present in spite of an absence of windows on the upper level. By controlling the views out, awareness of the occupants of the neighbouring houses is minimized, and a sense of privacy maintained on both sides.

The working space of the loft-style studios is illuminated by diffused light received from the glass block wall. A simple front door of panelled wood leads to the staircase joining upper and lower working areas within an open hall.

The concrete-and-metal staircase is an integral part of the room. Its bare slab side wall recalls the architectural forms of Japan, where concrete is widely used.

Abstraction from context is a preoccupation Chipperfield has explored in other recent projects, such as the Gotoh Museum in Japan (see pages 222–3). His control of views makes direct reference to Japanese architecture in the use of space to force the line of vision downwards, to achieve an illusion of spaciousness in a low-ceilinged volume. These have always been central features of traditional Japanese building: within simple wooden houses, with large roofs and long eaves shaded from hot summer sun, the occupants maintain a close connection with the building's natural setting, and are able to observe the changing seasons via sliding (and opaque) panels which endow spaces with a contemplative and fluid quality. Chipperfield draws on this approach, to screen the studios but to encompass nature, blending it with his own language of more solid modern elements. He uses a modest repertoire of techniques and materials to produce a series of open, flexible spaces — an optimum environment for an array of creative activities.

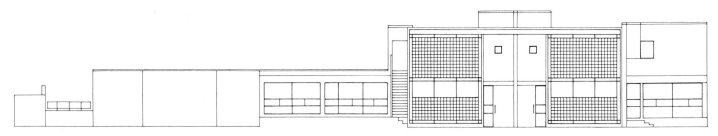

Front elevation.

Rooflights open up this sparsely designed loft-style space, incorporating a platformed corner portion, and side windows screened from neighbouring houses by a tall courtyard wall.

WORKSPACES, OFFICES & STUDIOS

A staircase projects down through the rear print workshop from a mezzanine area housing a graphics studio.

An industrial shed of subtle proportions: a custom-made steel-frame structure with infill concrete block walls, a pink stucco exterior and inverted glass-block walled façade is formed into two adjoining volumes, one behind the other on this very long, narrow site.

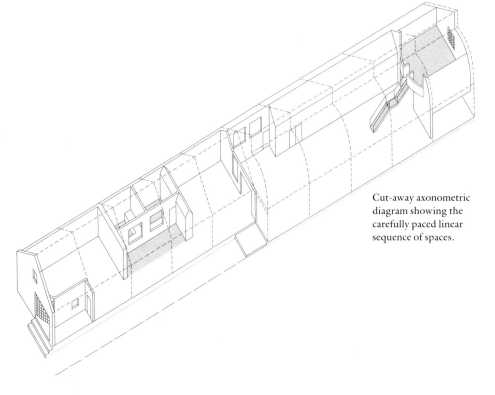

Cut-away axonometric diagram showing the carefully paced linear sequence of spaces.

WORKSPACES, OFFICES & STUDIOS

Houston Fine Art Press

CARLOS JIMÉNEZ
Houston, Texas, USA

The Houston Fine Art Press occupies an extremely narrow site (39 x 300 feet) on what was derelict land in an otherwise busy south-west area of the city. Faced with a wide range of restrictions, architect Carlos Jiménez succeeded in designing a building that could house no fewer than four main press work spaces, a graphic design studio, three offices, a photographic room, display area, offices for the curator and other staff, lounge, toilets and storage space for artwork, materials and equipment. The building's carefully structured, light environment

In the print workshop natural light is counterbalanced by a grid of custom-designed, fluorescent floating fixtures that provide task lighting over the presses.

also offers a calming retreat where the meticulous process of printmaking can be carried out.

A 10-foot-high wall shields the right-hand side of a long, slim, pink industrial shed formed into two semi-independent volumes. A strip of green courtyard between wall and building runs the length of the first, most narrow space, which contains offices and a long gallery receiving indirect light from the courtyard alongside. The building is set well back from the road behind high steel mesh gates with a striking framed façade. The main entrance is also set back from the east façade into which a curved, recessed wall of glass blocks has been set.

Jiménez's design both emphasises and plays down the building's formidable narrowness by introducing a progressive graduation in scale and volume along its length, which follows the printmaking's fixed sequence of activities. At the end of the gallery, the first printing press is located; the volume then expands, incorporating the main printing workshop, with three press stations, linear storage space and a photographic room. The white, functional environment continues in a broad sweep to an end staircase leading to a small mezzanine floor with a graphic design studio.

From this vantage point one can glance across at the composite volumes integrated as one single roof with differentiated ceiling heights. The semi-curved ceiling of the main workshop meets the cathedral gable of the building's front without tension. Both roofs interlock to create a generous and expansive space. Here, light forms filtering through the rooflight modulate from crisp to subtle as the day wears on.

Jiménez was allocated a very limited budget for the project ($43 per square foot), but still managed to ensure that most elements were custom-made. These

included the shed's steel-frame structure, the windows, cabinetry, lighting fixtures, ironwork and tilework. During the course of the work, he discovered that similar structures in the vicinity — available as standardized prototypes — cost the same as his own project.

It was a challenge to create such a subtle environment — even a sanctuary — allowing workers to focus clearly on the development of their craft. Jiménez's prototype for the Press was a self-enclosed enclave — a walled-in compound akin to a monastic environment. The process of printing one colour at a time requires a certain kind of commitment and faith which, he felt, in many ways paralleled the quiet fervour of religious devotion. Although Jiménez's other architectural projects reveal him to be an unerring colourist (taking inspiration from Latin-American communities and the work of architects such as Luis Barragán), in this fine art environment he has restricted colour to the pink stucco exterior, a contrast to the blue Houston sky.

Drawing on his early observations of the craft and motivated by the desire to 'transform reality into something sublime', Jiménez has created a simple space which is spatially rich without upstaging the work being created there. As a result, the Press has a calm, cloistered ambience enhanced by filtered natural light — optimum conditions for artistic work.

Metropolis' relaxed café spaces, with cane chairs from Maison. The padded angled end to the bar counter is perhaps a stylized reminder of the acoustic padding lining the rear of recording studios; the small window behind the bar a play on the apertures in the huge concrete façade.

An elegantly splayed series of maple-veneered panels provides both an acoustically proper and aesthetically pleasing solution to Studio A, which is flanked by adjoining spaces reached by heavy doors.

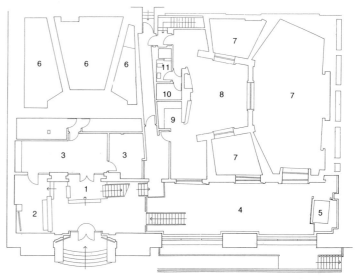

Ground-floor plan showing the double-height spaces of basement studios A and B below the café terrace and second-floor studios. In front there is a dramatic open space close to the side of the building. 1 Entrance. 2 Reception desk. 3 Administration. 4 Void. 5 Lift. 6 Void (within Studio B and adjacent booths). 7 Void (within Studio A and adjacent booths). 8 Reception room above Studio A's control room. 9 Kitchenette. 10 Storage. 11 Toilet.

Metropolis Recording Studios

**POWELL-TUCK CONNOR
& OREFELT LTD
London, UK**

An outwardly silent form of industry now drives the former Chiswick power station, a Grade II listed building in brick and Portland stone grandly designed by William Curtis Green at the turn of the century to power London's new tramway service. When the trams stopped running in 1952 the building became redundant, the generating equipment was removed, and it lay empty until 1984 when planning permission was granted for a mixed development of flats, office space, a film studio and car parking; subsequently the area designated for the film studio was approved for conversion to a recording studio complex. After a lengthy feasibility stage, Powell-Tuck Connor & Orefelt Ltd (PTCO) were appointed to lead the design project.

Metropolis is a highly specialized building. Reconciling the studios' functional requirements with an innovative aesthetic programme involved devising a number of alternatives, some of which proved too costly to undertake. Eventually phases 1 and 2, providing the first two studios, were completed in May 1989, backed up by recreation, maintenance and administration areas. On the basis of the company's early success, phases 3 and 4 were undertaken, adding three further studios on an upper floor, made ready for use from August 1990.

Set back from the suburban high road, the power station's historic status meant that the front and right-facing façades were sacrosanct, and they have been preserved intact. The interior of this evocative industrial building is, at the rear, a space of monumental scale, with original masonry and towering arched windows.

The front part of the building became offices designed by another architect, which have created awkward split-level floors close to the tall windows. Undeterred by the presence of this other style, PTCO created a new concrete structure within the lofty void at the rear — 'a building within a building' — set well back from the original windows, leaving an atmospheric, naturally lit space of atrium proportions punctuated by two new levels with solid timber and slate floors. With its hammered and polished surfaces, the new internal façade presents a physical and metaphorical toughness which holds its own against the original structure. Within the lower part of this powerful form are housed two large studios, surmounted by an open café terrace area. Above, three smaller studios are set back behind a jutting plywood vault with wide openings shaped like a set of upturned ramparts.

Triple-height stairs and a ramp way zigzag forcefully up through the expanse, scaling the concrete façade, and linking the lower administration areas to the café and upper studios. The stairs are linked half-way by a balustraded wooden platform close to the main windows which, high above the terrace, evoke the headiness of an exposed performing stage. Opposite, three industrial floodlights wink in traffic formation from the front of a grey, metal-framed lift, which hauls heavy equipment up and down the entire height of the space on an exposed winching track. The floodlit metal walkways become dramatic connective forms with a life of their own. Behind their tall façade, the studios are well lit internally, and their warmth glows through window openings 'like a ship in the night' into the colder 'atrium' space.

From a business point of view, Metropolis is part of the media services industry, and the added value of design should ensure that the quality and atmosphere of its facilities are second to none. Operationally, it is run like an exclusive hotel. The management have shrewdly applied niche marketing, and provide a range of specialist studios. The provision of state-of-the-art technology in such a rich architectural context makes it quite a phenomenon in the fast-moving music and media services industry, and yet the solidity of its architectural forms preclude any danger of the design being read as a short-lived, promotional, service component. The architecture powers the entire concept with an enduring dynamic.

Metropolis offers five studios, all well equipped for sound recording, but each offering versatile facilities and contrasting atmospheres to suit the whims of the most perfectionist rock and pop stars. Because music is now so technology-driven, artistes spend unprecedented amounts of time in recording studios, frequently over a 24-hour period. Unfortunately, interior recording studios are often abysmally functional cavernous burrows, cast in subterranean gloom, and strangely devoid of creature comforts like cafés, large leather sofas, kitchens, showers and relaxation areas. Metropolis, by contrast, is a civilised and atmospheric environment. What distinguishes it from other professional, but conventionally defined, studios created by acoustics technicians is the versatility of the design language applied. Acoustics, as managing director Carey Taylor points out, are a subjective area, and many types of sound-proofed rooms provide an arena in which a whole spectrum of sound can be created.

Throughout the five contrasting studios and their interlinking spaces, the architects' shrewd aesthetic strategy applies subtle layers of thought to the exacting brief. Seen as a whole, Metropolis is a group of highly controlled spaces balanced by their proximity to a large, open, more freely articulated space, its proportions and forms imaginatively invoking the original industrial function of the 'power house'.

The handsome proportions of studio A (1200 square feet, with a 1000-square-foot control room) are reached through time-locked double doors. Lined with 'flying' overlapping maple veneer ceiling and wall panels, with a matching floor, the studio creates a relaxed, unformidable space. Shapes and materials, as in all the studios, are chosen both for their acoustic and architectural performance. These are elegant interiors, generously proportioned, and their smooth, crafted wooden planes are evocative of beautifully finished musical instruments. Two smaller side rooms, each with different acoustics, are reached through huge, heavy, double-glazed sliding doors which can be kept open for larger sessions.

There is ample scope for two-way visual communication between studio and control room via a three-sided sleek, angled glass window which slants into the recording space. Technically an acoustic compromise, it effectively minimizes physical barriers so that band members and technicians can work closely together in individual rooms.

By contrast with the grandeur of the main performance space, the control room is a darker, more intimate, carpeted area with room for relaxation at the back as well as for the essential recording consoles. Layered wooden ceilings and walls provide surfaces with the required degree of reverberation within the studio environment; as the sound waves move back, they hit the angled glass window at the front of the control room, and are absorbed by the plaster ceiling and linen-covered padding on the rear wall.

The design of the studios efficiently excludes sound; at the same time, care has been taken to incorporate natural light through windows providing views of the atrium. This sense of openness extends to a reception room with adjoining kitchen and shower, with three angled windows overlooking the performance space. Here, musicians and technicians can unwind, entertain, or conduct business meetings in a relaxed, private environment.

Studio B is also a well-lit, tripartite complex, but more compact at 800 square feet, with a 600-square-foot control room. Here, a reception area opens directly on to the control room, and can be used with the door ajar as part of the sound-proofed area. Adjustable low-voltage lighting geared to a creative environment is complemented by precise task lighting for sessions which often extend into the night. Studios C, D and E are smaller, post-production rooms, with more intimate ambience, and orange or purple padded linen walls.

The open sweep of the café terrace provides a heady release from work in the studios, exhilaratingly spacious after their enclosed environments. Used as an atmospheric backdrop for modelling sessions, it did not stay a well-kept secret for long, but is still a hallowed preserve for musicians and their collaborators taking a break; like the studio complex, it is off limits to the general public. On good days, sunlight streams on to what could be seen as the ship's deck. Dispersed around the café Powell-Tuck's wooden furniture and cane chairs from Maison complement the main bar counter, with its padded leather sides.

Carey Taylor admits that a totally disproportionate amount of care and attention has been lavished on the project; now that it is up and running, the management's commitment to the £7 million project (of which £2.3 million was spent on design and construction) is such that the evolution process will continue. Plans are afoot for a small games room on the ground floor, and there are still 2000 square feet of additional space behind for future expansion. Powell-Tuck, who completed phase 2 with his independently formed practice Powell-Tuck Associates, has regenerated the power station with a rich, eclectic medley of forms which skilfully balance aesthetics and function — a genuinely Nineties place to play.

The wide-angled control room, with its hard glass front and maple-battened front ceiling, which is overtaken by perforated metal leading to contoured padding at the rear. The width of the maple battens is crucial for acoustic definition; screwed on to areas of navy blue linen, their visual effect is one of rhythmic order.

The more recently completed studios above the café terrace are reached by a ramp from a platform positioned high above the open space, itself reached by a lower stair.

PTCO have inserted a dramatic structure of open-tread stairs, balconies and a viewing platform between the original fabric of the turbine hall and new studio façade, linking upper and lower floors. There is a rich range of viewpoints from above and, seen from below, intriguingly juxtaposed forms animating the lofty space.

Outside, a glass-topped
bar and grouped tables
and leather armchairs
allow visitors to relax
and confer before their
meetings.

Floor plan.
1 Chambers.
2 Entrance/corridor.
3 Café/bar.

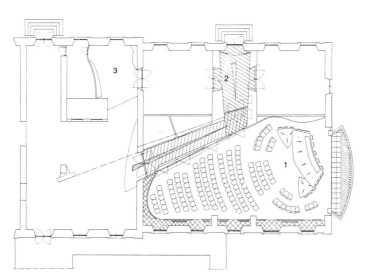

1.19

Chambers for the Conseil Général, Hôtel du Département

STUDIO NAÇO
Belfort, France

'Architecture is a call to the solidarity of things and of men. When it is merely a veneer, it provokes rejection, exasperation and refusal. When integrated with its environment, it is accepted and recognised: it works.' So say the young Studio Naço designers Alain Renk and Marcelo Joulia Lagares, who are exploring an open route between the fields of architecture, design and graphics in Japan, Mexico and the USA, as well as undertaking some high-profile government commissions in their native France. Whether designing furniture or entire interiors, they aim to use technology to give architecture and design a more expressive, open and human form.

In 1988 Studio Naço won a competition to design chambers for Belfort's Conseil Général within their local government headquarters, organised by the Contemporary Art Centre of Belfort and the Minister of Culture. In designing the project Renk and Joulia, with interior designer Denise Conrady, had two major factors to reconcile: the chambers were to be formal meeting rooms representing the state, but also to provide a forum with a relaxed ambience for the visiting public, so that communication between both parties could be conducted in an unintimidating locale.

The designers' interpretation of the brief provided a pragmatic solution, imposing a minimum of barriers. By creating a relaxed transitional space

between the building's main entrance and the conference area, they were able to dissolve the existing structural impediments to debate existing within the monolithic building, creating an accessible forum-type space with an appropriately unforbidding entrance. Although the implications of Studio Naço's proposal went much further than the requirements initially stated, its democratic impulse was fully embraced by the jury, which included many council officers.

Intended to be the largest open space in the building, the council's chambers are neither cold nor forbidding. Into a triangular space, Renk, Joulia and Conrady incorporated undulating lateral walls and rounded furniture expressing a calm, non-regimented vigour — an advanced design without ostentation or waste. Materials used are chosen for their 'classic nobility': marble, mahogany, leather, parchment. Almost all the furniture and fittings were custom-designed, right down to the chief of the council's telephone, the door handles, ashtrays, umbrella stands and toilet accessories. Prototypes were developed with the French national furniture office, responsible for furnishing President Mitterand's office at the Elysée Palace and those of French ambassadors. All these

are blended with the chamber's curved planes to create a 'second skin', inserted within the building's existing fabric. The designers intended their work to function on both a symbolic and structural level.

In order to establish a greater atmosphere of openness, the designers added reception areas with a bar and an entrance hall which connected with the chambers via multiple doors. Inside, there is a stepped marble platform and a sequence of stuccoed wall panels which gradually increase in height, ending with a wide curved panel facing the conference desk. As a result, no area of the room is relegated: instead of an imposed hierarchy, the thrust of the design, both acoustically and aesthetically, is towards the central conference desk, headed by the chief of the Council. This movement is emphasised by a series of sweeping metal lines inlaid in the grey marble floor.

The cumulative effect provides a subtle equilibrium in an arena where, it is hoped, democratic debates can be conducted. After the successful initial phase, the designers were commissioned to embark on an ambitious reconstruction of the façade to make sure that it too expressed the Council's desire to welcome the public.

Behind the conference table, a small atrium area is covered by insulated glass blocks which emit a blue-tinged light. Small spotlights set into the curved ceiling join with wall-fixed cast aluminium torches and back-lit parchment lights to create a dialogue between surfaces.

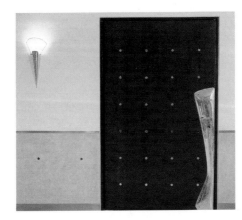

One of four mahogany copper-studded doors, with a cast aluminium frame, and gripped by a mighty aluminium handle.

Polytechnic of North
London Theatre Bar
(see pages 88–91).

Border Grill
(see pages 96–97).

La Flamme d'Or,
Asahi Building
(see pages 92–95).

2

Restaurants, Cafés, Bars, Clubs & Hotels

The 'World Fish' restaurant (in a former banking hall) features wooden chairs designed by Coates, with eight different backs evoking eight ports, including Hong Kong (red lacquer, in the foreground), Manhattan (drain cover) and Leningrad (lyre). Kate Malone's ceramic galleons sit on food trolleys, tables, and 'floes' of glass suspended above a long fish tank, with her ceramic corals and Simon Moore's glass icebergs. Fish shoals coast across the terrazzo 'sea bed floor' and, above, migrating birds fly in clustered chains on cropped lengths of net curtain.

Hotel Otaru Marittimo represents a rich cornucopia of artefacts gathered from around the world, at once an imaginatively interpreted global 'encyclopaedia' (as architect Nigel Coates terms it) of historical themes, and 'a potent microcosm of the city'. In this atmospheric environment, animated strata of fragments, images and objects – some used as unique elements, others as repeated forms or reworked themes – help to anchor a dynamic understanding of place.

Nigel Coates and Doug Branson of Branson Coates Architecture (BCA), together with project architect Allan Bell, bring to bear a particularly individual vision of harmony within diversity in this refurbishment of an early twentieth-century bank in central Otaru. Otaru, in the north of Japan, is historically Japan's second port and it forged a valuable maritime link with the outside world.

2.1

Hotel Otaru Marittimo

BRANSON COATES ARCHITECTURE
Otaru, Hokkaido, Japan

The stately fabric of the building has been redefined and animated by BCA's layered design, accommodating a five-floor hotel, with 24 guest rooms and suites on the top two floors designed around themes of eight world port cities, a 140-seat restaurant on the ground floor, a two-room museum and function rooms, bars and a nightclub.

Historically, the world's ports have operated as open, richly defined sites of trade and cultural interchange, connected by information networks, and used by a wide mix of individuals. BCA's fascination with process and global interchange is evident: trading is a metaphor for the exchange of ideas and artefacts between cultures, which have sometimes been scavenged, but mostly bought or bartered. Another global strand in the hotel's decorative surfaces is the migratory movement of natural forms of life which negotiate the seas and the skies in a patterned formation.

Branson Coates' encyclopaedic theme is applied to a multiplicity of expressive environments created within the building, which was unsuited to major structural change or the introduction of new architectural features. The bank provided a spacious shell in which a minimal design would have been hollow, one-dimensional and cold. With the support of eighteen of Branson Coates' regular group of artists and craftspeople who contribute key aesthetic elements, the hotel's layered design is both multi-dimensional and stably defined.

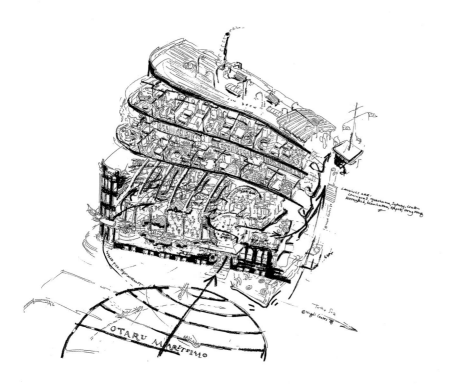

Nigel Coates' exploded drawing of the hotel.

The ground-floor reception establishes a playful début, rigged out like an early twentieth-century passenger shipping line office, complete with hide-bound video monitors for shipping news. In the largest space of the old banking hall BCA has designed World Fish, a huge seafood restaurant establishing a zoned environment ambitiously scaling the depths of the sea and the ether of the 'stratosphere' in order to present 'a composite visual mapping of the world'. The dramatically scaled proportions and robust row of columns allow full rein to the creative forms introduced. Shoals of fish dapple the solid sea-bed terrazzo floor, creating a directional flow under foot; Kate Malone's ceramic galleons coast along as table sculptures marking out sea level; layers of fin-shaped sails screen off serving areas, and diaphanous net curtains with migrating birds flying across the fabric screen one side of the upper-floor balcony. Even the corals (by Kate Malone) and icebergs (by Simon Moore) in the restaurant's prominent line of fishtanks function as works of art, as do set pieces like Tom Dixon's 'Solar' chandelier over the main staircase, Beverly Beeland's flying fish glass panels in the restaurant lobby, and Dirk van Dooren's fish video (played in the lift), beneath the fishtanks, and even in the toilets.

Up on the balcony, tables are made of bird migration maps. From here you can pick out chair backs designed by Nigel Coates which are part of a family of furniture individually customized to bring out the theme of the different ports: Hong Kong, Alexandria, Manhattan, Leningrad and so on. At the level of the pillars'

capitals, lighting is fixed to curved tracking carving out 'isobars' in the 'stratosphere'. Instead of frescoes which would give excessive weight and density to this unworldly upper level, the designers hang evanescent forms of delicate steel mesh, like clouds about to evaporate.

On the upper levels of the hotel, each guest room evolves conceptually from aspects of eight world ports, using colours, atmospheric qualities, objects and images to convey an iconographic tableau of one of four thematic strands. Bombay, for instance, is defined as Bombay Colonial, Bombay Palace, Bombay Market and Bombay Jungle, and has its own corridor bay.

BCA's thematic interpretations are never one-dimensional. Although some have a more boisterous impact than others (Manhattan's gas station room, for instance, with its yellow leather armchairs evocative of New York taxi cabs and blue-jeaned collage bedspreads), they all cut through the faithfully recreated period room approach in order to be evocative. After the initial photogenic image is glimpsed, the viewer begins to notice the ubiquitous forms of Coates' 'Tongue' armchairs, part of a series of armchairs and sofas, but here given individual surface treatments in velvet, leather, satin and other fabrics chosen for their associative qualities. The hotel's many carpets provide a dramatic collage or motif of forms. A flying porpoise, a girl riding a stampeding bull, Egyptian hieroglyphics, a plan of the Sir John Soane Museum in London, and a thousand-dollar bill are just some of the images which form a central nucleus on the floor of the hotel's more intimately proportioned spaces.

The majority of the works on the guest room and reception walls have been expertly sourced from London galleries and museums by BCA's Anne Brooks, who heads Omniate, the practice's second company, which also directed the gathering of all furniture, fittings, fine art, decorative art and antiques. With a £300,000 purchasing budget, she also

acquired a bespoke collection of historical maritime pieces, and natural history items for the second-floor Museo. Here the visitor can wander and muse on the eclectic spirit infusing the hotel, before diving into the vault of the bank next door, transformed into the Star Bar, its midnight blue sky resplendent with an ethereal fibre optic 'milky way'. A subterranean nightclub evoking the engine room of an ocean liner provides another layer of activity.

The hotel's great strength is its idiosyncratic vitality, which stretches the functional aspects of its operations to create an enthusiastic embrace of global and cultural associations. It pulls in a wealth of energetically explored cultural, historical, geographical and biological associations. There is a resonance to its plotted creativity which articulates itself in an engaging way, something the owners obviously aimed for, since a stay in such an environment is not cheap – but then it is beautifully 'value-added', something of which its former occupants would undoubtedly have approved.

One room of the two-room Museo on the first floor next to the Star Bar, which contains objects from natural and maritime history collected in London. Each room features three small cabinets at each end, interspersed with columns, and a huge, vibrant carpet, designed by Coates, below a suspended oval chandelier.

The 'Napoli, Ercolano' room is a rich red.

The 'Leningrad, St Peter's Square' room, with lyre back chairs, armchairs and sofa with an opulent patterned satin covering, and a carpet with a map of the room's thematic location. All rooms have oak floor boards.

Fixed seating and suspended table tops in Formica and swirled aluminium are designed and made locally.

Section diagram.

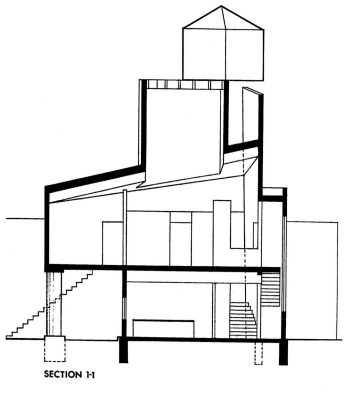

SECTION 1-1

Airiness and light pervade the restaurant space from finned windows at the rear. The main eating areas are given a tiled floor, set around a right angle of high windows overlooking the terrace.

2.2

Kentucky
Fried Chicken

GRINSTEIN/DANIELS, INC.
Los Angeles, California, USA

The challenge of bringing together Jack Wilke's burgeoning fast food franchise with inventive modern architectural forms was accepted with great enthusiasm by design partners Jeffrey Daniels and Elyse Grinstein. Both have a long-standing interest in the communication of ideas about art and architecture to a wider audience. Although the food here is economically priced, the architecture is not downgraded or disposable, but instead makes a pleasant change which breaks all the rules. Its forms and interior do not preach: they suggest welcome alternatives. Nostalgia for the Californian coffee-shop look of the 1950s, with its exaggerated sweeping roofs, huge signs and excessive lighting, provided the original inspiration for client and designers, but the theatrical allusions had to be worked in with a modern idiom to create a dynamic pull between the new and the old forms.

The building's exterior makes quite an impact next to the heavy traffic of Los Angeles' Western Avenue. Those driving around LA are accustomed to unrelenting visual stimuli. Buildings, advertising billboards and neon signs hold up a huge weight of images: 'vanity boards' groan with familiar faces of stars or ubiquitous brand identities, some with a human face. This time Colonel Saunders' famous physiognomy graces a rather unusual building: instead of merging with its surroundings, the structure is offered as Elyse Grinstein's colourful and humorous 'gift to the street'.

A 65-foot high curved stucco wall wrapped around a two-storey building is further enlivened by tapering solar fins which draw the eye around the corner.

Above, a floating cupola is surmounted by the corporate identity. The front of the curve, over the staircase, is shielded from the road by a rectilinear metal box, with large windows – 'a theatrical gesture addressing the street'. Here, passers-by can view people climbing the stairs and disappearing behind the curved wall.

On the ground floor is the kitchen, drive-through and customer-ordering counter. Above, the 65-seat restaurant and outdoor eating terrace and play area are reached by lift or a side staircase. A dumb waiter delivers customers' orders from the kitchen below. By separating the ordering and consuming functions, Grinstein and Daniels have given a greater dignity to the 'eating experience' which, although speedy by comparison with a visit to an *haute cuisine* restaurant, is not regimented. The restaurant is a strangely uplifting room, with high ceilings, white walls, large windows and a huge skylight allowing maximum penetration of light.

Mass catering of this kind does not usually coexist with good architecture: the combination adds further richness to Los Angeles' profusion of architectural forms. Even more importantly, Grinstein hopes that the success of this new relationship will convince more developers that 'good architecture is good business'.

Steel fins protrude from a curved white stucco wall, fronted on the road side by a corrugated steel box housing the staircase up to the first-floor restaurant.

One of Zsa Zsa's two entrance corridors: hard and soft face each other across a polished lumber floor. A collage of exotic carpet forms line one wall; on the other, exposed breezeblock surfaces cover acoustic insulation layers, against which rows of glass cases store liquor.

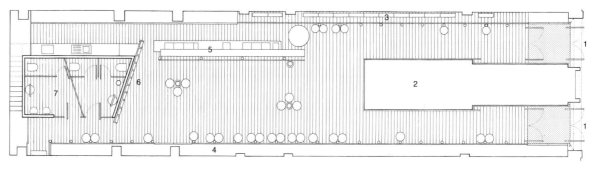

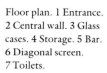

Floor plan. 1 Entrance.
2 Central wall. 3 Glass
cases. 4 Storage. 5 Bar.
6 Diagonal screen.
7 Toilets.

Bar Zsa Zsa

**DANI FREIXES AND
VICENTE MIRANDA**
Barcelona, Spain

This tiny but dramatic space is planned like a 'box within a box', in which the interplay of synthesized lighting effects and glass surfaces creates a dynamic, evolving aesthetic. Inside this box of tricks – a linear area measuring 180 square metres – six programmed lighting sequences can transform the reflective interior wall surfaces into mirrors, glowing panels and showcases. Such tactics create a subtly integrated environment, where the shapes of individual objects are blended into one overall form, and it is their relationships which become of paramount importance.

Freixes and Miranda chose the 'box within a box' structure principally to solve a sound problem. Initially, the bar had to be acoustically insulated to prevent music from disturbing neighbouring residents. Its ceiling is soundproofed, and the floor is made of layers of anti-vibration fibre and concrete topped with boards. Walls, sandwiched layers of acoustic insulation panels, are left in their raw state.

Within the hard box structure the creative roles of glass and light were then explored, becoming major players in an illusionistic game. The side walls are made of huge panels of reflective glass – a hard material which can be manipulated to create a sense of depth. Running along the length of the room, they screen glass showcases positioned against both walls which can be opened at each end, storing long neat rows of liquor supplies.

A rich collage of classical carpet covers the central wall dividing Zsa Zsa's two main entrances, softening reverberations from the rear of the bar. Made to measure on site by Peret, the graphic designer, the collage's decorative forms are emphasised by downlighters. Once the halogens and spotlights in Erco's sophisticated lighting system have been adjusted (via controls operated from a rear back room), the facing glass wall becomes a reflective surface. In this indeterminate space, the corridor becomes resplendent with sultry colours on both sides.

Behind the bar, thin sheets of birchwood back on to the wall which, when lit to full effect, become textured screens emanating a moody, autumn glow which bathes the bar in soft golden light. However, when downlit with an alternative mix of ceiling-mounted halogen lights and spotlights, the centre of the bar wall suddenly becomes illuminated by a stark white square of light in which three rows of bottles float. On the other side of the room, its reflection glimmers hauntingly on the glass surface facing the bar. By keeping this strong form geometrically pure the designers transfer the image with full force so that it appears to float in infinite space, surrounded by glimmering shadow forms.

In order to allow the lighting to work effectively, the designers have introduced serried rows of serial bar stools and circular table tops of stainless steel which create an illusory space which is uniform. Without drawing too much attention to themselves, the tables – which look like serving trays balanced on the side of small posts – underline the desired lighthearted atmosphere. Their forms are also put to work in clusters mounted on the central columns, creating small, circular, reflective surfaces for halogen uplighters. Stainless steel is hardwearing, and its reflectiveness substitutes form for image – all part of Freixes' and Miranda's masterplan for a total environment governed by light, not objects. In such a small bar, individually designed furniture would add excessive complexity to an area of mimimal size but maximum impact.

The illuminated display shelf is reflected in the glass facing. A gridded structure with square shelves allows visitors to leave their drinks alongside illuminated niches.

At the flick of a lighting switch, the glass panels are transformed into mirrors and the corridor space appears to double in width.

Behind the wooden
ledges the slate and
steel bar clamps itself to
the dark blue Marbo
tiled wall of the kitchen
area.

2.4

Dry 201

BEN KELLY DESIGN (BKD)
Manchester, UK

Manchester, which vies with Birmingham as England's second city, has during the 1980s experienced a happy revival in its fortunes. The vitality and independent enterprise which have characterised its music and entertainment industry over the last nine years have been sustained in the early 1990s, in spite of local opposition threatening club closures. The popularity and self-generating dynamism of its social scene has led to numerous international media dissections of the 'Madchester' phenomenon.

The Haçienda club, designed by Ben Kelly in 1982 and owned by record company Factory Communications, has been a prime mover in the Manchester scene. Dry 201 was instigated in 1989 by Haçienda manager Paul Mason to provide the club's clientèle with an early evening venue, and as an unintimidating place for relaxed conversation at any time of day.

space Kelly has exploited to address the dual bar/café function. The most striking aspect of the design is the use of multiple materials and the combination of rough industrial forms, used extensively in the bar area, with highly polished surfaces of metal, tile and glass.

Kelly's fascination with industrial materials and artefacts is demonstrated in many details. Telegraph poles act as columns, with small steel and wood bar ledges latched to their sides. Merged with existing structural steel posts, their rhythmic forms break up the wide space at the front of the bar.

The bar's façade is glass, 'carrying the daylight and the street into itself' with, at the right, an oversized Japanese oak door framed internally by steel and plaster partitions. Inside, the depth of the 450-square-metre space is accentuated by the main bar, which runs the entire 28-metre length, dislocated temporarily by the central Marbo tiled kitchen enclosure. The bar is made of solid, uncompromising stainless steel with a Delabole slate top, raised from the ground on steel uprights, revealing sections of drainage and support systems behind.

Above, the ceiling is animated by a series of acid-etched stippled glass panels, linked by lengths of suspended tubular steel rails in an articulated plane which runs from end to end of the room. These are in parallel with a metal lighting gantry which punctures front and rear glazing with its barbed spear ends.

Light from the glass façade penetrates the front of the long space, assisted by pendulum and gantry-mounted spot lights further back. On the right wall is the red fibrous plaster curtain rescued from the original building.

Kelly was again commissioned and in collaboration with his design team — Sandra Douglas, Elena Massucco, Denis Byrne, Peter Mance and Louise King — produced a solution which has quickly established the Dry bar as a focal point in city life which has revitalized the down-at-heel Oldham Street area.

Dry 201 is situated on the ground floor of a converted late nineteenth-century building, whose deep and narrow

By day, customers gather at linoleum-topped café tables at the rear, or at the front window against a side wall with a dramatic backdrop of *trompe-l'oeil* fibrous plaster curtain, taken from the original building, restored, and given a slick coat of red paint. Curved upholstered chairs, the occasional small sofa (designed by Jasper Morrison) and banquette seating provide flexible seating arrangements in striking tones of dark green, blue and rust. Blocks of wall and partitions painted in pollen yellow, orange, purple and red, set up dynamic but never overwhelming oppositions with Dry's array of forms and materials.

After dark, the bar accommodates a more boisterous clientèle out for a good time. They can make use of the spacious bar area, leaning in time-honoured fashion against its top, or gathered around in groups. Kelly has retained the original wooden floor, now cleaned and re-sealed but still retaining an authentic roughness clearly visible under the strong, semi-industrial, light fittings. A mélange of original timber, concrete and terrazzo by the door has been retained, together with other elements such as lead-framed windows — in order, according to Kelly, to maintain a sense of history within the bar's impressive spaces.

The design team's strong understanding of what Dry should represent and how it might function has manifested itself in many practical forms. Vague requests by the clients materialized as glass racking towers, underlit shelves for spirits and concealed areas for washing glasses. The cumulative effect is the result of controlled design, mixed with resourcefulness. It is appreciated and accepted by the fluctuating numbers of people who use the bar, which evolves throughout the day from relaxed café to frenetic pre-club bar, through changing but always congenial atmospheres.

Dry 201's glass façade with a Japanese oak door contrasts with the original first-floor frontage.

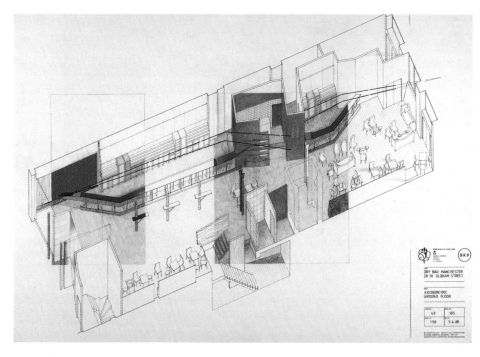

Rendered axonometric diagram drawn before the design was completed. A few details such as the treatment of the wooden poles in the bar area have been slightly altered.

The telegraph pole columns, with steel and wood ledges, are evenly laid out on the renovated wooden floor, adding a vertical contrast to the semi-industrial pendant light fittings, glass panels and lighting gantry.

The curved forms of Jasper Morrison's upholstered furniture contrast with the original sturdy metal girders. Vivid blocks of red and purple colour the inside of wooden partitions flanking the lift to the basement cloakroom.

The 'dragon' of cascading water, glass bowls and reflected light provides a dramatic central focus. The pipes and air-conditioning ducts in the ceiling have been left exposed.

Echoing the curves of the water cascade, the undulating glass screen inside the façade catches some of its reflections, providing a fish-tank effect.

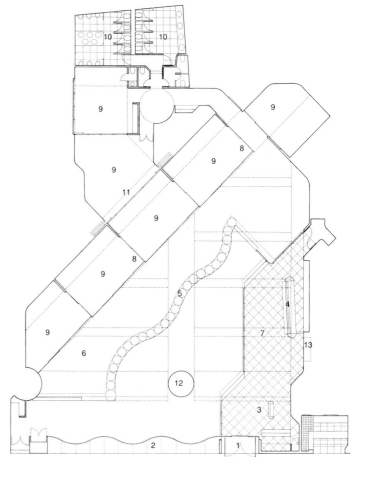

RESTAURANTS, CAFÉS, BARS, CLUBS & HOTELS

2.5
Zen Hong Kong

RICK MATHER ARCHITECTS
Hong Kong

Zebra wood and sliding
acid-etched glass panels
mark off the private
dining areas.

Floor plan. 1 Entrance.
2 Curved glass screen.
3 Reception. 4 Bar.
5 Water cascade.
6 Dining area. 7 Stone
floor. 8 Sliding glass
screens. 9 Private
dining rooms.
10 Toilets. 11 Wood
partitions. 12 Concrete
column. 13 Fish tank.

Having built up the highly successful Zen Chinese restaurant group in London, the owners called upon Rick Mather — creator of Zen W3, Zen Central and a third, more recent, London Zen and subsequently Zen Montreal — to design their flagship restaurant in Hong Kong. The competition was known to be tough: in central Hong Kong the result would have to work or the restaurant would be shortlived.

Located in a basement site in the centre of the city, Zen Hong Kong cost about £1.3 million, and owes its success to Mather's deceptively simple formula: 'You open the place up to the street, in this case to the shopping mall [the newly established, up-market Pacific Place, owned by the Swires Group], so that people can see the activity within, but also so that the street gives something back. And you try to give everyone a good table: against a wall, by a window, or within sight of a window. You need good lighting. You make the bar visible and easily reachable from the door, so that it's a hospitable focus. And then you emphasise the strongest features of the existing space: go with the peculiarities and you get something unique' (*Designers' Journal*, October 1989).

Mather's design encompasses all these tenets, as well as dramatic effects which give Zen Hong Kong its own personality. The essential twist is provided by a 21-metre-long 'dragon', based on the shape of a kite, made up of a series of frosted, shallow glass bowls suspended from stainless steel cables strung across the restaurant. Water is pumped continuously up to the highest bowl, then flows through narrow steel tubes, cascading from bowl to bowl down through the system, way above the diners' heads. A curved granite strip carves a diagonal path across the floor, serving as an anchoring base for the wires securing the bowls. This houses uplighters which

work in unison with low-voltage spots above, diffusing light through the running water, and throwing subtle, dancing reflections across the ceiling.

The restaurant's 11,000-square-foot floor plan is large enough to accommodate this potent thematic device which is 'woven' across its public spaces. Three main areas with varying levels of intimacy have been carefully delineated: a white marble reception; carpeted dining areas around the water cascade, and (unlike the first two London restaurants), private dining rooms behind sliding, acid-etched glass panels which can be pushed back to enlarge the public dining space. 'Every table should be equally desirable,' says Mather, who upholds this principle in his skilfully planned restaurant.

The absence of any ceiling reveals a dramatic view of the massive structure which supports the forty-storey hotel above. Mather has chosen not to cover this, but instead focuses attention upon the more refined materials used elsewhere — marble, rich green-grey carpet, mirror glass and zebra wood, as well as the dynamic *pièce de résistance*: the 'dragon' of water, glass and light, which warns away evil spirits, signifies the lively movement of money, and lures a discerning clientèle.

2.6

Hotel
Il Palazzo

ARCHITECT: Shigeru Uchida
HOTEL AND RESTAURANT DESIGN:
Shigeru Uchida/Ikuyo Mitsuhashi,
Studio 80
DESIGNERS: Aldo Rossi/Morris
Adjmi (Bar El Dorado); Ettore
Sottsass/Mike Ryan/Marco Zanini
(Bar Zibibbo); Gaetano Pesce
(Bar El Liston); Shiro Kuramata
(Bar Oblomova); Alfredo Arribas
(Barna Crossing; see pages 120–123)
Fukuoka, Kyushu, Japan

Japan is currently a conductive and invigorating environment for Western designers able to command the attention of far-sighted developers such as Mitsuhiro Kuzuwa of Jasmac and intermediaries such as Shi Yu Chen (the driving force behind Barna Crossing), who talent-scout for key prestige architectural and interior design projects. Cultural richness provides the definitive password within Japan's intensely competitive business climate, and the strategy of making architecture a vital element in speculative commercial activity has led to major investments in creativity, notably Hotel Il Palazzo.

Fukuoka is a prosperous industrial city in Japan's southern island of Kyushu, with few urban architectural assets to call its own. Haruyoshi, a seedy all-night entertainment area, is unpreposessing raw material for a cultural transformation, but it is here that Kuzuwa's new Hotel Il Palazzo is situated — a dynamic 'monument' to the present and the future, combining expressive design with a classy leisure development which, it is hoped, will serve as a long term catalyst for further urban aggrandizement.

The Italian architect Aldo Rossi was recommended by Shigeru Uchida who, with Ikuyo Mitsuhashi, undertook the hotel's interior design, and also assembled a prestigious team of architects and designers to create individual bars. By engaging Rossi, with his experience of Italian urban planning, Kuzuwa aimed to introduce 'an explosive factor' — a credible and grandly scaled master-plan which anticipates future development. For Kuzuwa, the art of good business can be fuelled by combining the right 'hardware' (the architecture) with the right 'software'

First-floor plan
(entrance level).
1 Piazza. 2 Lobby.
3 Reception. 4 Main
bar. 5 Main restaurant.
6 Kitchen. 7 Toilets.
A El Dorado.
B Zibibbo.
C El Liston.
D Oblomova.

(service and financing) to create an ambience which people are prepared to pay more for.

Il Palazzo occupies a water-front site, with its own white marble piazza. The impact of its huge façade of red travertine marble, devoid of windows, with a grid of eight columns crossed by green copper lintels, is one of grand and stately incongruity, like a warehouse for noble artefacts — an enigmatically regal presence among lesser mortals. From across the river, a motley collection of pitched roofs conceals a huge piazza and two smaller, symmetrically positioned buildings lying by its side. The plan has an urban quality: in anticipation of its symbolic role within Fukuoka, the hotel has been devised as a miniature city, and this image is reflected in the interior design.

The entrance hall echoes the strong symmetry of the building's façade, a rhythmic blend of stripes and grids in Chinese quince veneer and soft grey-green onyx terrazzo, which establishes a warm and sophisticated tone. Continuing the Italianate mood, a central colonnade of 'arch' columns set at regular intervals divides the space into an array of subtly lit smooth and polished geometrical forms. Upstairs in the restaurant and bar designed by Uchida, the same aesthetic envelopes the space with its subtle graduations of scale. The desire to give the hotel's identity a 'sense of communality' involved Uchida, as art director, in designing numerous ranges of furniture, lighting, clocks and other accessories. These are backed up by Ikko Tanaka's graphic identity scheme, installed throughout the hotel.

Bedrooms are smart, restrained and restful, and come in Japanese and Western styles, both of which employ Uchida's repertoire of soft woods (quince, cherry, shina, beech). In the shuttered Western rooms, the solidity of blue and earth-toned sofas provides a neutral backdrop to details such as beacon-shaped 'Dear Fausto' table and floor lights. In an exterior-interior connection, red travertine, a mainstay of the hotel's façade, is used on anteroom floors in both room types.

Uchida, sensing that the myriad of themed restaurants found in Japanese hotels was becoming a rather stale formula, decided instead to instal one restaurant/bar and no fewer than four bars, to attract both guests and locals. Their design was commissioned from a star cast of predominantly Western designers, each of whom was asked to create an atmospheric interior within individual spaces of identical volume in the hotel's 'outhouses'. Following the hotel's opening, the sequence of highly expressive interpretations brought an instant bout of bar-hopping until favourites were inevitably elected.

El Dorado, designed by Aldo Rossi with Morris Adjmi, largely retains the perpendicular lines of the original space,

in order to create a strangely mystical place with the air of a chapel, named after the mythical South American site made entirely of gold. Entering from the balcony, the visitor is greeted by a stunning gold wall, a miniature replica of the hotel's façade, an illuminated grid glowing behind the bar. By contrast with this enshrined image, simple red banquette seating with marble-topped tables running the length of the room have a modest air. The atmosphere is intended to encourage contemplation of the glittering promise represented by Il Palazzo's monumental splendour.

In giving Zibibbo (named after a sweet grape from Southern Italy) an Italianate slant on its romantic theme, Sottsass distinguishes his tiny bar from less salubrious associations with the numerous seedy 'love hotels' in the vicinity of Il Palazzo, a phenomenon he nonetheless found amusing. Specifically conceived as a lovers' retreat of an elevated and idealized kind, Zibibbo is firmly rooted in Sottsass' home territory and the sociable, easy-going and basic décor of Italian bars. Its somewhat confined space uses the full height to incorporate the forms of a miniature 'village': a marble-columned structure with a semi-enclosed upper area and an eyrie reached by stairways.

Under an azure blue ceiling painted with stars, interlinked parapets, windows, terraces and stairways at different levels provide a variety of suitably secluded

In a guest room, 'August', a laminated and formed beechwood chair with cherrywood legs, and a stained and lacquered Shina wood veneer side table, are illuminated by a 'Dear Fausto' light and translucent white glass and marble wall lights.

The entrance lobby combines quince veneer and onyx terrazzo for a warm and classically inspired appearance which continues the symmetry of the exterior. Uchida modified the insides of the columns (which hold recessed lighting fixtures) to emphasise the perpendicular lines of the colonnade. Soft grey-green onyx veneer is also used for table tops. The gridded wall and ceiling panels are made of quince veneer stained with clear matte polyurethane varnish.

The first-floor bar also employs a narrow repertoire of materials and shapes to great effect.

The entrance staircase of
Aldo Rossi's El Dorado
is made of riveted steel
panels with marble treads
and glass-and-steel risers.
Red leather banquette
seating and marble tables
are placed on a
diagonally set marble
floor: the atmosphere is
that of a tiny chapel.
Behind the bar, a
miniature, illuminated
version of the hotel's
façade in gold leaf on
wood decorates the wall.

rendez-vous (and perhaps a few voyeuristic vantage points?) to be explored. Using 'modest' materials such as terrazzo, marble, wood and painted metal in a primary colour scheme (a bright yellow panelled wood watchtower surrounded by blue walls and ceiling, and white columns with red furniture), Sottsass' design accentuates the bold juxtaposition of scaled-down architectural forms, which are subtly back-lit to create intimate, shadowy effects gleaming through the bar's many apertures.

The lure of El Liston, Gaetano Pesce's contribution (the name means 'to stroll' in Venetian dialect), can be

attributed to the soft, womb-like recesses of its labyrinthine spaces in which guests can linger for hours. Of all four bars, Pesce's is the one which most thoroughly disguises its basic rectilinear form, with an anarchically convoluted route layered with esoteric, intricate detail. The plan was generated from the profile of a drinking figure, with an anthropomorphically shaped bar counter at one end reached by a long stair linking three levels of intimate drinking booths. New materials and techniques are applied in dark and sultry tones bombarded with clashing lemon yellow and acid green. Pesce's crazy paving, looming ceiling forms and mottled ink blot walls, along with lurid silicon rubber lights, provide Il Palazzo with a den of stylized disorder to celebrate inebriation and spontaneity.

By comparison, Oblomova is a bright, double-height space with a few

synthetic than Pesce's but consists of a few pristine elements in subtly tinted acrylic and anodized aluminium. Here, the organic forms of nature are not allowed to generate energy, but are heavily stylized. A tall series of spindly 'lamp post' lights sprout even rows of curled aluminium halogen lights containing artificial flowers trapped in transparent acrylic. Designed as a rarefied place in which to consume vodka and caviar, and ponder on the tonal qualities of colour and form, Oblomova's ethereal presence is self-contained and completely divorced from both monumentality and voluptuousness.

Oblomova's pearlized
pink woodchip walls
contain a delicate and
unearthly series of
acrylic and aluminium
furniture and pillar
lamps, in stark contrast
to the other bars.
Kuramata described the
bar's open, sculptural
interior, reached by
quince veneered stairs,
as a 'temporary, false
and hypothetical place'.

beautifully regimented decorative elements which seem to float within sleek pearl-coat finished walls, made of OSB, a wood chipboard made to look like marble. Shiro Kuramata's design is no less

The labyrinth of
Gaetano Pesce's El
Liston features an
enterprising array of
materials, including
urethane in diverse
colours, epoxy resin,

rubber, coloured
papier-mâché stucco
and concrete paper,
used to fashion organic
forms which conceal a
structure made of
wood, metal and glass.

RESTAURANTS, CAFÉS, BARS, CLUBS & HOTELS

The brass surfaces of the bar reverberate with reflected light, assisted by small fluorescent strips set under the bar shelf. The curved panel set above the shelf also echoes the bar next door, but is rendered here in a warmer metal.

2.7

Polytechnic of North London Theatre Bar

ARCHITECTURE RESEARCH UNIT POLYTECHNIC OF NORTH LONDON London, UK

The Architecture Research Unit (ARU) of the Polytechnic of North London was founded in 1978, and combines teaching, practice and research. Directed by architect Florian Beigel, its specialist architectural practice is devoted to smaller-scale projects in the public realm with a high degree of research input. The Unit is selective in its choice of project work, and only pursues activities which engage its passionately held concerns for an architecture demonstrating 'gregariousness, conviviality, authenticity, simplicity and thoughtfulness'.

For a recent project for the Polytechnic itself the ARU was set the following brief: to design a public bar open to the street, where the general public and students could meet, with an adjoining saloon bar, as the first phase of a larger project to restore a large, barrel-vaulted Victorian music hall. 'The Great Hall', as it is called, will eventually provide a multi-purpose facility for drama, dance, music, sports, conferences and seminars. The bar creates a link between the ornate nineteenth-century building and a rather sober-looking 1960s building running alongside it.

The main bar is a long, low space with a metal-topped bar extending its entire length from the street to a glass door leading to an added staircase providing access to the theatre's main hall. A floor of concrete paving slabs continues from the front ramp down the length of the room, emphasising its openness to the street; above, a long strip of suspended aluminium sheet carries fluorescent lighting. New door openings have been made, and large windows installed with clear double-glazing (which can be covered over with sliding steel shutters). A bold, lower-case, neon sign announces the bar's presence, and creates a clear connection with the life of the street.

All the furniture and fittings have been designed, prototyped and marketed by Florian Beigel's own architectural practice to a very high standard of craftsmanship, attained with the help of sub-contractors. Using very basic materials — medium density fibreboard for benches, concrete paving slabs, various types of non-precious sheet metals — and plain, unadorned forms, the architects have created furniture with a dignified character which goes way beyond the confines of fashion, and gives the bar a timelessness rarely experienced in the

often aggressively themed pubs found all over the UK.

The austere forms and the juxtaposition of various treatments of metal and wood represent durable structures: the chairs combine a folded steel frame with a shaped birch plywood seat and back. Long, semi-partitioned benches running along the wall echo the traditional forms found in public houses from earlier eras. Small partitions and bar shelving in purple and red tones complement the metal and wood forms, contrast with the yellow walls and grey ceiling, and generally add an up-beat feel to this sociable space.

The old walls of the adjoining nineteenth-century building have been given a new finish in a subtle, two-tone shade of yellow-brown 'nicotine', providing a warm environment. In the smaller room, with its high ceiling, light plays on a number of reflective surfaces. There is a large arched window to the street, towards which a mirror on an adjoining wall is angled, reflecting the movement outside. Here, the tables are topped with brass, a traditional bar surface material. Long shelves of brass sheet on another wall reflect moving faces and create golden-toned versions of a long metal reflector behind the bar. The floor in this

The main bar seen in the mirror on the rear wall, showing the rolled steel frame of the bar, in front of plainly wrought shelves and a curved aluminium reflector. Running the length of the bar is a folded aluminium sheet lamp, with fluorescent lighting fixtures.

An original arch window lights the robust wooden furniture, parquet floor, brass table tops and wall mirror.

A closer look at the furniture designed for the bar: Vivonne chairs, with folded steel frames coated with polyester powder and shaped birch ply seats and backs; Burzet bar tables in folded sheet steel with matte brass surfaces; La Roquebrou benches in medium density fibreboard with a clear matte polyurethane finish and steel legs coated with polyester powder.

unassuming space is made of traditional herringbone parquet. Although there are no actual Victorian design details, the building's history is acknowledged and given a twentieth-century interpretation; it is made workable with efficient meeting and drinking spaces, and adjoining facilities.

Beyond the end of the long bar are telephone niches, a folded metal sheet staircase, and toilets on the ground floor (for the disabled) and the first floor. Combinations of materials continue to be used in an innovative way: wall panels in cement/sawdust composite and solid melamine, used together with aluminium angle frames and bent sheet ledges.

The ARU's desire to benefit a specific community led them to involve local people with the design, not just the results. Unusually for such a small project, over fifty locally based sub-contractors provided various types of craft skills, which were coordinated by the ARU. The various applications of folded sheet metal, for instance, were fabricated by the Holloway Sheet Metal Works over the road.

In their design for the two adjoining bars, Beigel and his extended team have shown a thoughtful understanding of the existing fabric of the respective buildings. In the resulting interior they have achieved a subtle and coherent balance between competing desires: to bring about an acceptable authenticity and to create new forms which are compositionally rich and based on advanced research.

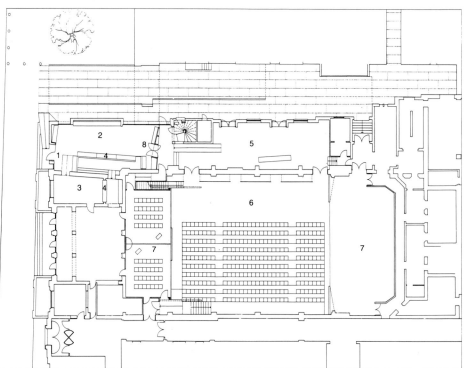

Plan of the 'Great Hall' theatre and bar. 1 Bar entrance. 2 Public bar. 3 Saloon bar. 4 Counter. 5 Great Hall foyer. 6 Great Hall with sideways seating. 7 Pavilion rooms. 8 Access to foyer.

RESTAURANTS, CAFÉS, BARS, CLUBS & HOTELS

The view from the
staircase, showing
Starck's velvet and
pearwood chairs and
padded grey velvet wall.
The curtain wall is held
back (far right) to
create an opening and
access to the toilets.

2.8

La Flamme d'Or, Asahi Building

PHILIPPE STARCK
Tokyo, Japan

As corporate identities go, the gigantic golden flame perched atop the Asahi Beer Company's new urn-shaped building is an unmissable symbol of corporate health in the downbeat environs of Asakusa in north Tokyo. This audacious architectural statement, built to celebrate the company's centenary and 'the promise of the twenty-first century', could not happen anywhere but in Japan. By choosing this particular location next door to the company's rather more low-key headquarters, Asahi is paving the way for the development of the whole area.

The powerful-looking building, rendered in polished black granite with a

luminescent 'plinth' representing energy. The large numbers of fashion-conscious visitors that queue daily around its massive form want to experience the dramatic forms of this latest project for themselves.

La Flamme d'Or's restaurant and bar areas, designed on two levels connected by a steep staircase, are precociously mixed in an exotic playground of design elements. The sheer height of the hall — and its subtly lit, curvaceous, bulbous columns like petrified globules sitting between floor and ceiling — immediately create for the visitor an exaggerated, stage-set atmosphere. The wall is a continuous half-curve on one side cut into by the upper drinking area. Starck's fertile repertoire of theatrical and organic elements creates a fusion of grand shapes and draped walls in muted grey-green shades. In this unique 'beer hall' neat rows of upholstered, high-backed chairs in orange, red and grey velvet sit around simple wooden tables, ready for the onslaught of Super Dry beer-drinking.

As an artistic creation, rather than a 'designed' space in the conventional sense, this is the venue for a rather saucy dream. Lacking the detailed trickery and enigmatic power of Teatriz, the towering spaces of the interior are glamorous and grand in scale, and the gestures playfully anarchic. Above all, its symbolism exerts magnetic pulling power.

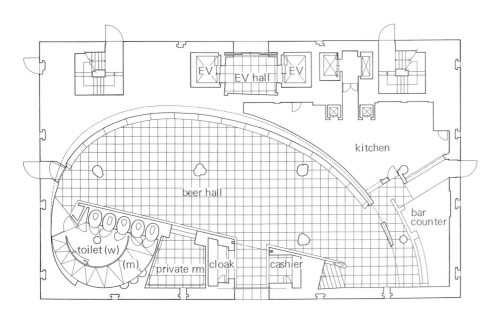

Ground-floor plan.

total square footage of 2705 square metres, contains a brasserie, restaurant, bar and a multi-purpose meeting room. It cost about 10 billion yen, including the expense of the reinforcements needed to carry the infamous steel flame.

According to Starck, the construction is based around a combination of symbols: the flame denotes passion, the urn mystery, and the flight of back-lit glass block steps form a

The decorative back of the curtain wall, painted by Jean Michel Alberola, marks the way to the waiting area.

Starck's black granite urn, topped with the gleaming gold steel flame, asserts an outlandish presence among the skyscrapers of Asakusa, and is a potent symbol of Asahi's revived fortunes.

A long staircase, flanked by a towering, organically shaped column, leads down to a white marble floor. Cornice lighting emphasises the height of the beer hall.

The women's toilets are warm red, with opaque glass cubicle walls, leaning taps in stainless steel tube which sprout from the floor, and small mirrors and hand driers on legs.

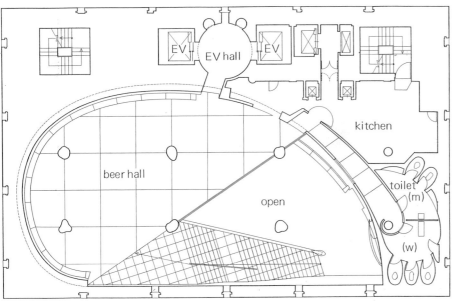

First-floor plan.

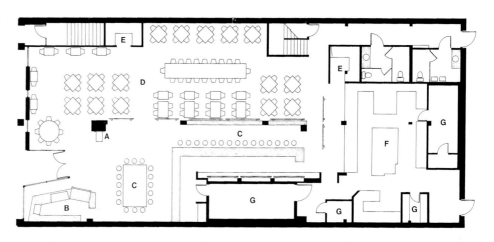

Ground-floor plan.
A Host station.
B Tortilla counter.
C Bar area.
D Dining area.
E Waiters' station.
F Kitchen. G Storage.

**SCHWEITZER BIM
Santa Monica, Los Angeles,
California, USA**

Both aurally and aesthetically, Border Grill is one of the loudest restaurants in Los Angeles. Although it has been awarded numerous accolades for its exciting cross-cultural cuisine, the Grill's acoustics are hardly the most sophisticated in town. But that is mere detail in a project which mixes wild murals based on Mexican folk-art imagery by London-based illustrators Su Huntley and Donna Muir with orange-red corral fences, midnight-blue water jugs and yellow pine school-house furniture. It is a riot of raucous but appealingly exuberant colours and forms.

Architects Josh Schweitzer BIM were well known to owner-chefs Susan Feniger and Mary Sue Milliken, culinary cult heroes in a city which takes its innovative restaurant scene very seriously. Schweitzer was an habitué of the original Border Grill on Melrose Avenue, a tiny and less extrovert space which packed in customers. His first job for the clients was the design, with David Kellen, of City restaurant in 1985, which was minimally decorated and served French, Indian and Thai food.

For Feniger and Milliken's newest venture, Schweitzer completely gutted an old, two-storey former brewery, and transformed it into a spectacular room partitioned by a series of rough-hewn 'cattle guard' fences painted the same vivid shade of blood-orange as one of the restaurant's exquisite sorbets. Made of lumber in jagged shapes, these fences screen the mezzanine, kitchen and bar area, allowing an irrepressible, Angeleno chumminess to pervade the space. The bar area incorporates a huge, square wooden table for communal drinking, while at the front of the restaurant is a counter with a station for making fresh tortillas. The building's original front façade has been replaced by a gold anodized aluminium grid filled with a jigsaw of glass and stucco panels, which draws casual clientèle into the spectacle of colour and movement within.

Schweitzer reconfigured the high, flat ceiling to eliminate any hint of austerity, making a low, undulating surface articulated into smaller trapezoidal panels. It does nothing to soften the noise resounding through the restaurant, but it does unite the murals on the ceiling and wall areas in an intoxicatingly giddy dance.

Just as Feniger and Milliken's enterprising menus are inspired by numerous trips to Mexico and Central America, the murals by Su Huntley and Donna Muir are a celebration of south-of-the-border ritual and fiesta. Intended to work from all angles, they show elongated forms from Mexican folklore, including the traditional Judas figure depicted as a low-life tom-cat puffing on cigars among alcohol-swilling and cavorting characters in a galaxy of eyes, hands and shooting stars. Napkins, ashtrays and publicity items also come from the same hands. The solid, deep-hued glassware — chosen by co-owner Gai Gherardi of l.a. Eyeworks — is set out on economical Southern yellow pine tables, designed by Schweitzer and fabricated by the contractor on site at a fraction of the cost of commercially purchased items. Low-slung bar stools, another of his economical designs, were made in Mexico, and existing school-house chairs were painted yellow ochre to complement the tables.

The rear bar area is an open working space strewn with hefty bowls of fruit and jars of juice and horchata.

Border Grill's bar, resplendent with blood-orange top and 'cattle guard' panels screening the rest of the restaurant. The bar stools, made from bent steel rods, add a further low-budget, high-impact effect. The ceiling panels hang at various heights, but show a continuous painting, by Su Huntley and Donna Muir, which develops various themes around the room.

A complex programme is accommodated within a constrained, elongated space by creating three integrated segments: bar, dining room and kitchen, each with a distinct character.

The dining room is a largely naturally lit space with a wide glazed street façade dramatized by a ceiling construction of curved steel beams and lateral wooden slats. Above this, an undulating ceiling of bent drywall sheets conceals ducting. Light plays on its ribbed forms, green-blue stained floor and marble tables embedded with fossils.

2.10
Angeli Mare

BUILDING
Marina del Rey, Los Angeles,
California, USA

The idea that the creation of architecture is based on the accumulation of stimuli which communicate its meaning is particularly attractive in Los Angeles, the city which 'brings it all together' (its official slogan). For Michele Saee and his fellow designers Richard Lundquist and Sam Solhaug of Building, the creation of an identity for a third Angeli restaurant — this time serving seafood at Marina del Rey — meant an engagement with the significance of its oceanic context.

The 4000-square-foot site, set in a shopping mall context, was thoroughly uninspiring: it was awkwardly proportioned, and also just down the street from the vastly superior site of Saee's new retail interior for Ecru (see pages 146–9). Saee took the elongated space (140 feet of façade × 30 feet), and divided it into three sections — bar, dining room and kitchen — with a street-facing entrance in the middle. Each section has a specific character, but the three are carefully integrated, and articulated almost as if they formed the head, body and tail of a fish, one facet of the oceanic theme applied through abstracted biomorphic forms.

The dining room has a relaxed ambience assisted by streams of natural light from the restaurant's wide glass façade. Saee throws out numerous conceptual readings of the effect he tried to create, which combine *al fresco* eating with an evocative suggestion of marine life (under water — even inside a fish, or a whale). The space's sculptural forms beg attention — for example, a curved ceiling of undulating wave-forms, which covers all the detritus of air-conditioning. Below this, a layer of curved steel columns and wooden beams evoke a dual association with fish vertebrae and skeletal boat frames. An overhead trellis effect gives an airy, outdoor atmosphere rare among LA's restaurants.

Blue-green stained wooden floors merge with textured grey upholstered banquette seats, against which are positioned dining tables topped with marble in which shellfish fossils are embedded; along the glazed front wall a 'water line' is incised. At the back, the kitchen is visible to diners eating under the protective framework of the ceiling ribs. Shielding the wine racks at the bar-end of the restaurant is a gigantic sculptural form in dark wood and steel like the archetypal reclining figure sited outside in a garden or park.

The contrasting tones and shapes of wood used in the interior and exterior, particularly around the more contemplative space of the bar, point to expressive curvilinear forms contained and concealed within a harder, more rectilinear shell. Instead of enjoying a wide, exposed façade, the bar is enigmatically shielded from the street by dark wooden panelling and a convex 'prow' of glass planes. Light-coloured concave wooden panels, cut off just below the table tops, reflect light drawn in from the convex glass window. A strip of light seeps in below, and between the bar and the concealed window tables a skylight draws light in from above, emphasising its height and length. Saee's wooden walls, partitions, entrance, bar counter, wine rack and ceiling structure are each individually shaped, custom-made constructions: their crafted forms set up a rich dialogue.

The bar is concealed from the main façade by inverted, blond wooden panelling. Parallel lines of lights clasped in tiny 'claws' extend over the bar, which is enclosed within a curved wooden pelmet.

The downstairs bar has a dark but intimate setting, articulated by a variety of subtle lighting effects. A polished black marble bar curves almost the entire length of the room.

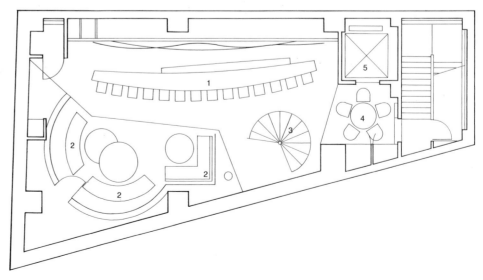

Floor plan of lower basement bar. 1 Bar counter. 2 Seating. 3 Staircase. 4 Enclosed bar. 5 Elevator.

RESTAURANTS, CAFÉS, BARS, CLUBS & HOTELS

2.11
Set/Off Nɔy

**TAKASHI SUGIMOTO,
SUPER POTATO CO. LTD**
Tokyo, Japan

Sugimoto, who calls himself a 'space environment designer', is an old hand at this amorphous discipline, with a roll-call of cafés and bars in Tokyo to his name: Radio; Old New, Be-in; Ex; Libre Space; Bar Set/Off. Now he has created a second version of the original Set/Off, in the Shinjuku district. It is a dual-option design, set in a two-level basement, with one bar nestling on top of the other, each with its distinctive atmosphere.

Descending a rugged stone staircase, the visitor enters the first bar, a modest 80.4 square metres including the kitchen, and is faced by a broad wood-and-stone collage which swathes the back of the bar. Intricate geometrical forms, echoing the wooden assemblages of sculptors such as Louise Nevelson, have been plucked from a variety of sources including offcuts and redundant objects. Processing these forms by hand, Sugimoto imbues them with a new significance, and gives the bar a unique quality. While the collage shows shadow-forms of new, untested products, the bar's furniture represents the smooth results of ideas united with technology. Solid walnut wood features in both, but the satin surface of the lacquer-painted bar top, table and chairs makes clear the distinction.

Below this bar lurks another, slightly larger (92.8 square metres) drinking area, with an altogether more ethereal atmosphere. Taking light as his theme, Sugimoto makes this the ordering device around which all the other, solid forms unite. He achieves his intention of creating a strongly lit environment by the use of subtle and indirect lighting. With fixtures which glaze, glimmer and create a shimmering wall of animated, illuminated pin-holes, he creates a variety of effects to add drama to this tiny space. Walls of polished black marble and a circular, frosted glass table add rich reverberation.

Glowing blue uplighters illuminate a frosted glass table, itself a reflective panel for a wall of glimmering pin holes. Above, a softer light is emitted from overlapping plaster board, cut in zig zags to fan its effects.

RESTAURANTS, CAFÉS, BARS, CLUBS & HOTELS

A sunny, enclosed, ground-floor dining area with a glass roof and an external shade cloth. The designers replaced hardwood beams with ones made of lightweight steel, laterally braced, without needing to remove the glazing.

Rockpool

D4 DESIGN PTY LTD
Sydney, Australia

The walls and ceiling of the first-floor Oyster Bar have been painted with an aquamarine pearlized paint finish. Mixed with this swirling effect are aluminium and wood veneer chairs, and an area of parquetry leading to the bar.

The brief given to D4 by client Neil Perry, one of Australia's most celebrated young chefs, was to 'create the best restaurant in the country'. Drawing on their experience in theatre design, D4 have created a dramatic solution.

Rockpool is situated in an area of Sydney known as 'The Rocks' which, in recent years, say the designers, has taken on a lamentable 'Disneyland' approach to history, with people in period costume parading the streets. The building itself dates back to 1870 — very old for Australia — and is situated minutes away from where the first European settlement was made. Its original fabric was in a very bad state, having suffered from numerous bouts of substandard additions.

Because of its historic location, the building was subject to a whole range of conservation requirements and building restrictions. Under the 'heritage maintenance' rules of the local authority, virtually nothing from the original structure could be demolished. Within the limited time available, D4 undertook basic restoration of the exterior. Termite-damaged hardwood beams were stabilized, and eighty years of paint scraped from the façade. Old wall surfaces which did not fit the proposed design were lined and 'entombed' intact. D4 avoided giving the building a fake vernacular, but concentrated on creating a wholly new design within the walls.

The plan is based on the original nineteenth-century layout of a master building linked to service buildings via a covered walkway. The restaurant is set on two floors, with a third for administration, and a basement storage area. The ground-floor walkway sets the principal arrival and service axis, and also provides a long vista through the building which can be seen easily from the street along with parading clientèle and waiters. The entrance is intended to present a dramatic introduction to the restaurant, in which the lighting, graphics and other special features have been contributed by other consultants.

D4 wanted to create a restaurant which was smart and upmarket, but unintimidating: a design to celebrate the indulgent spirit of the seafood cuisine created by Neil Perry, without interpreting the nautical theme too literally. It began with the distinctive, wide-backed Rockpool chair, with cast aluminium legs and frame supporting a plywood seat back finished in dark brown Palisander veneer. Particular care was lavished on this item, which is used throughout the restaurant. From it D4 evolved mobile waiters' stations, ice buckets, menu holders, tables, light fittings and other details using aluminium, chrome, stainless steel, wood veneer and mirrored panels. Four different types of lights were designed, each with spun aluminium dishes, laser cut and given a bright, anodized finish. In addition, a few of the lights originated from the air vent fittings from a yacht, which were modified with built-in standard lamp holders. All the freestanding elements relate closely to each other in terms of their materials, but retain their integrity as individual objects. Somehow the final effect is not quite cluttered, because the plan and circulation route are kept relatively simple.

Coming through the front door, the customer is confronted by a rampway, and on the right a steel-framed, carpeted staircase – dramatic 'devices' to which the designers wished to give prominence in order to provide a strong circulation route around the furniture and lighting. Dining areas are located throughout the building to accommodate 'the various psychologies of prospective diners'. The largest dining area is situated on the right of the entrance. Further along the ramp, variously sized and lit areas of a more formal persuasion can be found.

An emphasised sense of position is provided by mirrors positioned at strategic points in the restaurant; one in the front area allows a view of the back room. The entire right-hand wall of the restaurant functions as acoustic panelling, either wrapped with patterned fabric or screened with perforated customwood.

The client originally insisted on an open kitchen, but D4 – anxious not to have too much noise and light spilling out into the eating areas – steered him towards another solution. Curved screens and angled panels frame various kitchen activities, and divert diners' eyes to other areas of the restaurant.

The small first-floor Oyster Bar has, appropriately, a mother-of-pearl paint finish on the ceiling. A decorative sweep of

parquet flooring with a star motif creates a strong axis, leading up to the bar itself, where four dazzling headlights are set into panels between the bar stools. On the side wall, white neon strips divide silvered panels to give the bar a more dramatically lit ambience. 'Going to a restaurant is like going to a show,' say D4. Ultimately this unapologetic delight in drama is tempered with a disarming directness and practicality. Completed in March 1989, and the result of twelve months' work, Rockpool cost A$950,000, of which the building component was A$850,000.

The spacious kitchen area at the front of the restaurant is efficiently laid out, partially screened, and walled with acoustic panels. Freestanding mobile waiters' stations in aluminium and Palisander veneer can be easily positioned anywhere in the restaurant and equipped for precise needs. The staircase leading to the first-floor Oyster Bar is as unimposing as possible.

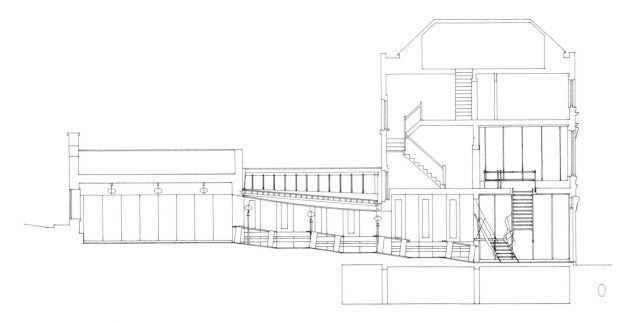

Section showing the long 'catwalk' ramp running from the entrance on the right through the building (ground-floor restaurant, and staircase to the first-floor Oyster Bar and storage areas).

One of the kitchen areas, partially screened with a reflective panel.

A wall of panels wrapped in Missoni fabric adds colour to the grey, silver and brown scheme used throughout. The bowl-shaped aluminium ice bucket is one of a family of custom-designed items.

Traditional ways of dining are presented in the second-floor room, with its raised wooden entry platform, tatami mats to kneel on, and red lacquer walls.

The austere forms of the ground-floor bar, situated at the bottom of the staircase in an open-plan area covered with rubber tiles. Black steel chairs are sleek and economical.

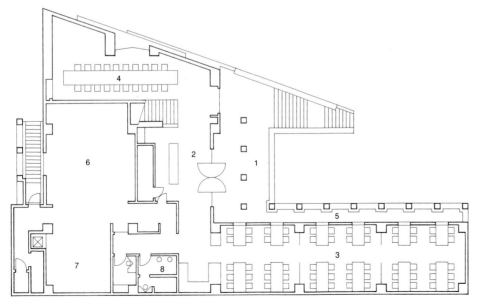

First-floor plan.
1 Terrace. 2 Reception.
3 Dining area. 4 Bar/
dining area. 5 Balcony.
6 Kitchen. 7 Staff
room. 8 Toilets.

2.13

Migoto

**SHIN TAKAMATSU
ARCHITECT & ASSOCIATES**
Kyoto, Japan

The restaurant Migoto is a relatively modest building compared with Takamatsu's other, intensely totemic projects in Kyoto and elsewhere in Japan. His tense and dynamic structures are characterized by the overwrought industrial 'musculature' of their exterior, and seem to resist the omnipotent and graceless forms of modern urban Japan with a strange, subversive language of their own. Although undeniably powerful and compelling, they are unpalatable to some Westerners, their conceptual origin appearing to be partly rooted in science-fiction fantasy.

The owners of Migoto, which specializes in *yakiniku* (Korean grilled meat dishes), like many of Takamatsu's clients, know that investing in new architecture can help increase their turnover, add extra cachet to their cuisine, and draw customers to a possibly hitherto unexceptional location. An architect with

Takamatsu's reputation for inventiveness frequently receives a fairly open brief, giving him the opportunity to create his daring forms unshackled by the restrictions regarded as normal in the West.

Migoto's 15-metre-high glazed tower is set in a triangle of reinforced concrete, and juts in front of the main building which is set back from the road. The tower's raised height is embellished from below by a curious splayed 'bird wing' in metal, an abstract sculpture with an ambiguous role. As a stylized 'defence mechanism', it protects the building's raised side entrance from the street, a common characteristic of Takamatsu's buildings, and its diagonal angle harmonizes the steep flight of stairs. The building's strong identity, however, ultimately derives from the cylinder of tall glass panels set in a robust, two-tiered metal frame, which makes it a landmark in a dull and anonymous streetscape.

Visitors lured by what Takamatsu terms an 'emphatic sign' see first the tower then, within, a large bronze patterned wall sculpture flanking the

staircase from the first to the second floor. Raised from the ground, the building has a floor area of 791 square metres, and incorporates a covered parking lot in the basement. At night the transparent, illuminated elements take on the prominence of an abstract 'sign' overlooking the city; its precise meaning may be unclear, but it certainly fulfils one role, which is architecture as symbol.

The interior, though made up of bold forms, has an inviting airiness and lack of pretension. The various restaurant areas are restrained and spacious, including two traditional adjoining spaces on the second floor with measured tatami mats, sleek dark red walls and low tables at which diners kneel. Only the expanse of mirror at the end of one room introduces the possibility of unreal space, repeating the room's unadorned simplicity.

Other eating areas feature a floor surface imitating the combed gravel of Japanese temple gardens, adorned with large rock sculptures. Plain white walls and chic black chairs and tables are the only other elements in this brightly lit room.

The staircase linking the floors rises over the kitchen below, and features overlapping diagonal panels bolted to an aluminium frame. This solidity is broken half-way up by a single opaque glass panel visible from the exterior: yet another tantalising sign to be unscrambled.

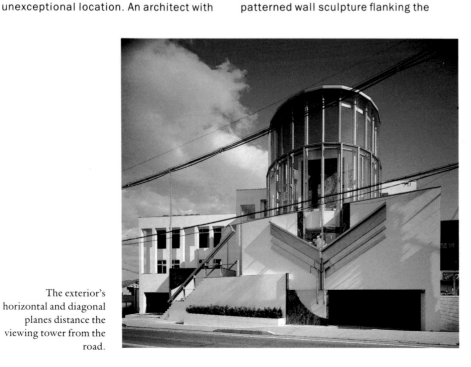

The exterior's horizontal and diagonal planes distance the viewing tower from the road.

In the bar, table tops of small squares of stained plane wood are held level by curved cast metal arms. Wedge-shaped stools in red, yellow or black leather are mixed with leather armchairs backed with wood. On the wall, metal bracket lights sit at intervals between purple leather-clad panels flanked by areas of polished burgundy stone.

Ground-floor plan with the main entrance on the right, and the foyer surrounding an oval lounge bar with a staircase leading to the basement bar/club.

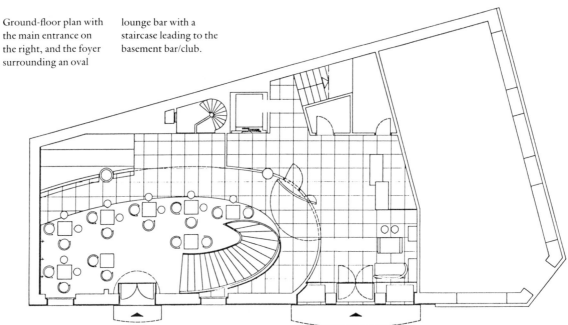

RESTAURANTS, CAFÉS, BARS, CLUBS & HOTELS

La Villa

MARIE-CHRISTINE DORNER
Paris, France

Based in St Germain des Prés, La Villa is the former Hôtel d'Isly (a small establishment dating from the 1750s), renovated, revamped and retitled by Marie-Christine Dorner for owners Vincent Darnaud and Alain Copet. Leaving the exterior relatively untouched, she has concentrated on giving a formerly bohemian but lacklustre family hotel a new identity with a wide range of furniture, an adventurous sense of colour and a great mastery of details.

Dorner designed the 1,200-square-metre hotel for regular travellers of some discernment who preferred a personal, individualized, even highly charged, atmosphere. Its façade features clear glass doors and windows with chic greenery. From the street, a painting is visible on the wall facing the entrance;

once inside, a yellow-and-purple patterned rug provides an immediate indication of the aesthetic of the hotel's more public areas. A small reception area is on one side of a curved space leading to the elevators, created by the introduction of a large oval wall encompassing the bar. Through a large sliding door in the wall, the bar, 'conceived as a place in which to dream' and decorated in regal violet and mauve, is resplendent with saffron yellow leather seating arranged in a long swathe around a cat's cradle of metal balustrading. The swirling metal forms duck and dive around a stairwell leading to a small nightclub below, designed in lurid shades of ochre, purple and crimson.

La Villa's bedrooms are varied in size, and their disparities are artfully accentuated by Dorner's use of different colour schemes in each room: red, cream and grey; red, cream and gold; light blue, dark blue and white; light blue, white and purple. Some are more sombre and ascetic; others more extrovert and sensuous. All have unusual details: leather headboards, two-tone leather-and-wood writing desks, sandblasted glass basins, oval metal room numbers. Even before the visitor enters his or her designated private world, there is a reminder of the room number reflected in light on the corridor carpet, a nice touch of trickery.

Not all visitors will find everything to their satisfaction: to see yourself in a long mirror you have to stand in the bath, and the light switches could confuse. Applying

Compared with the warmth of the bedrooms, the bathrooms exude a more restrained chic, as seen here through sliding doors of plane wood with splash motif metal handles.

a little basic psychology, Dorner understood that a traveller arriving in a foreign town needs to feel immediately secure, in a space he or she can easily identify with. As a result, she conceived each room as a cocoon, with the bathroom serving as the transition area. Consequently, some of the smaller, warmer-toned rooms are positively womb-like, representing a rather different (but equally valid) compositional approach from that applied by Écart at the Hotel Wasserturm (see pages 132–5). Here the senses are approached more directly: coldness and warmth are intermingled. The bathroom – cold, but comfortable – forms 'a metaphor of a natural landscape': a cascade of water flows down behind a sloping cliff of marble, and forms a pool in the hand basin, made of thick, sandblasted, luminous glass.

Although the colours and proportions of the rooms vary, the entrance, wardrobe and bathroom are all designed in the same materials (glass, mirror, marble, nickel), which helps to create a satisfyingly homogeneous space. The warm bedroom is isolated from the bathroom by a double sliding door made of plane wood.

Both ceiling and floor are inset by horizontal lines – a simplified version of the La Villa logo flashes contrasting colour across the carpets – and white lighting units, 'luminous clouds' into which small adjustable spotlights are fixed. They bring a sense of dynamic movement to the rooms; by contrast, the vertical surfaces are more sober, and painted in light colours.

Dorner, whose design work to date has been predominantly furniture, adopts a full-blown aesthetic in keeping with early twentieth-century French designers such as Robert Mallet-Stevens who espoused the cause of decoration. On a restricted budget, she has created a rich mixture of colours and forms for La Villa, giving its individual image a sensuous edge and an air of escapism. Beyond this, the design's strength ultimately lies in its imaginative detailing rather than in the imposition of any new far-reaching structure.

Colour combinations in the bedrooms vary from vivid to muted. Here, there is a suite of writing desk, armchair and stool in purple leather and plane wood. Taffeta-covered ceilings hold suspended, stylized cloud forms which house the lighting.

The bedroom furniture in this room has a monochrome dignity. The lighting can be adjusted to create a variety of effects.

The oval bar area, a dramatic combination of brightly coloured leather, stone, wood and cast metal.

The reception is a bare, low-key area with a functional air. Light is emitted from the sides of a suspended ceiling along the adjacent corridor, and from industrial spotlights.

Axonometric diagram.

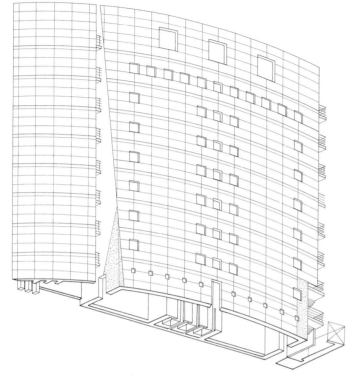

The raised bathroom area of one of the hotel's bedrooms, screened by a curve of opaque glass mounted on a concrete slab. Above the tiled floor, simple fittings for the basin protrude from a tall, slim mirror fixed in front of exposed concrete walls.

RESTAURANTS, CAFÉS, BARS, CLUBS & HOTELS

2.15

D-Hotel

D-Hotel's façade from the street shows the distorted perspective of its sharpened edges, which appear to be no more than leaning two-dimensional walls.

**KIYOSHI SEY TAKEYAMA/
AMORPHE ARCHITECTS
& ASSOCIATES**
Osaka, Japan

D-Hotel is located close to Dotonbori, the bustling centre of Osaka, Japan's business centre and second city. The hotel is part of a major redevelopment site, close to a new offshore international airport designed by Renzo Piano and due for completion in 1992.

Dotonbori, famed for its rumbustious nightlife and great concentration of restaurants, is now getting a more upmarket image at the hands of dynamic developers. D-Hotel, according to designer Kiyoshi Sey Takeyama, is 'a wedge driven into the area and pointing towards the future'. It is also a clear demonstration of the kind of building developers are prepared to introduce, and represents a radical contrast to Osaka's many Western-style hotels.

Situated on a narrow site, it is a hotel-in-a-wall, a concrete structure shaped like a fin with its point sliced off at the front. One end of its uncompromising façade is a windowless planed wall which stands independently from the main building, screening the end of the site from the road. Looking up at the two structures from ground level, they seem to lean together, the weight of the main block apparently being given greater solidity by its M-shaped pattern of fenestration. Next to the busy restaurants, *yakitori* bars and *pachinko* parlours of Dotonbori, it lurks like a large bird-wing, shielding its inner spaces. It is a building devoid of external signs, like a secret club.

The eight-floor hotel is built on a narrow plan encompassing 942 square metres. The bedrooms are hidden compactly away on five floors immediately above the ground which is, unusually, given over to public gallery space run by the company. Takeyama wanted to highlight the public areas of the hotel, and endow the bedrooms with the private, protected atmosphere of a retreat. The reception and lobby are situated in the basement.

The bedrooms are small in scale and elegant, in spite of their exposed concrete walls and ceilings. Curved panels continue the shield theme, marking off washing areas. Light is provided by low-voltage bedside spots, recessed ceiling spots and back-lit ceiling panels; natural light enters through square windows and a far wall of glass bricks. There is definitely a spartan quality to these rooms, but they are warmed by the careful juxtaposition of materials and the layering of planes.

Up in the eighth floor bar, a view of the seething metropolis is afforded from narrow-legged high stools set at a glass-topped counter. The sense of confinement imparted by a wire net screen fronting the window is relieved by a strip of floor in glass bricks – the very top of an enclosed area of glass wall carried vertically right through the building and visible on the lower floors as part of each bedroom wall. Further down the long room, a lower eating area affords less impeded views from larger windows.

Kiyoshi Sey Takeyama, born and bred in Osaka, has created the twenty-first-century equivalent to the hostel at the gate of the city: a retreat with little of the bustle and blandness of the themed restaurants and bars often found in city hotels. Unlike Osaka's other hotels, its 'cell block' overtones may be thought a little brutal for comfort, but release is found in its radically private spaces.

View from the kitchen of the huge coil protruding from the ceiling over diagonally slanting tables.

The fiery red and yellow orange-peel shaped forms of Hadid's ceiling 'furnace' unwind over a pit in the floor of the upper bar, emulating an ignited version of the grey coil which dominates the restaurant below.

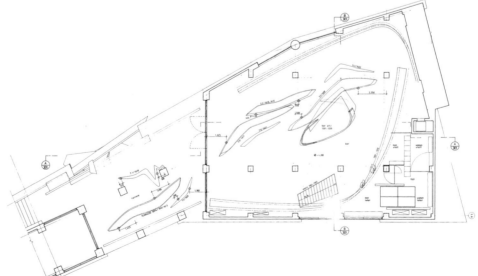

Floor plan of the upper bar area, showing seating to the side of the central open 'bar pit', and a terrace on the left. The curved wall conceals staff/service areas.

Moonsoon, Kita Club

ZAHA HADID
Sapporo, Hokkaido, Japan

While Masami Matsui's input as designer of Kita's basement nightclub fully conforms to the technologically mind-blowing aesthetic demanded of avant-garde clubs in Japan (see pages 118–9), it is Zaha Hadid's self-contained upper floors which truly enthral as an aesthetically subversive environment.

The developers Jasmac Co. Ltd chose the two designers to take the Kita Club in Sapporo to the outer limits. The constraints of its modern, but respectable, exterior instilled in Hadid a burning desire to break out and contradict its orderliness in her design for

fire and ice. Each area conjures up a strange, evocative and synthetic world — well beyond the pale of convention.

The ground floor is a cool, triangular space filled with narrow or angled forms in frosted, laminated or tempered glass, steel and stone — an array of contrasting grey and white textures. Inspired by the seasonal ice buildings of Sapporo, it features a vast glass splinter of a table running diagonally across the grey terrazzo floor. From the rear, other tables emerge, and their sharp fragments almost move across the raised level, drifting like ice floes across water.

The perfect venue for an ice-queen's banquet, the room is full of menacing, angled forms. One concession to comfort is found in the steel-framed chairs, arranged around the central glass dagger table, which have soft, white, sheepskin cushions. Applying the basic law that water expands when it freezes, Hadid's translucent surfaces look like water transformed to thick sheets of ice under pressure to break out. Walls of crushed glass, laminated to acid-etched plate glass and confined in steel frames, are backlit by explosions of fibre optic light: they lean back as if to brace themselves against added pressure. Like planes of ice frozen with tiny lumps of icing sugar, they envelop the room with a chilled static. Around the periphery, on non-aligned terrazzo steps into which recessed lights are set, frozen 'fingers' of tempered glass

Around the edge of the restaurant, angled walls are made of crushed glass laminated to acid-etched plate glass held within steel frames, and backlit by spotlights to create a shimmering surface.

Moonsoon, a restaurant and bar on adjoining floors. The result is a hybrid design combining a pressured sense of exterior static with a 'compressed internalized dynamic' — an approach which manages to stave off an actual explosion in great style. With all its theatrical power, Moonsoon is ultimately an environment equipped with a wealth of hot and cold stimuli to probe our abilities to respond to our surroundings. Hadid has given the formality of the eating area and the relaxed atmosphere in the upper bar two violently opposing characters based on

Interlocking sofas with movable trays provide an infinitely variable configuration of seating types in this elastic, sensuous lounging space, yoked via the bar pit with the forbidding angularity of the restaurant downstairs. The fire and ice imagery at Moonsoon envelops its unsuspecting visitors with a clever conceit of sensory devices.

form separate dining tables and benches secured to stainless steel supports, their translucent forms shot through with light like delicate, elongated boiled sweets.

The ceiling betrays a proximity to another, more quixotic kind of design dynamic generated above. In the centre a huge, grey, angular coil shape, set in a disjointed panel and apparently about to unravel under the pressure, appears to hold up the ceiling. At the rear an open-tread metal stair drops from a covered hatch. Something lurking above deserves a look.

Above the ice chamber whirls a veritable tornado of fire in brilliant reds, yellows and oranges — a vortex which tears through the domed roof of the restaurant below, spiralling up to a huge glowing furnace in the ceiling above. Inspired by orange peel cut into one long continuous piece, it provides a focal point of the most dramatic and gravity-defying kind. The surrounding environment is a relaxed and elastic zone of biomorphic sofas in grey vinyl leather decorated with bright lozenge- and flame-shaped cushions in velvet and vinyl. Tiny 'gold zinc' galvanized steel tables in a variety of cut-out shapes are spiked on to the elongated sofas snaking their way around the space. On the adjoining roof terrace, the biomorphic sofa forms continue, only here they are made of terrazzo.

Hadid's metallic spear forms and crushed glass-and-metal planes evoke an icy atmosphere.

Suspended pieces of marble serve as projection screens for images along the stairway to Ac on ca gua.

Maelstrom's long corridor bar with a water-polished marble floor has crazy-paving walls made of steel fretwork. The luminous reinforced glass part of the floor emulates a reflective water surface.

Ac on ca gua's ceilings are the site of Matsui's most spectacular visual effects. An array of steel shapes with reflective surfaces, including waves of steel mirror, creates a rippling movement. Each zone of the discothèque bar is divided by a glass wall – its transparency helps to create an integrated space.

Ac on ca gua: the lower basement plan showing dance floors on either side of the central seating area, and curved bar area to the right.

2.17

Maelstrom/ Ac on ca gua, Kita Club

MASAMI MATSUI/AXE CO.
Sapporo, Hokkaldo, Japan

Matsui is a club 'choreographer' whose comprehensive design approach extends to staff uniforms, tableware, menus, background music and sales pitches. With over a hundred establishments to his name (including Red Shoes, one of the first café bars in Japan; the Inkstick Club on the Tokyo Bay waterfront; Tango, Zapata and Strathisla), his creative business philosophy can be read in his books: 'Detail is the essence of space,' and 'Tokyo Nouvelle Vague.'

Two separate spaces within the Sapporo-based Kita Club come in for the Matsui treatment: Ac on ca gua, a lounge bar leading to a lower discothèque, and Maelstrom, a corridor-shaped bar. Matsui worked completely independently from Zaha Hadid, who was engaged by developers Jasmac to design Moonsoon, a bar and restaurant on the club's upper floors (see pages 114–7). The style of each contribution is very different, providing a 'multiplier effect' greatly sought after in Japan's larger club buildings.

Matsui aimed to introduce a range of quirky images and effects that would entertain visitors without relying on more formulaic solutions and materials. Inspired by Sapporo's Kamokamo River which runs by the Kita Club, he decided to use water, a relatively cheap element within the 4 billion yen project budget, to create unique organic effects in his interiors. In Maelstrom, a narrow corridor bar animated by light and movement, water tanks are fitted to the entrance, the wall of the bar counter, the partitions, and along the wall behind drinkers positioned at the bar. The constantly mobile spume of bubbles oscillates around spotlight beams, creating swaying, semi-opaque arcs of compressed water. The effect is enhanced by adding liquid crystal glass which can create both straight and scattered light in alternate movements.

At Ac on ca gua, which occupies a total of 724.72 square metres within a two-storey basement, guests are lured downstairs by a series of images projected on to huge marble slabs suspended around the entrance area. Down in the lower bar area, some of the lighting is

more conventionally space-age, but one disco lighting effect emulates, in a more stylized way, the effects of the bubbling water scattering the liquid crystal light forms.

Above the drinking areas, which each have their own decorative carpets laid out in sedate zones on the shiny white marble floor, a panoply of forms is suspended from the ceiling to catch and distort the light. Steel pipes, louvred boards and wavy stainless steel mirrors echo the reflections thrown up from glass and steel partitions. The furniture is mostly designed by Matsui himself, with a few chairs from En Attendant les Barbares. From the comfort of cosy armchairs one can experience the disorientating effects around the room.

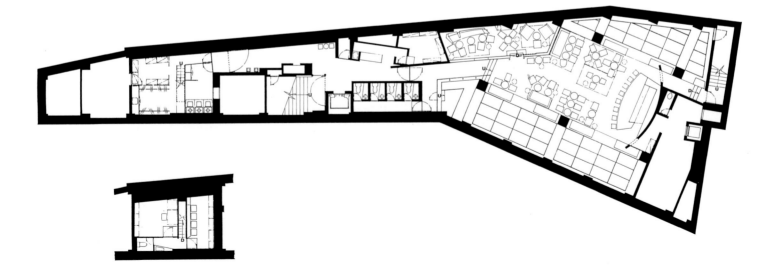

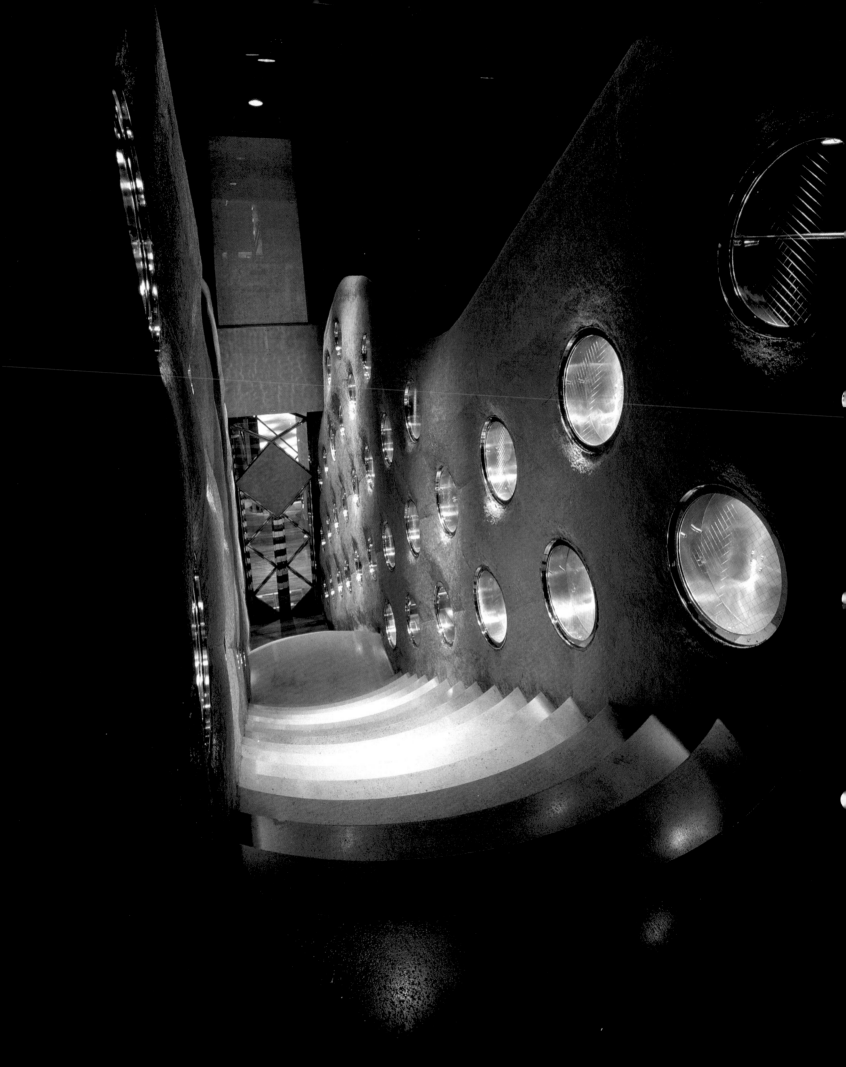

Barna Crossing

**ALFREDO ARRIBAS
ARQUITECTOS ASOCIADOS
Fukuoka, Japan**

The making of Barna Crossing – 'a gigantic twenty-first-century underground disco lounge' – was a major Spanish/Japanese cultural undertaking which, to judge by the credits (ranging from 'concept story' to 'cooking direction') given in the publicity material, was carried out almost like a film. Situated on the ground floor and basement of Il Palazzo Hotel (see pages 82–7), it is a tantalising, hybrid creature,

The warmth of the VIP bar area is enhanced by glowing, back-lit, yellow onyx panels behind the bar, and rich African wood floors. Gaudí chairs in oak, hand-carved in organic forms, are accompanied by tables by Mariscal of rough slabs of decorated alabaster.

A narrow, cavernous staircase leads down to the basement entrance. Its subterranean gloom is enlivened by recessed 'porthole' lights in the walls.

a fusion of innovative Spanish design and advanced Japanese technology. A creative team led by Barcelona-based architect Alfredo Arribas – working with Miguel Morte, artist-designer Javier Mariscal, and Juli Capella and Quim Larrea of ARDI magazine – was assembled for the project by the enterprising Shi Yu Chen, the 'driving force' of Creative Intelligence Associates (CIA), for client Mitsuhiro Kuzuwa of Jasmac Company Ltd.

The architecture of Il Palazzo represents a miniature city: within it, Barna Crossing is a subterranean

playground which forms an up-beat contrast to the brooding intensity of Torres de Avila, Arribas' other collaboration with Mariscal (see pages 136–9). The concept exploits the 'organised chaos' resulting from the metaphorical 'crossing' of the energy and activity of its creators and participants. An area of 1567 square metres in total, the two-storey space with a mezzanine floor incorporates a wealth of materials, finishes and imagery. Instead of the typical zoning of areas into dance floor, lounge, bar, restaurant and VIP rooms, an attempt was made to open up the space, and give it a free-flowing sense of communality found elsewhere in the hotel. In this way, the design team hoped, people at the 'crossing' (of east and west) could become part of overlapping activities taking place simultaneously, rather like being at a grand festival. In keeping with this, the music played is from cultures all over the world.

Arribas has covered the basic shell left by the hotel's architect Aldo Rossi in a lining of aluminium panelling which contains all the service elements (including ashtrays, signs and dustbins) in an expressive wrapper. It plays a dual role, as it is not only a practical container, but also establishes a strong context for a rich variety of finishes and treatments (flat, relief, castings and perforations). Within this lining, about thirty different strategically located architectural elements take the form of sub-themes within the whole. These include individual

Beneath the mezzanine restaurant is a more casual eating and drinking area with rows of flip-down aluminium bar tops.

The raised restaurant within a self-contained glass-sided box provides unrivalled views of the discothèque floor (to the right) and the bar areas below. A whole range of bar stool designs are scattered throughout the space.

designs for at least twenty styles of bar furniture, using painted wood, marquetry, stone, brass, steel, velvet, wood and leather in a profusion of patterns. Although they possess contrasting atmospheres, the self-contained mezzanine restaurant and the open bar areas with their smooth wooden floors are both treated as expressive art environments. The ultimate art object is the dance floor itself, encased in an artfully reinforced glass box. Only the bravest creatures venture into this area, which can be viewed from the intimacy of the glass-fronted mezzanine projected above a trio of bar counters on the basement floor.

Barna Crossing's lighting makes great use of the reflective qualities of the aluminium-lined walls. The dance area contains a wealth of special effects such as a state-of-the-art laser beam 'shower' and a computerized, moving, mirrored wall set above the dance floor at mezzanine level. Other elements less orthodox in this 'neuro-pleasure city' include a glass aquarium of tropical fish.

The ornate mix of organic Spanish forms and patterns extends to decorative screens by Javier Mariscal and menu cards and other printed material by graphic designer Alfonso Sostres. The artistic 'programme' even includes staff uniforms designed by Chu Uroz. Menus feature predominantly Catalan and Japanese dishes (some mixed), served as *tapas*; they are chosen from a rice-paper and bamboo fan menu, and eaten with thoughtfully provided dual-function chopstick-forks. Barna Crossing is, ultimately, a highly ordered environment, one that is entirely appropriate in Japan's relatively formal culture. Its precisely planned and distanced conceptual design proposes new forms for the practice of modern social ritual.

RESTAURANTS, CAFÉS, BARS, CLUBS & HOTELS

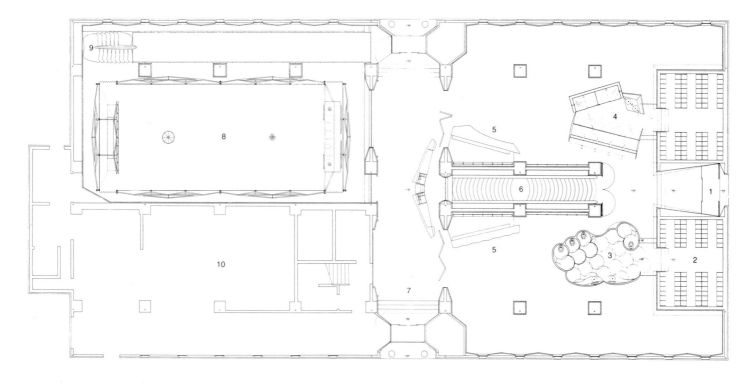

Ground-floor plan.
1 Entrance.
2 Cloakrooms.
3 Women's toilets.
4 Men's toilets. 5 Bars.
6 Staircase. 7 Private
members' entrance.
8 Void above dance
floor. 9 Staircase to
upper gallery. 10 Staff
room and office above
bars with dining areas
and kitchens on
basement and
mezzanine floors
below.

Vast aluminium-wrapped columns at the periphery of the dance space flank glass panels held up by an elaborate series of struts. A state-of-the-art laser light system in a decorative circle and square formation animates the glass box.

Finished steel panels form a curved metallic backdrop to the entrance desk in what is the most brightly coloured wall in the restaurant. Tiny recessed spots in the floor mark out small changes in floor level at the end of the entrance corridor.

Axonometric diagram of the 215.8-square-metre restaurant, with the entrance on the left.

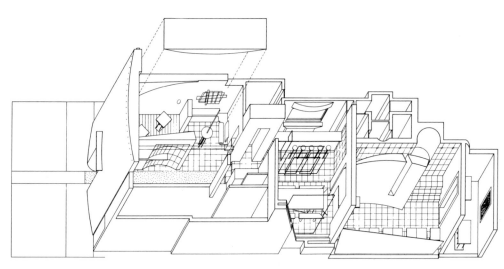

2.19
Tambaya

SOICHE MIZUTANI
Tokyo, Japan

The introduction of contemporary art to a traditional Japanese eating house is a rare phenomenon. Tambaya is situated in Shinjuku, in the centre of Tokyo. In undertaking a re-design of its interior, its owners had its 300-year-old reputation to maintain as a *unagi-ya* or eel restaurant of the first order. Its distinctive image had been synonymous with a traditional eel cuisine, but a drastic up-date was now needed. Having broadened the menu to include *kaiseki* (a set meal of dishes), the client accepted that a new aesthetic formula, proposed by designer Soiche Mizutani, would revitalise the restaurant's existing image.

Not only are there works and hangings along Tambaya's walls for diners to contemplate while eating, but the restaurant's very forms — the overlapping tinted glass screen, curved internal walls with finished steel alcoves, solid glass-topped drinks table hung from the ceiling — all speak of a desire to establish an appropriate setting for and a dialogue with contemporary art.

Mizutani did not wish to create an ephemeral style, rather a 'timeless' design 'which will last for the next hundred years'. Whether this ambition can actually be achieved remains to be seen, but judging by Tambaya's track record as a company it is easy to see where the motivation for longevity comes from. Where Mizutani undoubtedly succeeds is in endowing a cultural tradition with modern, sculptural and unadorned aesthetic forms. In this way, says Mizutani, the past can be reinterpreted through a relationship with the new.

The practical rationale for the restaurant's design relates to the nature of the premises. Relatively old by Tokyo standards, the original 1930s wood structure of the three one-storey houses needed extra support and unification with forms added in the 1960s. Working with these existing elements, Mizutani added new columns and beams, and reinforced the roof. He created a unified space for the restaurant by connecting the different floor levels and ceilings of the three houses; however, their distinct qualities are enhanced rather than erased. There are three defined eating areas: one of smaller café tables on the lower level of limestone floor, backed by a long sofa seat; one on an elevated level of stone floor with trestles, for larger parties; and another at a higher level of oak floor, for groups of two to four.

The bar is a simple, deep counter made of black granite with wooden bar stools. Behind it, instead of the almost obligatory shelves of exotic liquor, is a window providing a view of bamboo in a miniature Japanese garden located at the back of the restaurant — a sign of natural life and a visually compelling abstract pattern. The drinks are kept out of sight beneath the bar.

A warm and vivid, but never overwhelming, use of colour creates distinct tonal areas. From the crimson entrance wall one passes through into the main restaurant with its mix of white with sandy coloured plaster walls, deep blue upholstered seating and aquamarine glass screens at the bar.

The brightly lit bar area has a limestone floor, and seating upholstered with blue polyester velour fabric. Simple effects such as the slatted wooden wall panel and the red painted niche break up the expanses of curved plaster wall.

The aluminium bar stools, fixed to the floor with steel springs, form an undulating line in front of shelves of irregularly shaped slabs covered with stretched aluminium plates. Their form allows some movement of the upwardly directed rays of light, which creates architectural decoration on the bare walls.

Stout, static, metal columns at the edge of the dance floor, with illuminated 'capitals' of translucent fabric, inflated by circulating gusts of air.

The dramatic tongue-shaped bar is given as much prominence as the dance floor. The bar counter has a 10mm iron top, which has been sandblasted and chromium-plated.

Epsylon

DENIS SANTACHIARA
Reggio Emilia, Italy

Santachiara's work, mostly avant-garde product design, has always attempted to provide a dialogue between the object and the end user. Approaching the Epsylon discothèque the visitor is, so to speak, struck by lightning: the club's sign features a sharp, crackling flash created by a common voltage jump. Once inside the entrance lobby, one walks across a narrow portion of glass floor below which the air conditioning plant room is visible – a truly unnerving but intriguing threshold to this unusual club. Above the cash desk a distorting glass recessed into the metal wall dilates the face of the cashier – providing another, suitably surreal, introduction to an animated space which thrives on the designer's ability to play with the user's sensory and spatial expectations.

Epsylon needed 'to become a fashionable venue of superior quality'. The club, set in the historic heart of Reggio Emilia, is distinguished from the mass of typical discothèques in the Romagna region by Santachiara's engaging interplay of animated forms and 'hybrid spaces'.

The carefully soundproofed club occupies 800 square metres; its entrance area, bar and dance floor are the most distinctive features. The steel counter of the bar thrusts its long, sinuous form down the centre of the room, allowing visitors to move freely on either side, with enclosed serving area suspended from the ceiling by metal bars. Cash registers sit on each side of the bar's forked end.

Dotted around the bar and the perimeter of the room, against ledges for resting drinks, are rows of aluminium stools. They are little more than perches for a roving, playful, but definitely not sedentary, clientèle.

On the dance floor, overlays of electronically created images are projected by spotlights on to the 25-metre-long wall behind the DJ's desk. Their animated, synchronized action appears to expand the space. In the toilets, there is a further reworking of expectations: instead of the usual sinks, there are just two black holes above which automatically operated taps spurt water from behind a mirror.

On the second floor, a mezzanine corridor runs around the dance floor, providing a secluded area with columns covered with ridged sheet metal. The illuminated 'capitals' at the top of each

are draped with a transparent fabric that 'breathes' jets of air around their glowing forms. Separating the bar from the dance floor are platforms made from sheet aluminium with transparent resin inlays. Fitted with comfortable armchairs, they move slowly, doubtless an unnerving experience for the inebriated. Both here and in the bar, the furniture is based not on constructed volumes, but on light, animated, unfixed supports, 'as if everything were made to move or be moved'.

Instead of a 'dark ambience with a lot of flashing lights', Santachiara has created a soft, twilight atmosphere. The lighting effects are not exclusively concentrated on the dance floor (which, except for projected images, is quite dark) but spread all around the venue as 'performances'. From the perimeter of the bar area, powerful beams of light shoot up from the floor, crossing the slots in the narrow bar ledges, and reaching the bare wall where they act as *trompe l'oeil* architectural decoration.

Although designed to exacting technical requirements for effective soundproofing, acoustics and ventilation, Epsylon goes way beyond mere schematics. Although initially Santachiara was considerably more knowledgeable about technology than dancing, his inventive approach to what is intended, after all, to be an area for play is laced with a healthy irony which cuts across the users' expectations. The result is strikingly original.

Axonometric diagram of the L-shaped room, with the entrance on the right, the bar, platforms, dance floor and columns.

The restaurant waiting room retains many elements of the old theatre lobby, facing large luminous photographs leaning against a new curved wall.

The theatre's original cupola above the restaurant, with added gold leaf decoration; Isometrix's theatrical lighting simulates a furnace high in its dome.

RESTAURANTS, CAFÉS, BARS, CLUBS & HOTELS

Teatriz

PHILIPPE STARCK
Madrid, Spain

Teatriz is situated in an elegant area of Madrid, occupying the former Beatriz Theatre, a grand, atmospheric, turn-of-the-century rendez-vous for the middle classes. Philippe Starck, himself a practised master of dramatic gestures applied to restaurants, bars and hotels (see La Flamme d'Or, pages 92–5), was recommended to owner Placido Arango of Sigla by Ian Schrager, client and owner of one of Starck's earlier incarnations, the Royalton Hotel in New York. In this, his first Spanish-based project, Starck has taken his cue from the building's own inherent theatricality. He has wisely left intact the theatre's original stage with its dramatic relics adorning the upper walls. His treatment of the residual forms of its auditorium structure is subtle. The theatre's baroque spirit serves Starck's

Ground-floor plan.

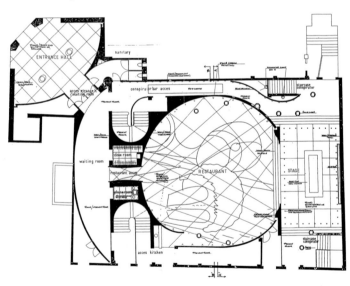

own grand gestures and concealed devices.

Teatriz operates as a series of image-based set pieces linked to a central core of operation: a circular restaurant based in the high void of the old theatre pit. Starck's design conjures up no one theme or consistent atmosphere; rather, wide realms of fantasy are evoked – from mysterious severity, slick elegance, ironic

comedy to sensuous opulence – at every turn.

Within the fabric of this house of culture, Starck makes numerous references to art. Two-dimensional works of art have to convey their effects with the minimum of means, and he sees no reason why a three-dimensional interior space should not also generate its impact through super-charged emotional effects. Starck gives Teatriz a sense of place, not by a conventional engagement with architectural form, but through a more sign-based cinematic process which sets up a carefully orchestrated psychological play on meaning.

In order to prepare the visitor for the dramatic variations of scale that lie within, Starck provides various entrances: one, on the exterior, is over-scaled and forbiddingly monumental; another, cushioned in black leather and riveted in red copper like the entrance to a sado-masochistic brothel, is suggestive, but misleading. These decoy doors represent the peeling back of layers to a centre of stimuli to entertain a changing audience – business clientèle at lunchtime and the 'movida' in the evening.

Starck often introduces a curtain within his interior projects, 'a synthesizing object' to provide drama, mystery, simplicity and economy rolled into one design component. Here it appears in gathered folds of grey velvet which hide the hall's original balconies, and hang voluminously around a cylindrical space 20 metres across and five floors high. It is held open by a Dalí-inspired crutch, revealing the balcony bar area, high above pearwood walls, with huge blackboard columns which guests are encouraged to 'customize' with grafitti.

Positioned on the stage opposite is a luminescent onyx slab of a bar, almost like an altarpiece straddled by a huge pearwood frame. A mirror behind the bar reflects another rich touch: a mahogany balcony holding an upper bar and restaurant from which diners can eye the competition down below and the more ostentatious drinkers approaching the raised stage bar. Starck has cleverly retained the theatre's hierarchy of positions, manipulating it with his own aesthetic order of forms. Above the altar-like bar a filmy net curtain beside the towering frame adds an air of bathos. The theatre's original prop equipment, dusty with age, is just visible behind its semi-transparent drapes. The central sphere of floor space is an elegant, sociable arena, overlooked by the original gold-leaf patterned cupola. Above its hollow form, a circle of red light smoulders enigmatically. Tables are scattered around a huge granite mosaic floor, its fragmented forms based on the masks in De Chirico's 'Two Sisters'. Each table is given one tall backed chair: another stylistic play on scale.

The theatrical expanse of the main restaurant is contrasted by a series of much smaller, womb-like spaces around its central core, whose soft forms present a surreal and strangely menacing form of hyper-luxury. A telephone booth is lined with pink cushioned walls which engulf a coquettish mauve armchair on a small area of chequered carpet. Down in the basement, a lounge bar piles on sensuous layers of puffed-up velvet sofas, parquet floor, veneered walls and bookshelves, and roman blinds around a cosy, fake log fire, creating a perfect pastiche of a sensuous, domestic idyll.

Like the toilets at Café Costes in Paris and Manin in Tokyo, those at Teatriz

Gold leaf columns add a gaudy touch to the neo-brutalist appearance of the Conspirator bar, with its rough concrete and exposed brickwork, and unnervingly backlit wall panels with engraved floating shadows.

are not merely services: instead, they are dimly lit repositories of conceptual devices. The haute-couture door handles are designed by Christian Lacroix in the form of a Spanish arabesque, but the toilets are housed in two regimented tiled blocks, which Starck likens to monolithic Carl André sculptures, with red and blue lights set in their frosted glass doors. In the adjoining washroom, free-standing basins represent a dramatic stylistic antithesis: two Louis XIV tables are topped with hollowed-out slabs of pink marble, while three metal water pipes lean against their sides like canes. Starck's sleight of hand continues its roving gestures: a mirrored wall adjoins the upper bar, from where shadowy moving forms of visitors going about their ablutions can be discerned.

There is a method behind such apparent madness. Although conventional notions of beauty do not concern him, Starck stages his effects not at random but to unleash carefully orchestrated perceptual environments where the visitor can never afford to be complacent, but must be braced for a repertoire of visual tricks which invert customary visual and functional associations. His ironic devices play with our prejudices about taste.

The telephone booth is luxuriously furnished, with domestic trappings on a small scale, and oyster-pink padded walls.

From the balcony, the vast mosaic floor of Teatriz's restaurant is inspired by a De Chirico painting; it is skirted by a voluminous grey velvet curtain held back by a wooden crutch to create an entrance aperture. A pearwood veneer balcony with a clear glass railing incorporates stage lighting.

RESTAURANTS, CAFÉS, BARS, CLUBS & HOTELS

RESTAURANTS, CAFÉS, BARS, CLUBS & HOTELS

Wasserturm Hotel

ÉCART
Cologne, Germany

The solemn façade of the historic water tower.

A Putman-designed 'W' high-wing sofa in one of the hotel's duplexes, which is lit by a large, back-lit, plexiglass screen shielding the entrance. Natural light enters from an original circular window.

Breathing new spirit into old industrial buildings is a growing preoccupation of architects and designers: the challenge is to give their tired and worn fabric a redefined role which nonetheless respects their original *raison d'être*. Apart from the saving on the excessive costs involved in building from scratch, converting historical relics and monuments can create assets of great value both to clients and users, and for posterity.

The impressive nineteenth-century water tower on Kaygasse in Cologne, now revitalized as a hotel, represents one example of this growing trend. Monumental and austere, with restrained decorative elements, it is the largest structure of its kind in Europe. The cylindrical, fortified tower was designed by Charles Moore, an English engineer, and served the city of Cologne for some decades until the late nineteenth century, when the invention of underground water systems made its technology redundant. Used as a bunker in the Second World War, it escaped excessive damage; later, as one of the few monuments left in the city, it was preserved as a historical landmark.

Reinvigorated by Écart's design, the Wasserturm now holds a prominent position among the hotels in Cologne. Planning regulations dictated that the new work had to preserve the original structure of the 34-metre-wide tower, so Andrée Putman of Écart (with Bruno Moinard and Georges Grenier), in conjunction with Cologne architect Konrad Heinrich, sought to draw out the industrial character of the building, while creating within its walls a sensual and comfortable hotel environment.

The original floor plan of the strictly geometric monument shows three concentric rings made of bricked pillars connected by arches, with blind windows throughout. The designers restored the surviving façade, unblocking windows to let in as much light as possible. The top part of the tower, which had been damaged in the Second World War, was rebuilt to provide additional floors, including a roof restaurant with views over Cologne.

The cylindrical tower's ten floors are carved into 'segments' around a great entrance hall with exposed brickwork — the tower's central public space; its 10-metre-high arches give access to the various functional areas via high, low-lit balconies. The interior spaces radiating from this point of arrival are trapezium-shaped, which necessitated much creative play with curves to provide comfortable bedroom and lounge areas. 'The tower itself is so overbearing that we wanted to keep the rooms simple,' says Andrée Putman. She is stimulated by such challenges, and aims always to infuse her design work with 'the audacity of oppositions, the mix of rich and poor, formal and informal.'

In the Wasserturm, solidity and austere architectural forms were already in place. The primary intention, therefore, was to give prominence to comfort, softness and sensuality to 'break the strange solemnity of the building'. The formal and dignified elements of Putman's interiors are combined with a rich but not overly opulent palette of colours: beige and oyster mixed with saffron yellow, and luminous blue and green in the bedrooms; dove grey and marine blue in the bathrooms. The presence of structural bronze coloured brick was the main factor in the colour choice of other, softer materials, such as velvet upholstery.

Ninety bedrooms range from singles to two types of mezzanine suites and a grand Presidential suite. Underlying their strong aesthetic is Putman's view that international hotels should aim not to offer homeliness, but to present a daring and creative environment which will stimulate visitors who are often in town for only a few days.

The curved 'half-moon' forms of the upholstered furniture, porthole-shaped windows and tiled bathroom alcoves all echo the strong shape of the exterior. Space within the Wasserturm is a valuable commodity, so all the furniture and fittings had to be compact as well as elegant. Sofas were designed to fit into vaulted niches; armchairs are club-shaped; in the bedrooms, dressing tables are designed to double up as comfortable desks. Details build upon judicious choices of form to create a full-blown effect which could only have been achieved with custom-designed furniture and fittings. Original artworks add their contribution, hung throughout in strategic positions. On either side of the reception lobby are placed imposing sculptures by Dan Flavin

and Donald Judd; a Tom Wesselmann painting dominates the rooftop restaurant.

Since no more windows could be added to the existing fenestration, Putman designed sanded glass panels in the bedrooms, which are back-lit with dimmer switches to add luminosity. Various surfaces are incandescent — vanity table tops, recessed reading lights — and there is virtually no overhead lighting.

Downstairs, the soaring, narrow, bricked arches of the entrance hall add to this unifying rhythm. Illuminating the cavernous hall are semi-circular lights placed on the pillars at ground level. Higher up, the gangways between bedrooms exist in an atmospheric half-light (assisted by small spotlights), which accentuates the vivid nature of the spaces beyond.

Putman's earlier schemes involved the revival of the work of previously overlooked designers, such as Eileen Gray and Roger Mallet-Stevens. Converting the monumental Wasserturm involved yet another uncovering which, in the process, has revived a formerly redundant historical artefact without compromising the integrity of its original conception.

Part of an en-suite bathroom, tiled in matte blue-grey, bordered with a black diamond mosaic.

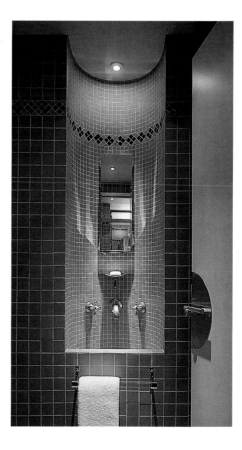

Floor plan of the hotel's duplex suites: on the left, the sixth-floor salon areas and bathrooms; on the right, the mezzanine floor with bedrooms, some with en suite bathrooms. Around the centre runs a balcony and upper, adjoining bridges.

The furniture exudes luxury and timeless classicism. A yellow velvet armchair is juxtaposed with a dressing table with a glowing top.

Wide, full-length mirrors provide the illusion of extra space in the bedrooms, which feature incandescent light fittings which give a soft glow, rather than directional light.

The bronze-coloured brickwork inspired the choice of colours used within the smaller spaces elsewhere. The texture and decorative elements of the masonry are particularly stunning in the great entrance hall.

Luminous panels are incorporated into the bar and lounge areas, furnished with more distinctive curved sofas and armchairs.

Within the moon tower, a high planetarium volume made of polyester is covered with skeins of optic fibre cells which look like stars and constellations. This volume turns through 180 degrees high above the bar below.

This project presented an unusual challenge: the conversion into a nightclub of two run-down, fake mediaeval towers at the entrance to the Pueblo Espagnol, in a relatively isolated spot of Barcelona. Even Arribas and Mariscal, seasoned multi-media designers, admitted to being initially daunted, but were intrigued by the bizarre space on the edge of the park where reproductions of traditional Spanish buildings can be seen and which, in a sense, is Barcelona's forerunner to Disneyland. The place had lain empty for some time, until Teatriz SA, owners of a restaurant in Madrid designed by Philippe Starck (see pages 128–31), decided to breathe new life into its sturdy forms. The nightclub is a stage set with disorientating visual effects: light-generated, kinetic

and spatial tricks exploit the soaring height of the towers and strange, wall-inscribed symbols.

Torres de Avila was a long project: expensive, difficult to draw, and difficult to construct. The easy part was developing a concept for the club which was based around symbolic oppositions applied to the two towers, providing a strange kind of coherence to a complex space. The left tower is intended to represent night and femininity, the right, day and masculinity – contrasting spaces topped by emblems of the moon and sun, and joined by an intermediate area which combines these oppositions with no less a sense of artful unease.

The two tall spaces are individually defined by forms which extend vertically above the bar areas and tiered balconies, levitating within the old walls, but without making contact with them. This mobile effect is emphasised by the faint reflections of the lighting and the multitude of shining points.

2.23
Torres de Avila

ALFREDO ARRIBAS ARQUITECTOS ASOCIADOS AND JAVIER MARISCAL
Barcelona, Spain

The main bar in the moon tower on the left is a darkened space with symbols, animals and figures inscribed on its walls. It is dominated by an elongated balloon of sheer fabric, wreathed in skeins and glinting particles of optic fibre light, which appears to hover above the bar, attached to a circular seated base. Below, a spindle structure contains a glowing, iridescent circle of contrasting light effects, echoed by rows of lights around the bar.

The other bar is a tall, spacious, golden-toned void, overhung by a luminous stressed pentangle suspended from the ceiling and open in the middle to the sky. Through the opening, a light-studded sphere slowly moves up and down, reaching the entire height of the tower.

To bring a degree of comfort to Torres' disturbingly ethereal splendour and induced vertigo, sensuous materials are used for furniture and wall and floor surfaces: suede-covered drum-shaped stools, high-backed sofas, and velvet and leather curtains.

Several open-tread metal staircases and walkways at different heights, which cover the rear of the rough-hewn towers and the area adjoining, offer a range of vertiginous perspectives. In the space between the two towers, a glass-walled bar above a glass pyramid roof is furnished with suede-covered stools and a huge wooden bar like a ship's prow. From the lift which runs up the right-hand tower

Up at the top of the intermediary space, a small area with a prow-shaped wooden bar provides dramatic views of the interlinking metal staircases situated at the rear.

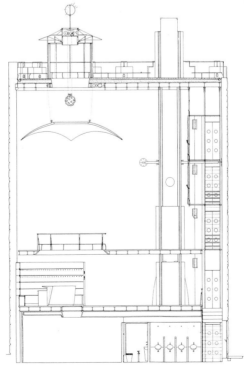

Section through the sun tower, with lift shaft and staircases on the right.

The darkened environment of the moon tower's bar incorporates some stunning lighting effects, including illuminated 'wrap-around' shelves within an African wood structure.

to the roof terrace, panoramic views of Barcelona can be experienced by the visitor, by now immersed in special — and spatial — effects.

A black dome, topped by a moon, illuminated with white symbols, covers the apex of the left-hand bar. The sun on the other tower is the pinnacle of a cylindrical structure from which the studded sphere dives into the warm void below.

The club's innovative design derives its force not from static forms, but from ethereal and ambiguously dramatic effects. Arribas would like to think of their seductive power as being akin to cult, or magic, but ultimately it is the exuberance of the participants in this unworldly setting which causes the sparks to fly.

Arribas and Mariscal have aimed to establish a compelling narrative in their design, setting up changing atmospheres at various points around the structure where half-hidden signs can be discovered. The computer-programmed lighting effects, in particular, add a spontaneous, self-generating dimension to the club's unnerving design. The hand of the artist is never far away: Arribas' and Mariscal's joint venture harmonizes art with design, employing urban languages, modern technologies, old codes and ancestral traditions, which are realised with a rich array of materials and means.

The warm, honey-coloured sun tower contains two suspended moving elements: an encrusted, illuminated sphere and a curved, luminous white volume. A narrow tiered balcony is dotted with leather stools, and slabs of alabaster attached to the wall serve as tables.

The roof terrace, showing the tops of the sun and moon towers, complete with Mariscal's illuminated symbols.

RESTAURANTS, CAFÉS, BARS, CLUBS & HOTELS

Instant access to the pavilions' individually landscaped gardens can be had from the ground-floor bedrooms.

Hotel-Restaurant Saint James

JEAN NOUVEL
Bouliac, Bordeaux, France

In stark contrast to the stylized and intimate urban spaces of Hotel La Villa in Paris, the design of Nouvel's hotel for the renowned chef of *nouvelle cuisine* Jean-Marie Amat knocks on the head any pretensions possessed by wealthy lovers of fine food searching for an opulent setting. Instead, the Hotel-Restaurant Saint James is a simple country retreat, but there is nothing naive about its interior design. On the contrary, it manifests a knowing urbanity which has been neatly absorbed into the breathtakingly beautiful surrounding landscape.

The hotel is situated in the small hamlet of Bouliac, just off the village square, on a high ridge facing Amat's newly planted vineyard on the southern slope of the Garonne valley. Four new

independent buildings, housing eighteen bedrooms and a new restaurant on a modestly sized plot, extend in a splayed row from a restored one-storey seventeenth-century villa. Nouvel took care to adapt the new elements of the design to the scale and volume of neighbouring houses.

Each of the four buildings is uniformly clad with a metal gridded structure, overlaid with panels of rusted metal grating which give them an abstract, slightly mysterious air and industrial aesthetic: Nouvel was inspired by the ventilation system used in tobacco warehouses in the region. The resulting double skin serves as protection from the elements, as well as adjustable shuttering. Whole panels of grating can be hoisted up (by electronic jacks operated by controls at the head of each bed), exposing adjustable panels of clear glass.

The pavilions are separated by small

gardens and linked by a covered pathway. The restaurant nudges the corner of the old villa in which Amat's exquisite concoctions are prepared in enlarged kitchens. To emphasise its exalted position above the horizon, Nouvel has followed the line of the sloping site with a three-stage stepped effect. At mealtimes the rusted metal shutters are cranked up to forty-five degrees above the glazing on the south and west sides so that visitors can take advantage of panoramic views over the valley from the comfort of white upholstered chairs. These are Nouvel's own design: squashy cotton seats, with arms and back rests like resilient lumps of bread dough, attached to a thin curved metal structure.

At the end of the day, Amat's wealthy clientèle withdraw to bedrooms above the restaurant, or in each of three smaller pavilions. Nouvel has sub-divided floors into a variety of shapes: some up to 60 metres square with a bed in the centre of the room; others narrow, triangular slices, 15 metres long, widening to incorporate bathrooms, with beds close to the south-facing windows. The space taken up with lobby and circulation areas has been minimized to allow as much private room space as possible.

Walls of off-white plaster and polished concrete floors catch reflections from the gridded shutters, which when

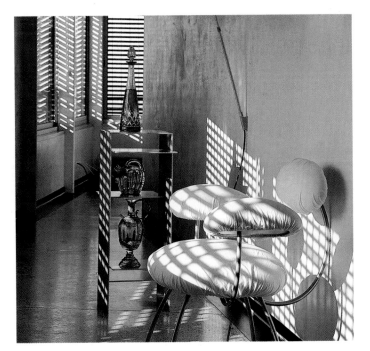

Antique glassware adds decorative forms to the light-filled bedrooms. The organic forms of Nouvel's white chairs achieve great stature in the sparsely furnished interiors.

Glass panels enclose
white and silver
bathroom fittings so
that smaller rooms
maintain a maximum
degree of openness.

Interior and exterior in
flux: a panoramic view
of the Garonne valley
from the hotel's airy

ground-floor
restaurant, seen here
with metal shutters
raised full height.

raised give the rooms a refreshing sense of openness, dazzling views and contact with nature's noises and smells. When closed, their roughness is hardly discernible from across the room, but is replaced by an impression of transparency and lightness in some of the larger rooms. The beds, designed by Nouvel, are raised platforms of bleached wood – higher in top-floor rooms to take advantage of the views. The bathrooms are compactly fitted into the rooms, with sanded glass partitions to maintain an open-plan feel. Mirrors, silver taps and white fittings exude high-performance efficiency.

Apart from the curvaceous white forms of Nouvel's chairs and other light-coloured soft furnishings, there are exposed grey funnel radiators along the skirting boards, and graceful lights by Paolo Rizzatto. Amat is gradually adding to the rooms antique glassware, ceramics or rugs to give each an even greater individual quality. Meanwhile, his guests – most of whom leave considerable trappings of material culture at home – revel in their unencumbered spaces where life, at least in some respects, can be pared down to basics (good food feeds the soul, so that does not count). Nouvel's ingenious, light-filled spaces and sensitively absorbed architecture, like Amat's food, refresh the jaded palate.

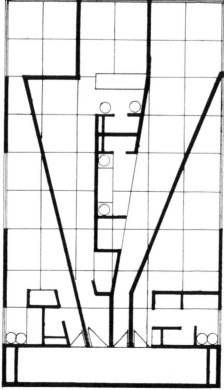

Restaurant building: first- and second-floor plan, with elongated bedroom shapes. Bedrooms in the other three blocks offer compact, rectangular variants, giving each its distinct character.

Across a newly planted vineyard, Nouvel has inserted new hotel buildings which respect their context, their
metal cladding overlaid with adjustable rusted grilles reminiscent of Bordeaux tobacco warehouses.

Elementer
(see pages 166–167).

Joseph
(see pages 160–163).

Leon Max
(see pages 170–171).

3

Stores, Showrooms & Retail Centres

At the front of the shop, a wedge-shaped wood-and-glass display case is cantilevered from a huge curvaceous plywood column, in a dramatic locking together of forms. In the foreground, Saee has carved a seat in the end of a display unit to accommodate the human form as well as the goods on display.

Ecru

BUILDING
Marina del Rey, Los Angeles, California, USA

The architectural projects of Michele Saee of Building are the result of an unusual and laborious making process which provides an insight into how form evolves. His passionate belief that architecture should be felt as much as seen leads to a close engagement with constructional techniques that explore craft processes. As a result, his work extends the expressive possibilities of design.

Ecru is situated in a two-storey shopping centre at Marina del Rey, minutes away from the seafood restaurant Angeli Mare, another recent project designed by the practice (see pages 98–9). The space Saee took on was an empty container within an uninspiring steel frame building. His conceptual starting point came from the immediate context of the marina, with its interplay of curved and moulded shapes, and from the techniques of boat construction. Their formal richness is linked with a challenge potently explored in his earlier design for the Ecru boutique on Melrose Avenue: how to translate images into architectural space without a two-dimensional, graphic result.

Clothing relates closely to the human body, echoing its curves and planes in a way that geometric forms could never emulate. It was the inspiration provided by a stylized Indian figurine which led to the scaling up and application of its gracefully contoured shape to the boutique's undulating walls, ceiling, columns and display units. Their organic structures carve out an expressive language of form based on natural structures, and are sheathed with curved plywood to emulate the effect of clothing on a human body.

The interior is made primarily of plywood, a basic construction material rarely used for dramatic ends. Instead of producing detailed construction drawings, Saee and his team drew full-size templates in the studio for free-standing, chevron-shaped walls, display counters and the equally asymmetrical forms of the façade. The templates were then used by carpenters to build ribbed frames of ¾-inch plywood, sheathed with ¼-inch plywood, which are positioned along either side of the shop, concealing the changing rooms.

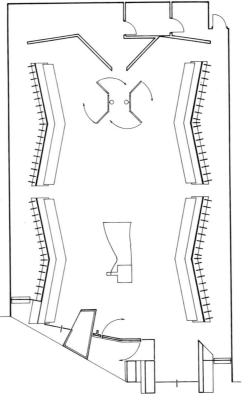

To bend the plywood into curves, each piece was placed in water and scored. Once mounted on studs suspended from a gridded beam in the ceiling, they dried and set into their contoured shapes. Not being machined forms, their tolerances were low, but the additional effort required to ensure that the panels fitted together smoothly did not deter Saee from attempting even more complicated juxtapositions — for instance, a wedge-shaped display case cantilevered off a figured column, which almost looks as if it grew that way.

By a similarly laborious process, the ceiling is shaped like the ribbed bottom of a boat. It proved too expensive to make in wood, so moulded gypboard was used, to create a dramatic, angled surface which merges smoothly with the plywood panels. The contoured forms are reminiscent of musical instruments which express sound through their shapes both literally and metaphorically.

The smooth surfaces of Ecru's curvilinear forms are played on by 'boom' lights, set in rows like tiny whiskery oars, or heads of wheat. Rippling pools of light splash across the surging, wave-like contours of the ceiling. A line of spotlights runs across the façade, positioned like eyeballs within oval recesses carved into the concrete canopy, and giving a suitably human introduction to the space beyond.

The bold, sculptural forms of the glass-and-plywood façade demonstrate a desire to engage with the urban context, to

Floor plan, with the four chevron-shaped plywood panels and display case protruding from the window plane.

Long 'boom' lights are suspended over the boutique's sinuous structure, picking out reflections in its curved surfaces. At the rear, two stands of V-shaped, pivoting mirrors cast their own reflections. On stained and sealed concrete flooring, two stained display units incorporate faceted benches into their even structure.

assert a presence which breaks up the blandness of the boutique's boxy, shopping mall context. A dramatic floor-to-ceiling pivoting convex glass door sets the tone, creating a double-width entrance open to the street; next to it, a rectangular glass display case protrudes from the window plane, as if proudly offering up goods to its surroundings.

Saee has aimed for a totality of design. He tried to imagine the interior of Ecru divorced from its mall context – as a space which predated its construction, in order to maintain a more direct link with the marina and its boats. Within this idealized context, Ecru can be seen as a block of wood which has been carved, forming a space designed without the distraction of sourced elements – except, of course, the clothes, which blend in effortlessly within his environment of strong, painstakingly crafted forms which embrace their tactile nature.

A pivoting, convex fin of structured glass swings round to open up the façade, a series of asymmetrical forms set at an angle, and seemingly disembodied from the dramatically warped contours of the interior, which are themselves virtually independent from the rectilinear cement plaster 'box' which contains them.

A view from the changing rooms situated behind the huge plywood partitions, which are reached by gaps between the chevron-shaped constructions. The horizontal scoring which allowed Saee to bend the plywood sheets is left visible, to expose the method of their making.

The changing rooms have metal-framed doors in opaque glass set into the rear of one of the stone columns.

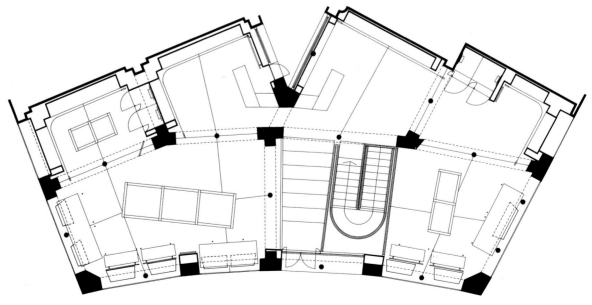

Ground-floor plan: the shop is arranged in three main display areas which provide a broad, curved façade on Place des Victoires, and radiate into four smaller, more intimate spaces at the rear, marked off by original stone columns.

Esprit

**STUDIO CITTERIO/DWAN
Paris, France**

The philosophy of these architects is powerfully demonstrated in their latest retail project for Esprit, situated on one side of the oval-shaped Place des Victoires. Antonio Citterio and Terry Dwan look back to a time when 'technology implied a moral rigour' not an 'ominous future': the language of high tech should involve an exploration of 'the inventiveness and optimism' of the industrial revolution.

The shop has a broad front, a curve of display windows exposed to the bustling piazza which give the interior display areas a fair amount of natural light. These spaces radiate away from the exterior, articulated as a series of interconnecting but intimate rooms: it is a forceful confrontation of urban and interior space.

The central metal staircase, set close to the window, imposes itself immediately on entering: it connects the ground-floor area with the display, changing room and storage spaces in the basement. There is a rugged feel throughout this space, with its subfusc tones, rough cement-finished walls, and stucco-painted cast-iron and stone columns. The architects' desire to show much of the building's original structure made it difficult to incorporate the air conditioning and lighting, but they persisted until they were satisfied: the

lighting was accommodated within the strong forms of the space without relinquishing its own identity. Three types of lighting tackle various functions: low-hanging, trough-shaped lamps for ambient light, spots to illuminate hanging displays at the rear, and incandescent under-shelf fixtures to pick out horizontally positioned merchandise.

The use of raw materials, humble in origin, is an established part of the architects' repertoire of architectural details, used to great effect in their previous work. However, this project demonstrates an alternative application in its allusion to a high tech language that avoids any slick, over-worked clichés. References to the factory floor of old – the solidity of materials before they meet the indomitability of technology – include the machine-like rolling ladders, heavy oak tables on cast-iron wheels, durable concrete floors, and 'indestructible' stainless steel finish to the staircase.

The clothes are displayed in niches, furnished with illuminated, fixed shelves;

they are boxed in rather than flaunted, and give a homely ambience to the spaces. The rigorous visual appearance of what the architects soberly term a 'retail laboratory' is not, however, imposed heavily on the visitor without relief. Its honest-to-goodness impulse is softened by adding rattan chairs, ecru canvas sunshades and a subtle palette of colours. There is also a certain earthy air of domesticity provided by the rough-hewn wooden furniture.

Aesthetically this is a long way from the white heat and harsh metal prevalent in earlier Esprit shops, and light years away from the company's original, post-Modern, flagship emporia. There are no gaudy, laminate-clad 'beach cabanas' or nougat-styled terrazzo features here. In fact, Esprit's stylistic twists and turns have reflected closely the changes that have taken place within a wider sphere of design practice. The growing use of wood, stone and metal that is treated rather than shiny suggests a low-key return to basics and, in the sense of embellishment, under-design. Now that the style-saturated 1980s are over, this is a refreshingly holistic approach, which respects the fabric of the building and creates a dialogue between the power of its original and of its new forms.

One of Esprit's generously proportioned display windows showing the solid oak tables and sturdy, low-hung lighting fixtures.

Taut, tent-like structures provide modest, mirrorless changing-room space, but within Koshino's zip-up neoprene 'cubicles', stretched to fit over metal frames, you could be squeezing yourself into a garment in the durable fabric she greatly favours.

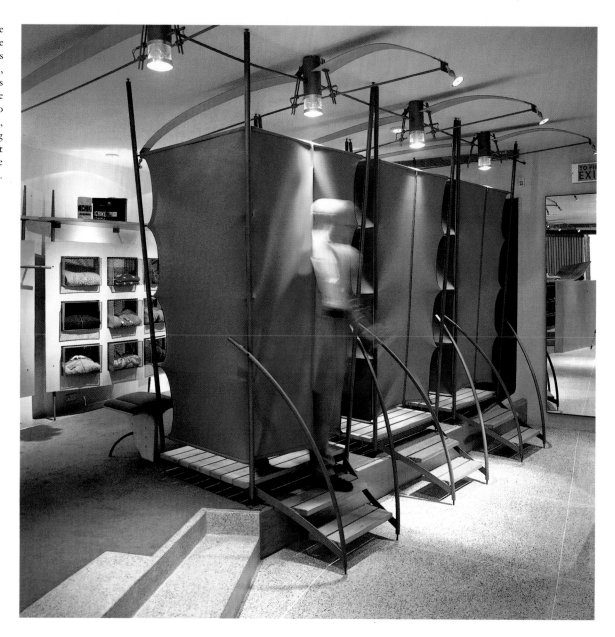

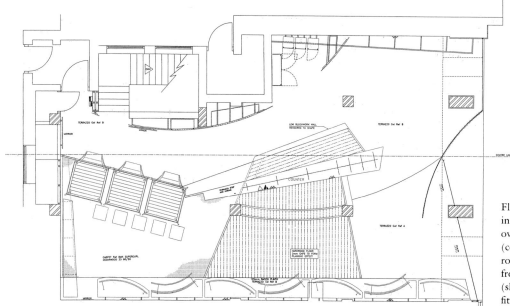

Floor plan: zoned areas in different materials, overlaid with angles (counter, changing rooms and glazed frontage) and curves (sliding door and wall fittings).

152

FERN GREEN PARTNERSHIP
London, UK

The Japanese fashion designer Michiko Koshino has lived in London for a decade. In recent years she has enjoyed cult status for her neoprene jackets, suits and sportswear with their highly conspicuous logos. She is an established name in Japan, but as a specifically British-related fashion phenomenon, a designer who draws her inspiration from UK club and street culture. Koshino is well aware of the internationalism of her appeal, and was adamant about steering clear of a design solution for her new Neal Street shop that displayed any obviously Japanese references. Instead, she aimed for 'a total environment', a concept that her followers could identify with, but which at the same time would satisfy her backers in Tokyo that she could make the grade commercially.

For this high-profile space in one of Covent Garden's pedestrianized streets, her brief to Fern Green stipulated a centrally positioned cash desk, to provide a focus of interest for the customers. Its raised end thrusts diagonally upwards towards the window, adding a touch of wit. A concave frontage, angled inwards, incorporates a three-metre-high curved, sliding door faced in wide oak strips. The design gives a clear view of the interior with no distracting elements. 'The shop is the display,' explained Koshino: in fact, the only item ever put in the window is a record console, wheeled out on occasion, with a live DJ playing records.

The walls and ceiling of the interior 'shell' have been created as one single colour backdrop in neutral, earthy tones which support seasonal changes in the colour of the clothes. Dramatic, custom-designed lighting helps to give the space its individuality. On the ceiling, a curved metal 'spine' connecting the light fittings creates a swirl of movement, with a series of plywood panels held in tension by metal rods. The designers used adapted car headlights, with smaller lights on each end of the plywood 'fins', to focus on the merchandise. Materials combine sportiness with natural organic forms, but avoid too raw a finish. The cash desk, raised on an oak platform, has a sandblasted mild steel frame clad with natural MDF panels and a walnut top. The changing rooms, reached by neat wooden stairs, evoke beach-hut cubicles.

The main display units are curved MDF panels. Suspended on sandblasted epoxy-coated mild steel uprights which form spikes at the top to support curved shelves for accessories, they disguise the rectilinearity of the wall surfaces.

The layered floor finishes add interest to the small (100-square-metre) space which is sensitively 'zoned'. Once past the terrazzo floor and the raised wooden platform, the visitor is greeted by a raised section of carpet running under the changing rooms and up the rear wall for about two metres — a visual pun which adds another dynamic element to the ingredients. This is a popular, accessible, inviting and stylish interior, achieved on a budget of £120,000.

The curved oak front door on a concave runner, flanked by clear glazing through which the inner life of the shop can be viewed.

STORES, SHOWROOMS & RETAIL CENTRES

Nicole Farhi

DIN ASSOCIATES
London, UK

Rasshied Din, the retail design specialist, cut his teeth on most of the UK's Next shops of the late 1980s. He is also an accomplished theatre designer and, with the retail scene experiencing a protracted downturn, he will certainly develop his repertoire in such diverse areas in the 1990s. Over the last two years, retail designers and managers in the UK have had to change tactics drastically to adapt to a climate of recession, thoroughly examining how customer satisfaction can be achieved in more low-profile and economical ways. Ultimately, however, there will always be the need to create a highly charged atmosphere conducive to purchase, even if the budget used is smaller, and the exercise happens at less frequent intervals. At the wholesale end of high fashion, less is having to work much harder to persuade cautious but powerful retail buyers to support a designer's latest collection. Din's London showroom for Nicole Farhi is a masterpiece of evocative working (i.e. selling) space – a light, calm, relaxing, durable and finely structured advertisement for the company, possessing all the characteristics for which Farhi's classic clothes are renowned.

'Timeless and classic with a contemporary edge,' was the primary objective of Din's brief to transform an area devoid of any natural light. He introduced daylight over the whole space by removing the roof, and then proceeded to refine the elements that were revealed.

Through a small entrance, the showroom is reached by a narrow staircase which opens up into a bright and spacious double-height space 6,500 square feet in size on the first floor. Surrounding this space – designed specifically for shows of ladies' fashion – and on a mezzanine above are incorporated storage and changing space, a smaller men's showroom, a cash-and-carry retail area, ancillary offices and a meeting room. The showroom sells clothes both to the fashion press and direct to buyers, by means of shows held within the main showroom space.

Taking out the roof was a happy experience, but initially there was much discussion on how to get the 'correct architectural feel' with what remained. Finally, a 6.5 × 13.5 metre rooflight was made of crossed steel trusses and an 'I' beam frame. Any potential problems of heat gain or loss from such a large area were prevented by double glazing and a well designed air handling system.

The initial design ideas included adding to the mezzanine level and designing a secondary staircase, but these were discounted because of the cost and complexity of structure in what is already a well defined space. Running along two sides of the main showroom are uninterrupted rows of 3.5-metre-high doors with laminated glass panels, screening an L-shaped corridor where the ladies' collection is located on a simple shelf-and-rail system. Models reach this area from a changing room, located at the corner of the two arms of the L, away from the main showroom itself.

The showroom is intended to be a salon, but one with a fresh atmosphere obtained by employing natural materials, such as bleached oak for the floor.

Natural light and light tones provide a restful environment in the main area for the fashion shows, akin to a nineteenth-century conservatory.

On the third side of the showroom, a separate room displays Nicole Farhi's recently introduced menswear collection. This is a small rectangular area, with a large oak-framed mirror and oak-planked table designed by Matthew Hilton, and a display system. The floor is made of natural honey-coloured paving slabs, normally used only outdoors, which also appear at the reception and entrance stair well. Together with the bleached oak used throughout the showroom area, these materials warm the white space, and provide a subtle contrast with the pale green metalwork, furniture and lighting.

The reception area is separated from the showroom by a 4-metre-high screen of timber-framed laminated glass panels with centrally positioned doors. This screen encourages a sense of anticipation before the visitor enters the openness of the showroom. The main challenge was to ensure that visitors' expectations of the sharply contrasting scale of the entrance and the main atrium space were fulfilled. It was achieved by exploiting the natural assets of the space, harmonizing its proportions, and

introducing diffused overhead lighting, together with simple materials and carefully planned details.

The showroom is designed to be left relatively empty, and no clothes are seen except as part of the shows. The light, upholstered, tub armchairs and small circular wooden tables give it a homely ambience. In the absence of merchandise, structural features, volumes and light command centre stage.

Inspired by nineteenth-century iron-and-glass shopping arcades, railway stations and glasshouses, the showroom demonstrates an imaginative interpretation of these traditional forms. The vertical lines of the showroom doors emphasise the height of the showroom; their forms intersect with the roof trusses, creating a rhythmical pattern across the space, particularly when the light casts narrow shadows.

Special effects have been achieved with economical means in this space, which was designed for a budget of approximately £100 per square foot.

A room adjoining the show area is devoted to Nicole Farhi's new menswear collection, displayed on a wall-mounted rail and a satin chrome frame supporting a simple, chrome-finished bowed rail and etched glass shelf. The oak-framed mirror and oak-planked table are by Matthew Hilton.

STORES, SHOWROOMS & RETAIL CENTRES

View of the reception area, where white timber-panelled doors continue the pattern set in the atrium, creating a civilised point of arrival for the trade.

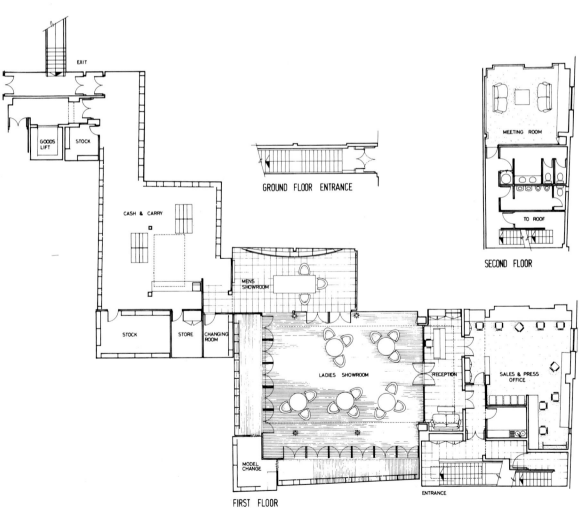

First- and second-floor plans of the showroom, and adjoining offices and changing rooms.

EXIT

GOODS LIFT   STOCK

CASH & CARRY

GROUND FLOOR ENTRANCE

MENS SHOWROOM

STOCK   STORE   CHANGING ROOM

LADIES SHOWROOM   RECEPTION   SALES & PRESS OFFICE

MODEL CHANGE

FIRST FLOOR   ENTRANCE

MEETING ROOM

TO ROOF

SECOND FLOOR

Set back from the street, the shop is fronted by glass, with an elegant green-and- white patterned marble pavement adding a decorative threshold to its tiny space.

Looking from the rear of the shop, the trio of vaulted ceilings divides the space into three main sections, with walls lined by wrought iron-and-glass display units.

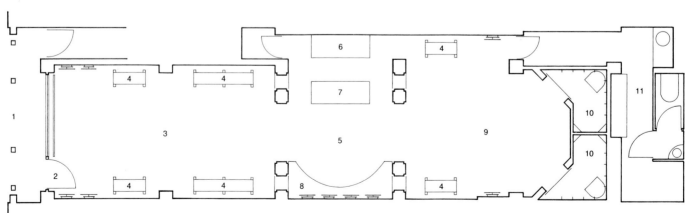

Ground-floor plan.
1 Covered marble pavement. 2 Entrance.
3 Women's collection.
4 Display units.
5 Central vaulted area.
6 Wall cabinet. 7 Cash desk. 8 Seating.
9 Men's section.
10 Fitting rooms.
11 Staff rooms.

Jasper Conran

This project developed from a previous collaboration between designer and client, which produced Conran's showroom in Great Marlborough Street. After long discussions, both parties agreed that Conran's first shop should epitomize their shared sympathy with the classical forms of English and Italian culture. Not all retail projects spring from such fortunate agreement, but this coincidence of aims did not necessarily make the job any easier. Indeed, the challenge for Leonard of working with a client who is himself a designer with strong ideas, coupled with the task of successfully interpreting the brief within a limited retail space, demanded just as much as any of his other, larger projects.

The initial inspiration came from Renaissance Venetian architecture, a favourite period of Conran. However, both Leonard and Conran were careful not to follow this theme too literally, as the results could have been contrived and gimmicky. Instead they attempted to unite the architectural forms of fifteenth-century Venice with a medieval spirit of a more English nature, which would complement Conran's clothes.

The threshold of the tiny (85-square-metre) shop immediately evokes an Italian mood, distinguishing it from its neighbours at the heart of Brompton Cross, a select area of fashion boutiques. The shop's all-glass frontage is set back, and the Conran patch is tastefully marked out by green and white marble set into a new area of pavement. Inspired by a Fra Angelico altarpiece, its effect is heightened by external footlights focusing on the internal window displays.

Although it is a hard-working fashion emporium, there are no harsh edges or icy monochrome design values here, but instead an intimate scale and a warm atmosphere. Three adjoining areas, each with vaulted ceilings bounded by arches, divide men's and women's clothing and changing rooms, adding interest to what would otherwise have been a boxy space. The divisions provide a sense of walking through an arcade, which gradually dissolves as the space becomes more 'private' and loses its symmetry towards the rear. Leonard claims that the lack of perfect symmetry 'allows the more English elements to work successfully', avoiding a space like an exquisite Quattrocento painting that is not functional on any level other than the spiritual.

The front section of the shop carries the bulk of the merchandise on custom-designed wrought iron-and-glass display units. Leonard's love of the English vernacular in design leads him to use traditional materials which provide comfort and stability in his furniture designs. The limed oak cash desk and planked oak floor blend well with the cool walls and vaulted ceiling.

A centrally placed, rotunda-inspired area with an oak block floor, built-in banquette seating and pilastered walls, faces a video screen set into the front of the cash desk, breaking up the overall soft and sensual feel of the space.

Other elements contribute to the dramatic, but dignified atmosphere: full mirrors provide a focal point at the rear of the shop and help create a feeling of extra space; Conran's curvaceous wicker mannequins add wit and, of course, a practical way to present key items. Simply designed wrought iron display units add to the carefully crafted elements, and give a time-worn appearance heightened by the arrow-head beaten into the end of each rod.

The lighting units, designed by Shiu Kay Kan, provide a subtle touch, hanging from each rib of the vaults. Their curved stainless steel forms, held by strung low-voltage wiring, bow over the space to create a tension with the arches.

The central cash desk area, showing part of the curved banquette seating and the unobtrusive display units.

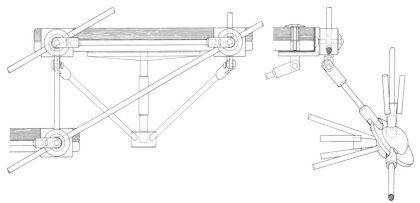

Looking through the carefully engineered support system of the staircase at a backlit display set into the smooth grey plaster walls.

Detail drawings of the staircase's cable support system.

Around the staircase, the ground floor has the aspect of a gallery, with furniture and beautiful artefacts, including vases by Philippe Starck on shelves or behind glass-fronted display cases.

3.6

Joseph

EVA JIRICNA ARCHITECTS
London, UK

The famous relationship between Joseph Ettedgui, redoubtable retailer and purveyor of all kinds of chic, and Eva Jiricna and her eminent practice, renowned for its rigorously elegant designs, has an enduring nature. Both have learned a considerable amount about high-fashion retailing during their eleven-year collaboration — a period when the fashion industry was evolving into a powerful consumption system that was constantly regenerating itself. Although in the late 1980s retailing slumped badly in the UK, and some of the latest fashion phenomena have arrived all dressed up with nowhere to go, the Joseph shops still hold their fascination for what has been termed their 'combination of rationality and sensuality'.

For Joseph's previous shop at Brompton Cross, Eva Jiricna Architects created an appropriate aesthetic to meet his request for a retail space with the feel of an Italian palazzo, eighties style. A metal-and-glass staircase — the distinctive signature of Jiricna's practice — was to be its major feature, joining together the many elements in a difficult 1000-square-metre space. The project was designed on a budget of £750,000 (£937 per square metre), and constructed in eighteen weeks, partly through the help of trusted subcontractors, allowing Jiricna to maximize the time she spent on project development. The discipline of this schedule determined many design decisions.

Joseph's latest shop in Sloane Street was designed once again to a tight timetable: having bought the building,

Joseph needed to have this prime site up and running as soon as possible. Fortunately, Jiricna's experience and vision allows her quickly to evaluate, cohere and clarify even the most unprepossessing raw retail space. The shop is a little smaller than its Italianate predecessor at Brompton Cross, and possesses a comparatively limited shopfront area. It occupies three floors of differing sizes, totalling 800 square metres. Joseph wished to display both women's and menswear combined with accessories, furniture and other high-quality objects, and to situate a small coffee bar on the second floor for his clientèle.

The existing geometry of the spaces available had little unity, and the shell was rather monolithic in nature. Jiricna replaced a badly positioned spiral staircase with a centrally located one to ease circulation and link up previously constrained floor spaces. Its design is a development of the staircase at the Brompton Cross shop, but this time conceived on a much larger scale. A separate team was responsible for it: Jiricna and her team member Duncan Webster collaborated with Matthew Wells of the creative engineers Dewhurst MacFarlane on the design — their most intricate one to date but which maintains structural integrity. As with earlier examples, it has a consistency of detail in its 'kit of parts' which forms a dynamic focus, with which the various retail spaces on each level can work in differing ways. On entering, the staircase salutes and draws the visitor further in, providing a visible orientation point for movement from one floor to another. To the regular visitor, it takes on the appearance of a resplendent three-dimensional sculpture

Ground-floor plan showing staircase, cash desk, oval display tables and glass wall cabinets.

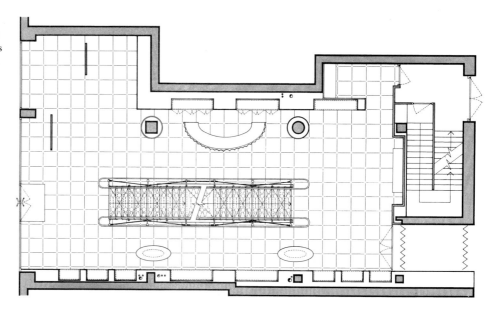

lit from above and below, emphasising its central position and its distinct qualities. These include opaque glass treads supported by 8mm rods which form a sinewy maze of structural members, each reduced to the minimum required thickness. The overall structure has a delicate appearance which belies its solid central suspension.

Each floor of the shop is divided into regular bays creating show-cases for small objects or hanging systems. Free-standing walls are used to increase merchandizing space, and glass shelves are chosen to display items in a clear and elegant fashion. Nothing is overloaded. Satin-polished stainless steel hanging brackets, as used in the Brompton Cross project, are combined with cantilevered plaster shelves to provide a contrast with the floating quality of the glass.

Cash tables made of brown stained maple are curved in plan with a dished profile front to soften the geometry, echoed in oval display tables, skirting, ceiling and wall details. This calm fluidity enhances the otherwise monolithic character of the space. Scattered about are chairs by designers including Tom Dixon, Mark Brazier-Jones and Kevin McCloud which, as at Brompton Cross, are changed from time to time.

To harmonize the various display systems, a restrained palette of finishes is employed. After sampling various prototypes, the practice chose a beige Spanish sandstone floor tile throughout to provide continuity. Walls and ceiling are a natural grey plaster sealed with an interesting mixture of beeswax and white spirit, to give the desired degree of

warmth. Ceiling details in timber are painted grey to blend in with the plaster.

Upstairs in the café, just a step away from the retail area, are eight tables designed by Jiricna. The black café chairs with backs like mussel shells and the bar-stools with curved metal stamen-shaped legs were designed by Philippe Starck.

An assured calmness and subtlety permeate the retail space, providing a restrained but not unwelcoming backdrop which does not fight with the shop's stylish merchandise. This is always carefully positioned or folded by a poised and uncrumpled sales team, ready to satisfy in equal measure the tactile and the visual senses of the participants in this ritual.

Such an aesthetic requires considerable imagination and planning. 'Atmosphere is function,' says Jiricna, 'You have to create it and make sure it is going to be right for the type of merchandise to be sold there. Function is also to do with what material is right as a background for certain types of clothes. The quality of the lighting is also a function in this sense.'

The lighting is a mixture of low voltage and metal halide for the display areas, concealed wherever possible behind the ceiling trough. Halides are hard, bright lights; softened by low voltage tungsten halogen, they give the effect of natural light without damaging the carefully contrived aesthetic effect. Fluorescent lighting at the rear of the display recesses highlights the glass shelves, and backs up the natural daylight from behind translucent glass screens.

The front entrance, with a full view of the stainless steel-and-glass staircase suspended from the second-floor slab. The design of the balustrade is incorporated to create a composite structural system.

In the first-floor display area, freestanding walls help to increase the merchandising space, but their position is carefully planned so the calm atmosphere is maintained. Exposed light fittings in the main areas have sandblasted glass bevels which give a soft, diffused light.

The main changing room: a small and eccentric space with more couches by de Portzamparc and a white carpet with red arrow insets.

Floor plan. 1 Entrance. 2 Cash desk. 3 Changing room. 4 Column. 5 Metal 'conque'. 6 Display space. 7 Office. 8 Men's department. 9 Perfumery. 10 Lamps. 11 Free-standing circular mirror. 12 Statues. 13 Doors to perfumery.

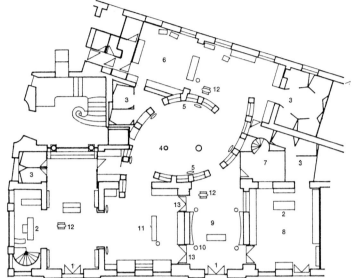

Boutique Emanuel Ungaro

CHRISTIAN DE PORTZAMPARC
Paris, France

The headquarters of Emanuel Ungaro's fashion house is situated in a grand nineteenth-century mansion building in the heart of the *haute couture* district of Paris off the Champs Elysées, at the end of avenue Montaigne. The street is lined with the salons of the high and mighty: Christian Dior, Valentino, Balmain. Four floors of the building are taken up with space for Ungaro's international business activities. On the ground floor, designed by Christian de Portzamparc, is the company's main showroom for clothes, perfumes and accessories. His brief included all the furniture and fittings which, as an integral part of the total design, it was hoped 'would clearly express and complement the spirit of Ungaro's work'. The project represents a departure from de Portzamparc's larger-scale work; its eclectic forms also break with the traditional aesthetic of many *haute couture* salons.

The 400-square-metre boutique faces avenue Montaigne, with the entrances and display windows in the retained façade. The geometry of the site and the existing structural divisions generated the layout of the interior, with an *enfilade* of rooms along each street front, each housing a particular line of clothes and/or accessories. The largest and most dramatic space is in the centre, formed by a *conque*, or shell shape, made of two curved, dark blue, stove-enamelled metal walls punched with openings to the outer areas. Its dark colour and strong

form lend it a dominating presence, and de Portzamparc has scored the shiny metal surfaces with wild scrape marks which break up their solidity.

De Portzamparc's aim was to emphasise the division of the shop into 'rooms', each with its own specific character. However, it was equally important that a clear layout was created: this is achieved by the large metal curves of the *conque*, which acts as the heart, and into which the other rooms have access.

A white marble floor throughout is shot with small black arrow insets which sweep in grid formation across the entire space. The walls are lined with painted wood or stuccoed panelling, and carry recessed hanging rails for the display of clothes. In the blue metal walls, the niches are backlit and lined with wood panelling hand-painted with a textured finish to complement almost every conceivable shade of garment.

Outside the inner sanctum, a vast circular mirror rests on a black marble base, flanked by two period oak doors. It gives the viewer a long vista free of merchandise, and is matched by a smaller, strategically placed mirror suspended on a steel pole for essential

back views. Should the customer need extra stimulation, a small circular area set in one side of the mirror provides room for a video screen.

A similarly aesthetic approach characterises the lighting. De Portzamparc brings together a variety of light sources which add drama and wit to the surroundings: ambient lighting is provided by false skylights, and by his 'Le Soleil' range of deep white saucers, recessed into the plaster ceiling and held in place by a curved metal arm. A perfume display set in mirrored niches is thrown into dramatic relief by four undulating tapered lights, made of sandblasted glass on tall conical black wooden bases.

'La Ligne', de Portzamparc's own range of furniture (sold exclusively through Ungaro) animates the showroom's cool chic, with squat oval couches and stools in upholstered black and white fabric, and playful wooden fittings. In the main ladies' changing room, ceiling-height sycamore chests with decorative handles and a table of bent metal legs add a decidedly wacky tone to the serious task of selecting outfits.

The intended spirit of the shop is also conveyed by a number of curvaceous resin statue forms, prominently positioned as if in a temple. Their striking symbolic presence, either on plinths or standing the entire height of the shop (to hide structural columns), emphasises the beautifully stylized body forms of Ungaro's clothes.

The showroom's curved blue metal walls form a shell shape at the heart of the room. Clothes are displayed in illuminated niches lined with pearwood and hand-painted in a textured finish. Two statuesque resin shapes dominate the space.

Reflected in a huge circular mirror on a black marble base is a smaller, artistic tailor's dummy perched on a brushed steel stand.

The reception seen from the showroom, connected by a glass walkway and stainless steel balustrading. On the right is a wide, pivoting, sandblasted glass door which allows the sales office to be opened up to the showroom for larger events.

The basement administration area is vertically connected with the ground-floor showroom by a new maplewood staircase inserted along the length of the space.

Split level elegance: across the void is the new staircase leading down to the administrative area. On the right, the showroom is screened from the sales office by the pivoting glass door.

Elementer

ARMSTRONG ASSOCIATES
London, UK

This showroom is Armstrong Associates' second project for Elementer, a UK company which markets high-quality Danish ironmongery widely used by architects. The refined simplicity of Armstrong's design of the company's headquarters in Slough met with unanimous approval, and has assisted the company's development. When Elementer's managing director Peter Thorley decided to relocate his small London office one floor down, to a larger ground floor and basement area within a Victorian warehouse in Southwark, partners Ken Armstrong and Jenifer Smith were once again brought in to design the interior — this time to function as a showroom as well as offices.

The 120-square-metre space had to incorporate a showroom, meeting room, sales area, general office, private offices, storage space, and kitchen and toilet facilities, on a limited budget of £95,000. In order to maximize the available floor area, simplicity had to be the governing principle. The architects removed the existing side staircase and covered the

remaining void. They then removed a beam to create a long opening in the dividing floor that runs the full length of the space, and is crossed in two places by glass-topped walkways. At the far end of the ground-floor area, a new wooden staircase has been inserted. This not only links upper and lower working areas, but allows light into the lower floor. Consequently, the interior has been given another intangible dimension, enhancing the feeling of space and freedom of movement between floors.

Elementer's various facilities have been housed with great care. As the offices were also to function as a public showroom, the entry needed to create an immediate impression using design elements that were in keeping with the client's flexibly modernist sympathies. The ground-floor reception area features a large maplewood desk facing a circular cut-out in the main staircase wall. Through this two glass screens in the other side of the staircase offer views through to the sales office and showroom, reached by a glass-topped bridge over the stairs. Orientation is carefully paced; once in the showroom, the visitor can take advantage of a flexible area, designed to expand if necessary. Receptions and other events

held in the adjoining showroom can extend quite naturally into this office (kept free of clutter), via a huge pivoting door in sandblasted glass. Wall-mounted display panelling appears on both floors.

These strategic decisions have involved astute choices of materials: the stairway is framed by a stainless steel balustrade and etched glass screens. Elsewhere, glass is sandblasted, or clear on door panels, screens and over the bridge walkway leading from the reception to the showroom. The flooring throughout is maple hardwood, which is also used for the reception desk. Door frames in mild steel contrast with the array of Elementer products used throughout. Recessed lighting provides subtle enhancement of the geometrical forms of the showroom, and spills down the maple stairs, adding atmosphere to the administrative areas situated below.

The simple, unadorned execution of elements within the showroom emphasises their tactile quality and their differing forms, but not at the expense of efficiency and comfort. The design's confidently expressed guiding principles have produced two interconnecting floors which work well for employees and also show Elementer's products to best advantage.

Upper ground-floor plan. 1 External entrance. 2 Entrance to showroom. 3 Reception desk. 4 Bench. 5 Stairs to lower ground floor. 6 Glass screen. 7 Sales office. 8 Pivoting door. 9 Bridge. 10 Showroom. 11 Void.

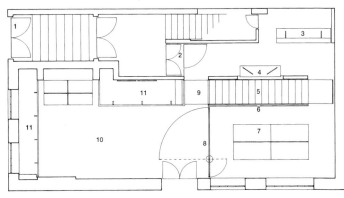

Between the sound and the substance: a conscious decision to use very few materials results in the creation of a small arena of calm, in which the tonal values of the acrylic set the atmosphere.

3.9

Yoshiki Hishinuma

SHIRO KURAMATA
Tokyo, Japan

Using the same unique qualities of coloured acrylic which make the Oblomova Bar at Il Palazzo Hotel such a symphony of colour (see page 86), Kuramata has created a tiny but dramatic fashion boutique in Tokyo. In just 54.2 square metres, tucked into the ground floor of a much larger building, there was hardly space to accommodate bulky display systems or complex overhead track lighting. An extended session of lateral thinking produced the solution: to 'un-design' the defining elements of the space – floor, wall and ceiling – so that the 'soft' qualities of colour and tone are given full range.

Kuramata often experimented with formal and aesthetic values in this way, to heighten the psychological impact of his

interiors. Obviously the basic elements of the space have to exist, but their impact as separate components can be extinguished. By presenting acrylic's delicate colours and its quality of semi-transparency blended in simple blocks, he has created a bright and rhythmical atmosphere, visually emulating the effect of music. Numerous diodes within the acrylic are activated by a conducting film, and give an ethereal, coloured glow to its slim forms.

Because the backdrop is so neutral – large white diagonal floor tiles and smooth, anodized aluminium walls – full force is given to the play of the bright-toned acrylics. The functional elements within these walls exist only as a series of unimposing horizonal lines. Running from one side to the other are anodized aluminium and steel hanging rails. Shelves of aluminium-covered wood hug a curved wall which marks off the minuscule stock-room. Elegant matching aluminium coathangers with non-slip rubber corners embellish the rails, small details which are the low-key carriers of the coloured acrylic's vibrant 'tones'.

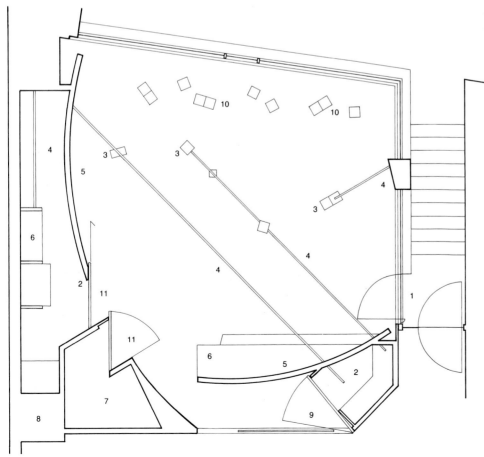

Floor plan. 1 Main entrance. 2 Stockroom. 3 Column. 4 Hanger. 5 Wall. 6 Shelf. 7 Fitting room. 8 Cash desk. 9 Display area. 10 Display columns. 11 Doors.

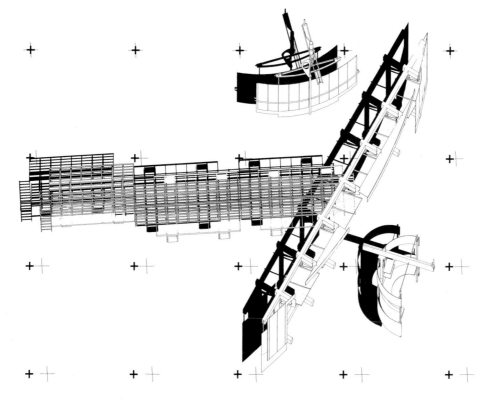

Four freestanding objects, suggestive of the machinery of the production process, within the grid of the concrete columns. From left: runway (open)/clothing display (closed); screen for conference area/model changing area (top); client waiting area/ overhead lighting; reception desk.

The overhead lighting fixture defines the entrance area leading from the reception desk to a conference room in the corner, and introduces a more arbitrary feel to the horizontal layered partitions arrayed behind the central structural columns. The floor is rough sandblasted concrete.

The wide, curved metal reflectors of the 'plane wing' sweep diagonally across the end of the catwalk/runway.

3.10
Leon Max

MORPHOSIS
Los Angeles, California, USA

Morphosis creates a potent architecture 'of movable parts'. Those with a keen eye can discern in each project by Thom Mayne and his partner Michael Rotundi tantalising references to (and adaptations of) furniture and other elements previously applied. Not a recycling of ideas, this recurring repertoire of forms represents a continuity of independent and evolving research and development.

This has two major effects. Firstly, their forms, predominantly made of wood and metal, frequently resemble sculptural assemblages signifying the constant weighing up and testing of ideas – ideas which are often left hanging in the balance, but which represent questions which are always addressed. Secondly, the architects are able to retain a healthy distance from the commercial function of the project in question. Their continual enquiry through form produces interiors which explore and question basic functions and processes all too often taken for granted.

Leon Max's main fashion showroom in downtown Los Angeles is the site of fast-moving activities – a selling, meeting and display space rolled into one. Leon Max wanted an aesthetically strong, hardwearing and flexible interior to accommodate fashion shows, visits from buyers and other clients and fluctuating quantities of his latest lines, to be stored but readily accessible. Morphosis took the opportunity to analyse the fashion marketing process, and the resulting interior bears witness to the tactics of concealment and revelation.

Leon Max is a strongly rectilinear space, lined with aisles of semi-independent units storing merchandise and marking off private offices. These gridded, yellow-tinged, plywood partitions in turn partially conceal outer blocks of geometric blue window blinds at the periphery. Within the central arena are four elements which animate the space: a reception, catwalk, conference room and waiting area. Their materials, construction and aesthetic evoke a sense of the machinery and process of industrial production, but at the same time allow them to function as mobile props.

The movable modular units reinforce the showroom's spatial boundaries. Their perforated surfaces play on the storage/display theme: fabrics reveal their contrasting colours before they become fully visible. A central maplewood catwalk dominates the space: attached to its sides are adjustable metal flaps, modelled on hydraulic planes which, when fully raised, fence off the catwalk almost as if it were a high-performance runway. At the side are skeletal chairs, with frames made of steel sections and perforated sheet metal seats. The front is a simple rigid seat, and the back a complex, articulated support structure.

Behind the central expanse of sandblasted floor, sliding partitions of Douglas fir plywood and steel frames conceal a conference room with a long, frosted glass table. Even this space can be broken down and joined to the centre, by moving the frames, which turn on elaborate metal hinges. Breaking the rigorous symmetry imposed by the partitions is a 30-metre-long lighting unit which slices diagonally across the space, superimposed on to black, L-shaped structural elements which can incorporate occasional seats.

Throughout the project Morphosis strove to 'eliminate traditional architecture', and avoid the banality of the one-dimensional showroom archetype. In its place they generated resonant forms which propose and suggest a multiplicity of functions. Avoiding a wide repertoire of materials, the project achieved its hard-won objective on a budget of $390,000.

The showroom chairs are designed by Morphosis: an ingenious interplay of a frame in steel sections, and a flat seat which is a single plane of perforated sheet steel. In the background are the steel 'flags' attached to the sides of the catwalk/runway, seen here in the upright position.

Standard lighting tracks, set in a customized metal fixture, run in a rhythmical line across the tilted triangular ceiling plane. The cherrywood cash desk on the right is followed by a succession of blue-panelled bays in which different displays can be established. A terrazzo floor provides a durable and textured base.

Ground plan of the L-shaped space, with the triangular ceiling plane running from the entrance on the left to the rear of the shop, across horizontal floor strips marking out six bays.

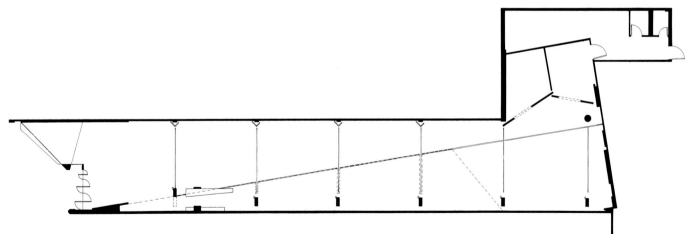

Domain at Burlington Mall

SCHWARTZ/SILVER ARCHITECTS
Burlington, Massachusetts, USA

Detail of the back wall, a sculptural tableau of forms which draws on De Stijl. The intensity of the orange pillar marking the end of the ceiling plane gives it greater prominence when seen from the front of the shop, from where it looks way off centre: it is in fact centrally placed in the hidden rear space.

Domain is a chain of shops established in the US over the last three years to sell contemporary European furniture to discerning 'baby boomers'. Schwartz/Silver has designed all twelve shops to date, evolving a dynamic design language based on bold colours and contrasting materials such as wood, metal and terrazzo. It is a singularly unfussy formula, and highly appropriate for a target market of young professionals.

The architects have avoided imposing notions of style; instead, they have defined a flexible, non-regimented, retail space with strong geometrical forms. Dual architectural elements are used to break down the barrier between the customer and the retail space: a display platform projects through the clear glass of the angled front façade, and three doors made of pivoting panels emulate large, abstract canvases. These are both familiar devices seen in earlier Domain shops.

The Burlington Mall shop is a narrow, L-shaped space, divided into a series of 15-foot grids by deep blue columns along the perimeter walls. No further fixtures have been added to the walls, allowing minimal intrusion into a space that will display an eclectic and frequently changing mix of modern furniture. A triangular panel cuts across the ceiling in a diagonal sweep, emphasising the length of the room and directing customers towards the concealed end. Fine black strips are inlaid horizontally across the floor to make further delineations; the lighting track and narrow grooves cut into the ceiling panel add to the sense of a sequence of spaces or bays from the front to the rear of the shop. Translucent panels on a track system can be moved into various positions, breaking up the open space.

The 5000-square-foot shop was completed for $325,000, a mere $65 per square foot, so a judicious choice of materials was essential. Construction costs were minimized by using standard building materials and methods – for example, the 'bow and arrow' lighting track, but this was then combined with a custom-made metal fixture. Walls are gypsum drywall, some with custom paint finishes, others with reveals of aluminium channelling. Cherrywood fin details on the columns and desk serve to add warmth and character with minimum use of expensive materials.

At Politix, Cleveland, a large, busy format incorporates a complex structure of industrially inspired wooden and metal armatures expanded to a dramatic scale to hold clothing. Across the ceiling, taut and controlled sets of wires run parallel, holding spotlights on the underside of curved cast aluminium forms. Display tables of wood and sandblasted glass and steel are positioned along the length of this rectilinear space.

3.12
Politix

MORPHOSIS
Cleveland, Ohio, USA
Portland, Oregon, USA

Morphosis' work for Politix demonstrates the successful application of conceptual architectural forms within a retail context. The brief called for improvements to two separate properties owned by Politix, a progressive men's fashion retailer. One is a 1000-square-foot space in a new commercial mall in Portland, Oregon; the other a larger, 1500-square-foot space prominently positioned in a renovated shopping mall in Cleveland, Ohio. As with the Leon Max showroom (see pages 170–1), Morphosis' ambitious aim was to apply an imaginative, technology-inspired approach to a retail brief, while distancing themselves from its commercial aspects.

The concept explored is the making of objects: in particular, the making of a garment, a high-speed process and, with its high level of skilled labour, very craft-intensive. With their abiding love of analysing process, the architects saw that clothing on display represents the

creatively applied their sculptural forms into structures for the display of men's clothes. It is an unusual and imaginative idea, beautifully executed, and sufficiently strong to address itself effectively to the display and selling function of the shops.

At Portland, a huge, diagonally positioned display unit dominates the brightly lit space, a direct translation of an antique loom with an intricate wooden structure woven with fine, taut metal. There is a sense of mechanical movement emphasised in the fine threads of wire which shoot off the loom to a higher metal frame.

At Cleveland, the loom imagery is fragmented but applied on a magnified scale. Armatures of spindles and cables are established along opposing sides of the shop in clearly marked zones, their bases serving as display units for clothes. On one side, the industrial structure is set forward from the outer wall and extends the whole length of the shop, in front of rows of changing rooms and storage space. Above, parallel rows of taut wire — more disciplined than at Portland — underline the rigid tension of a machine in action. The powerful metal-and-wood structures set on polished slate floors and lavishly adorned with merchandise establish the larger shop's more extrovert atmosphere.

At the Portland shop there is less space, and clothes are displayed in large, square, back-lit recesses, leaving room for the evocative loom — a single object

Beneath the towering armatures of Douglas fir and steel ranked along the periphery of the shop, one gets a sense of being in an industrial workshop, but at the same time among the fruits of the loom.

culmination of a process of making. The industrial forms of their display units therefore suggest the beginnings of such a process and provide a strong theme to which all the main display areas are connected.

To both spaces Morphosis have applied images of the industrial production of textiles gleaned from Diderot's eighteenth-century sketches of workshop machinery. The architects have studied the looms, warps and wefts of textile manufacture — as well as the shapes of fabric pattern cut-outs — and

POLITIX

175

and main focus of attention – under an uncompromising grid of cold fluorescent lighting fixtures set in the black ceiling. However, its imagery is extended to the dramatic window display, and given a human dimension. Four mannequins dubbed 'loboto-men' stand at an angle to the window, legs akimbo, dressed in Politix's lastest outfits, with headless faces on necks supported by a triangular wire structure above. Where their heads should be, curved mesh metal containers hold flourishes of coloured fabric, like party hats. Looking more closely at the figures, one sees that their metal 'antennae' are connected with the top of a high, rectangular, transparent, wired panel behind, emphasising a structural and conceptual link between all the major parts of the display systems, which refer back to the origins of the making process – the mighty loom.

At Politix, Portland, splayed wire spins off the cold rolled steel rockers of the loom structure, lit by recessed fluorescent light and supported by rows of spotlights.

The 'loom' holds clothes in niches and on rails; it is the only central display unit in this tiny shop. The bulk of the storage is in cast aluminium hardware shelves, set in backlit recesses around the sides.

Facing a clear glass frontage overlooking the shopping mall, the mannequins are industrial players, their heads deconstructed and attached to wires.

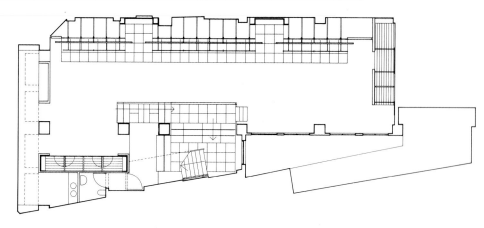

Floor plan of the basement retail space, with platform and double-height stairwell leading to street level.

Simple pieces of furniture such as a reproduction of the fifteenth-century painter Paolo Uccello's 'Tomasa' chair (also displayed in the men's shop) provide a contrast in scale. The changing-rooms on the right are backed by a frameless glass door, which forms a relationship with the glass balustrade, and lets light in through the main staircase and the double-height window.

Issey Miyake Women

STANTON WILLIAMS
London, UK

Issey Miyake's instructions to Stanton Williams for their first commission were simple: 'Just make me a beautiful space.' The designers, inspired by Miyake's clothes, reacted by 'demonstrating a concern with objects' in their finished design for Issey Miyake for Men, London. They treated the goods as exhibits, creating a 'conversation' between space, materials and light which won them the prestigious UK D&AD Gold Award in 1988.

This acclaimed dialogue, the result of a close and trusting relationship with the client, led to this second commission, a sister-shop facing the original across the Brompton Road in South Kensington. This time, the basic requirement of the brief was to transform a small ground-floor retail space into a single, integrated retail unit. The result is a scheme which clearly links the new lower retail space to the street level by the removal of most of the ground floor, creating a grand, double-height stairwell.

This link is amplified by the visual

connection between a single linear ceiling coffer and rooflight with a double-height (7-metre) translucent window facing the staircase. These vertical elements 'concentrate the movement down the lower area', adding an air of ceremony to the descent below. It echoes the concept behind the smaller, more vault-like men's shop, establishing a formal relationship between the two.

Lines and forms are carefully modulated throughout. Sealed plain white plaster walls emphasise and define the structure of the space without an excess of rhetoric. With a series of modular planes space can be organised effectively, providing a freedom of movement and capacity for change, qualities the architects feel are inherent in Miyake's clothes.

Natural materials in the lower retail space — oiled and whitened oak, raw silk and canvas blinds, a pale grey granolithic floor with *pietra laro* stone and limestone paving — emphasise tactile qualities. As well as Stanton Williams' carefully crafted oak tables, there are items of furniture by specialist wood craftsmen such as John Harwood and Jeffrey James, which reflect

the level of skill that goes into the creation of the clothes. Sally Greaves Lord's occasional mixed-media wall hangings add further individually crafted elements.

A second phase of the scheme adds a planted garden area in a small rear courtyard, visible through glass, throughout the year. Natural light is let in through this space, linking interior and exterior, and transforming the appearance of the shop.

The designers' desire for flexibility in use is reflected in the shop's generous proportions — a wide staircase, a studio-type space in the lower retail area, a large wooden table and display tops. They convey a self-assured openness rarely achieved in a retail context, where space for stock is generally treated as almost holy ground. Here, the designers have respected the strong forms and subtle layers of the fabrics of Issey Miyake's clothes, and have given them pride of place against the subtle tones of the shop. This ability to draw objects out of a background is derived from Stanton Williams' exhibition and gallery design projects, in which they learned both to develop their distinctive vocabulary and to experiment with form. As with good exhibition displays, you need to slow down to appreciate fully the relationship between objects and context. Although subtle in appearance, much is at work in Stanton Williams' spaces — this is not design for people in a hurry.

From the lower retail area, floored with limestone leading to terrazzo, a timber staircase leads up to the main open-tread staircase and double-height entrance. The basement has been transformed and given a generous sense of space, such as that found in a studio.

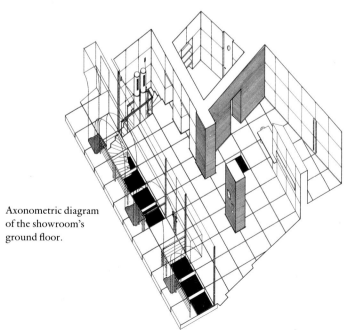

Axonometric diagram of the showroom's ground floor.

Between the old wide brick arches and walls, new glass and aluminium elements are picked out by spotlights.

STORES, SHOWROOMS & RETAIL CENTRES

Downstairs, a huge, blue-tinted anodized aluminium table commands a central position. It is lit through aluminium grilles above and below, the floor grating being given a translucent, blue-textured appearance by the underfloor lighting.

Set within a seventeenth-century building located in the historic centre of Toulouse, the new showroom for Technal – which manufactures aluminium industrial products – combines archaeology and invention to dramatic effect. Dedicated to demonstrating the creative applications of aluminium, it combines exhibition spaces, a library, projection room and a seminar room within original brick vaults. Managing Director Jean-Michel Martineau understands the valuable role of design – in anticipating new products, in endowing technology with new forms, as well as in providing an imaginative and progressive context for Technal France's products to be displayed and explored.

In spite of the modest nature of the site – a ground floor and basement area

totalling 200 square metres, previously a shop – designer Jean-Michel Wilmotte has overcome its structural difficulties. The interior thrives on the contrast between the archaic character of the old brick fabric, and the technical sophistication of the aluminium forms both applied and displayed.

The light, supple quality of a modern material like aluminium is given a context through its juxtaposition with warm red banded stone arches, walls and pillars; in the process, the historic stonework is revivified and its forms become abstract compositions. Aluminium is applied in a number of ways: for inlays in the concrete floor slabs, and as a wrapper for the air-conditioning ducts which run vertically through the space. It is also used for the showroom's architectural hardware – banisters, doors, window-frames, illuminated display windows, door handles – and, on a larger scale, to create a long,

3.14
Technal

JEAN-MICHEL WILMOTTE
Toulouse, France

imposing table.

New and old, rough and smooth – brick and aluminium are juxtaposed to highlight their contrastingly rich colours, textures and forms. In his approach towards the rough, banded brick of the old structure, Wilmotte is an archaeologist, cleaning away old layers to expose the basic architectural forms. Between the brick flag-stones, he inserted aluminium inlays which, strangely, become like *objets trouvés* in their context, only newly created ones. They help to create a subtle disorder of contrasting scales, textures and forms.

In bringing coherence to this disjointed space, the imaginative introduction of light accentuates the new volumes and textural relationships, without destroying the spirit of the original building. Daylight penetrates Technal's numerous openings and arches, and the rugged and imprecise forms of the brick vaults are given new clarity of form by a subtle mix of natural and artificial lighting. This is particularly striking in the basement meeting room, empty except for a huge anodized aluminium topped table, which seems to float on the aluminium grille flooring with its translucent blue glow emanating from concealed lighting below.

On the ground floor, the low wooden ceiling beams were cleaned and retained. Their rough dark forms keep traces of old grey paint, providing another structural and textural contrast with the inventively applied aluminium forms found in Technal's vaulted spaces.

In the basement the air-conditioning ducts look like metal totems alongside the staircase, mixing modern curved forms with traditional brick arches.

3.15

Cassina, Collezione

**MARIO BELLINI,
WITH GIOVANNA BONFANTI
& MARCO PARRAVICINI**
Tokyo, Japan

This 300-square-metre showroom is positioned on the top floor of Tokyo's Collezione, a commercial building designed by Tadao Ando. Its internal space is formed by two separate volumes: a double-height gallery defined on two sides by glass, and by concrete walls on the other sides which converge outside the space; and a low-ceilinged upper area which overlooks the gallery and opens on to a terrace facing the street. The entrance opens directly into a big double wall in stunning Pompeiian red, which unites the two areas and creates a bridge at the upper level which links it to the passageway around the balcony. The wall, punctured by deep windows at which visitors can stand, is a key element of the space. It is lit from above and behind by scenographic lighting which, by creating strong contrasts of light and shade, imparts the allure and grand scale of a theatrical set piece, day and night. Bellini

quaintly likens it to 'a fragment on an endless aquaduct', but there is nothing of the found object about its crafted quality. A curved sandblasted glass-and-steel reception desk, equally pristine, sits on either side of the wall, 'mounted like a jewel' within its two sides.

The wall acts as a filter towards the gallery and adjoining showrooms. It stands at 45 degrees from a large staircase faced with hefty panels of galvanized iron, which forms a strong triangular 'intervention' that makes a similarly scaled counterpoint to the wall. This leads to the open space of the upper gallery, from which three partitioned showrooms are accessible. These interconnecting, adjustable spaces have been deliberately scaled down in proportion to allow the creation of set rooms with a domestic ambience, replete with elegantly laid out dining and living room furniture.

From the exposed concrete beams of the ceiling is suspended a *trompe l'oeil* painting of writhing forms by Sandro Chia. It is pointed out by a single spotlight, and provides a neat, ironic gesture in place of a real Italian fresco.

One of the adjustable upper rooms.

Working drawing: the double wall positioned behind the building's façade, reception desk, showroom and staircase to the viewing gallery and upper spaces.

The colliding geometries of the wall and internal bridge which runs at an angle to the front window, providing a vantage point for viewing the gallery areas.

Iron staircase in the main gallery area, leading up to a raised level and full view of the main wall.

The intersecting planes of the dramatically lit double wall and its more low-key neighbours. Encircling the foot of this structure are glass-topped reception desks. On the left, a sculptural staircase faced in galvanized iron rises from the cherrywood floor.

STORES, SHOWROOMS & RETAIL CENTRES

Shonandai Cultural Center
(see pages 232–235).

Cité de la Musique (west side)
(see pages 200–203).

4

Cultural &
Public Amenity
Buildings

4.1

Horst-Korber Sportzentrum

CHRISTOPH LANGHOF ARCHITEKTEN
Berlin, Germany

The completion and opening of the Horst-Korber Sports Centre coincides with the beginning of a new era in Berlin's history. It took three years to build, and five years to plan and achieve the necessary permission. Now that East and West Berlin are reunited, the Centre provides a facility which can be used by sportsmen and women from all over the city and from further afield, for competitive sporting activities of the highest calibre. In the long term it is also hoped that the Centre will assist in the development of Berlin as a world-class venue for sports.

With this project, Christoph Langhof, with collaborators Thomas Hanni

to the quality of Berlin's built environment is unstinting.

The architects worked closely with Bernd Trabert, the owner and manager of the building, a 'discriminating and dedicated client', and involved a range of consultants including Ove Arup & Partners on structural and environmental aspects, landscape architects and acousticians, to ensure a high-powered result that would fulfil both current and anticipated future needs.

The Centre is set close to Berlin's Olympic Stadium in an attractive stretch of forest and, although complex, is so well integrated into this verdant environment that its dimensions can be gauged only from the air. The effect is achieved by sinking the buildings into the ground with the help of over five hundred anchors, which support walls that would otherwise be crushed by the build up of soil.

Comprising two separate parts, the Centre houses a range of sports halls which cater specifically for handball, hockey and volleyball, with a weight-training room and changing rooms. To the north of this, the second building incorporates administration and seminar rooms, plus a sauna, whirlpool, medical centre, café and single-bedded accommodation with south-facing rooms for up to forty athletes during long training sessions. The two buildings face each other longitudinally, creating a 'corridor' between their façades.

The 88.5 × 45 metre main sports hall can be subdivided into three smaller halls, one of which can be divided again into three smaller training areas. High on the right are the press booths.

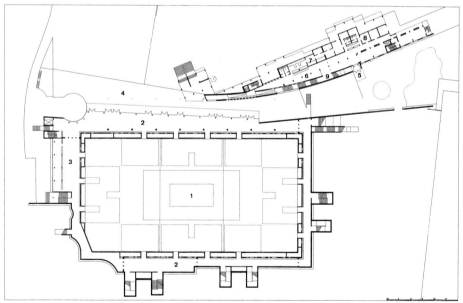

Ground-floor plan of the two parts of the complex, connected below ground. 1 Sports hall. 2 Foyer. 3 Café. 4 Spectators' entrance. 5 Players' entrance.

6 Restaurant.
7 Kitchen.
8 Manager's office.
9 Corridor/staircase access to changing rooms and sports hall below ground.

and Herbert Meerstein, has attempted to take a sports venue beyond the realms of the purely functional, by creating a building of a more general cultural nature. It is named after a prominent government minister who, until his death in 1981, had worked to advance sporting activities in Berlin. It represents both his passion, and that of the architects, whose commitment

Getting into the main sports areas is a journey to the depths. A long stairway leads down to the lowest floor of the building, opened to the south by windows letting light into the various rooms.

The main sports hall has a ceiling height of 14 metres. It seats 3,450 spectators on telescopic stands made of beechwood strips, which are also used for the wall surface throughout. During training, the stands can be moved back into the walls of the hall, adding a substantial area to the playing courts, which can be divided into two or three sections for simultaneous matches. This versatile space is covered by a curved glass roof, which appears to hover over the floor. Four hundred and twenty dome-shaped lights sit on the roof to ensure that the light is regular, non-dazzling and natural — ideal conditions for high-performance sport. During fine weather, the rooflights can be opened, giving the players an open-air atmosphere. The roof is made of steel, suspended from four 30-metre-high pylons, with 'fingers' linked by cables under tension supporting the roof. The pylons — part of a light and delicate-looking construction — provide a strong identifying feature of the building.

The centre is a steel construction, covered with tinted stainless steel riveted panels which reflect the light. Langhof has used tropical timbers for the outdoor terraces and beech on the interior sports hall walls; the main changing room areas are floored in red rubber, and all fittings are in stainless steel. The design invests the Centre with the elegant dignity and austere grandeur of a cultural building, without compromising its high-performance requirements.

The stairway leading down to the sports hall and changing rooms, with access on the lowest floor of the building.

Bright patches of colour interspersed with grey in the weight-training room, which is lit by a combination of industrial uplighters and natural lighting through large rear windows.

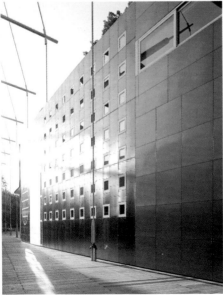

The steel façade of the block adjacent to the main hall of the 15,800-square-metre sports centre, viewed from the terrace. On the left are the sides of the 30-metre pylons from which the roof of the hall is suspended.

The small wards are sympathetically lit, and screened to encourage natural light to fall on to the reflective floor surfaces.

Cross-section through building. From left to right: ramp connecting garden and patio, wards, lightwell, consulting rooms and forecourt to chapel.

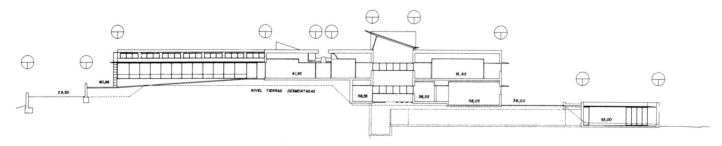

Móra d'Ebre Hospital

JOSE ANTONIO MARTINEZ LAPEÑA & ELIAS TORRES TUR
Tarragona, Spain

The new hospital built for the provincial government of Catalonia overlooks the town of Móra d'Ebre, and the large orchards and river beyond. Sensitively designed by Jose Antonio Martinez Lapeña and Elias Torres Tur, it is a relatively low and horizontally extended building on a 25,000-square-metre landscaped site which integrates well with the surrounding landscape. It is traditionally constructed, without any prefabricated parts. Working with a relatively low budget, Lapeña and Torres have achieved professional results with simple materials used on both exterior and interior.

In front of the wide building, a huge triangular landscaped area crossed by a small projecting block distances the hospital from perimeter roads. The site is encompassed by low rough-hewn stone walls, emphasising that it is raised from the surrounding terrain, but not to the degree that the low-level horizontality of the building is lost. Its low white façade presents a briskly efficient demeanour, emphasised by a large blue clock on the top right-hand side of the entrance block, which is square like a postage stamp. This is unmistakably a public building, but it is not over-imposing, and it is beautifully scaled to fit its environment.

Between the clinics and treatment rooms at the front and the wards at the rear are closed, terraced lightwells. Breaking up the light source are taut strips of fabric roof, some at a higher level than others, in blue or orange canvas. It is here that the obvious Scandinavian influence (the silhouette is blended with nature, and comprises forms combined to fulfil human needs rather than to create beautiful geometry) meets more local influences, in the form of decorative brick paving and orange trees.

At the rear of the hospital the long, angular planes of the front elevation become smaller recesses, in order to provide both visual access to and protection from the elements. Here, the hospital wards are designed in units around small patio areas overlooking the river, and connecting via ramps to a terraced garden.

The wards are orientated towards the best views to the north or east. Their atmosphere is calm and light, with smooth surfaces. The light sources are carefully judged and the wards are sited close to the Ebro river. This provides another positive and psychologically uplifting dimension to the hospital's interiors: landscaping is a factor often not considered when prefabricated hospitals are sited, due to planning constraints, restricted urban sites or lack of funds. As this hospital is run privately, it enjoys small, secluded wards, some accommodating just one bed with another for visiting relatives, and all wards have private bathrooms.

The specialist medical units, clinics and surgeries are ranged longitudinally, their heights adjusted specially to suit each space and to ensure an optimum amount of natural light. All services, including washing rooms, kitchens and boiler rooms, are situated on the north side around a closed service courtyard on the fringes of the site. A compact west-facing block, with internal courtyards, houses other services. At right angles to the main façade, a projecting wing houses a state-run outpatients' clinic. Also situated independently from the main building is a lower-ground mortuary chapel, a semi-circular space on the edge of the landscaped site.

The hospital is a well-proportioned building on a generous site with an abundance of natural resources. Its rationally planned interiors show a scrupulous attention to ease of use and maintenance, but it is flexible enough to allow an empathy with the surrounding landscape. Sunshades along the windows and canopies over the internal courtyards, for example, allow naturally filtered light to illuminate the humanely designed spaces.

Two tones of grey wall tile are applied to a sleekly curved stair wall leading from the main entrance lobby.

Looking through the maple-floored gallery towards the entrance, which admits light down the central axis. Cameras and photographic equipment are displayed in Perspex units suspended by metal rods.

Schematic perspective (bird's-eye view) showing the mezzanine-level bridge crossing the length of the double-height galleries, connecting the café/terrace with the rear gallery spaces. The 'camera obscura' is positioned on a second-floor balcony, within the museum's façade.

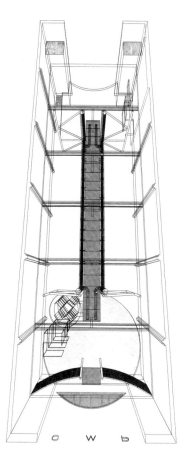

The main staircase set within a light metal wire cloth cylinder framed with tubular steel which gives a mobile, spiralling effect. The staircase itself has risers and treads of bent steel plate.

4.3

California Museum of Photography

STANLEY SAITOWICZ
Riverside, California, USA

The remodelling of the former Kress department store into a museum of photography for the University of California dramatically reverses the aesthetic values widely adhered to by architects of art museums. Saitowicz's conversion is based upon 'the idea of a museum of photography as a camera in which people are film'. However, the strength of the solution owes as much to the inspiration provided by the building as to his conceptual response to the contents of the museum.

The Museum's cut-out exterior, with giant 'pin-hole camera' and new columns and perforated metal canopy framing the entrance.

On visiting the site, Saitowicz, a painter as well as an architect, was immediately struck by the lens-like space of the building, in which light entered from both ends. This theme shapes every aspect of the project: 'I wanted you to walk into a black room…to be in the harsh mechanical darkness so that you are constantly aware of the mechanistic nature of the photograph.'

The building is conceived as an instrument, an apparatus for the display of appearances. A camera is a box for transporting appearances, but the word also means 'room'. The original camera was a black room with a pinhole which produced an inverted image on the opposite wall. Saitowicz's plans which, appropriately enough, are rendered in white on black, show a giant pin-hole camera apparatus, large enough to enter, positioned on the first floor café terrace, and approached by a bridge forming a strong central axis from the façade. This affords visitors a preview of the street 'before the camera'.

The lens device is incorporated into the façade of the museum, its presence announcing the beginning of photography. The glass in the existing windows were removed, to make frames for the lens behind. Columns were added to frame the entrance, and three holes cut in the parapet which frames the sky. A new perforated metal canopy was added over the entrance.

Inside, Saitowicz achieves the desired atmosphere of gloom and harshness by using steel throughout, and carefully directing the ambient lighting. However, the open-plan nature of the space means that circulation does involve human encounters, which takes the edge off any hard qualities. A bridge divides the darkened space into two galleries, permanent and temporary, carrying fixtures which throw beams of light across

and along the length of its perforated steel structure. At one end is a gallery, at the other it joins a mezzanine floor, on which there is a circular café with a small balcony overlooking the front of the Museum. Technical servicing is deliberately exposed, covered with heavy metal ducting, and the diagonal beams of the bridge structure add further elements to the extended metaphor of the photomechanical process used throughout.

Large enclosed circular areas throughout the building create analogies with the human eye, or with man-made ocular devices — the café above the entrance, the auditorium, and a spiral staircase enclosed in fine mesh which tunnels through the 23,000-square-foot building.

In each of Saitowicz's projects he 'aims to convert the site into a state of mind by constructing ambiences which integrate and interpret the given conditions'. A good site and a handsome building, but combined with a restricted budget ($74 per square foot for a 23,500-square-foot project) meant judicious planning was needed to achieve the desired results. This museum is the antithesis of the bleached white walls and light of the celebratory spaces of many art museums; it emphasises photography's reliance upon mechanical reproduction for its very being, by using sensory effects and guiding metaphors. The result is an architectural 'apparatus' of great interactive power.

Warm, flexible and intimately scaled: the walls of the proscenium theatre combine oak panelling with painted plaster finishes in a restrained but lively resolution of form and function. The semi-circular auditorium has two curved rows of balcony fronts in red perforated metal, with a long swathe of oak capping and intervals of polished brass rails. Larger areas of green perforated metal acoustic panels frame the stage. The forestage is adaptable: it can either function as a thrust stage, or as an orchestra pit with the help of an electrically operated lift.

4.4

Center for the Performing Arts, Cornell University

JAMES STIRLING, MICHAEL WILFORD & ASSOCIATES, IN COLLABORATION WITH WANK, ADAMS, SLAVIN ASSOCIATES
Ithaca, New York, USA

At the opening of Cornell University's Center for the Arts, James Stirling admitted that the first time he had to perfom on stage was in front of architectural students in a cramped room at the University of Venice, and he felt as if he was in a Marx Brothers film. Perhaps this early experience indirectly influenced the design of the Center's proscenium theatre, a beautifully proportioned space with an excellent balance of form and function. The architects envisaged the Center more as a Tuscan hill village than a Hollywood stage set, an analogy made all the more potent by its close proximity to the vertiginous, picturesque Cascadilla gorge. They have had to perform an architectural balancing act, reconciling an economical budget and a complex programme, without stifling the lyrical vitality which permeates the Center.

The Center provides a teaching facility for theatre arts and a performance space for the University. Architecturally, it serves as a gateway to the central campus, its position symbolizing a point of informal congregation for town and gown. At the same time the ensemble of buildings manages to relate both to the small town character of the avenue along which it lies, and the dramatic landscape of the gorge.

The programme included a 456-seat proscenium theatre, flexible theatre, dance performance studio, black box/laboratory theatre, auditorium for films or performances, plus various classrooms, studios, faculty offices and back-stage facilities. Its realization has been fraught with difficulties and the building had to be constructed in two phases. It cost US$168 million ($148.54 per square foot), an evidently inadequate budget for such an ambitious programme. The 113,000-square-foot site was also too cramped: the clustered volumes had to be accommodated within a prominent, but narrow, 1-acre area wedged between an apartment building and a college dormitory close to the bridge over the gorge.

The necessary compression of volumes has created solid forms with an unusual combination of 'a front side and a

Ground-floor plan.

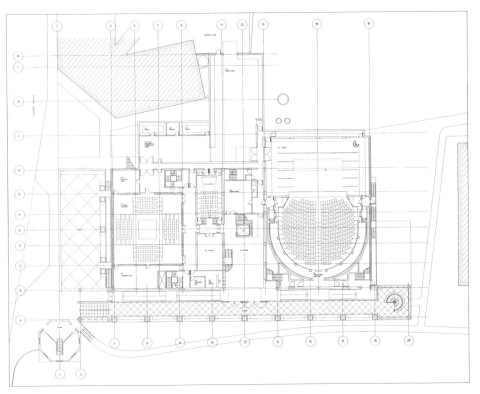

side side and two back sides'. The solidly massed theatrical facilities are configured by a steel-framed loggia which runs the length of the building on the right of the front gable. With its porch-like trellis (echoing details of houses in the town), it provides a covered and scenic route along the edge of the gorge to the main entrance – a well-scaled balance of formal and informal elements.

Through double doors set in a glass wall is a three-storey-high lobby separating the proscenium theatre at the rear of the building from the studios, classrooms and offices at the front. The colonnade of the loggia provides an attractive promenade approach with views across the gorge and towards the lake. Part of it is enclosed to make a covered route for bad weather.

The entrance hall also serves as the main foyer for the theatres – one which, like so many theatre foyers, is easily congested with interval crowds. However, it allows the glorious freedom of being able to stroll out through the main doors to take the air and experience the view from the marble-paved loggia.

A bell-tower containing an elevator shaft rises from the entrance hall upwards like an Italian campanile; it also echoes the many other towers at Cornell. Floodlit at night, it dramatically announces the Center's presence, emphasising its Italianate nature by its horizontally striped stone. Instead of brick and stone cladding, the exterior has a compromise combination of open-jointed Vermont marble on the pavilion wall and loggia, and stucco on the other elevations, limiting exterior richness to selected surface areas. The masonry is clipped and hung to exterior surfaces, without mortar.

The 743-square-metre proscenium theatre is horseshoe-shaped, and reached by two entrances from the foyer. Its interior treatment creates an intimately scaled performance space with seating for 515; the backstage areas are spacious. Fixed seating on the ground floor has parallel aisles; loose seating on two tiers of shallow balconies extends around the room, drawing audience and performers together in a convivial atmosphere, enhanced by oak panelling and smooth, painted plaster finishes.

Other smaller performance spaces are geared to various activities. The 180-seat 'flexible theatre' has multiple entrances which allow arena, thrust, alley or proscenium seating on adjustable platforms. Seating in the dance performance studio below the proscenium theatre can also be composed in a variety of configurations. The upper dance studio has adjacent open terraces facing the gorge and plaza, as well as a triangular bay window jutting like a prow over the plaza, flanked by bold coloured banners. A two-storey octagonal 'lighthouse' structure at the end of the colonnade anchors the edge of the site close to the gorge by the bridge, providing a campus information centre and a grand bus-stop shelter.

When designing the Center, Stirling tried to envisage a rich medley of performances animating its solid, Italianate forms. He aimed for a 'village' environment which would allow, for example, a Mozart opera in the proscenium, a three-ring circus in the flexible theatre, a topless gogo dancer in the bay window of the dance studio, grand kabuki in the loggia and street performers in the plaza – though not necessarily all at once!

The completion of the project left the architects with some wistfully imagined 'what ifs', clever devices that they might have woven into the language of the architecture to enhance its scenographic aspect. A huge *trompe l'oeil* mural was planned for the car-park wall of the stage house, sharing the view across the gorge to Lake Cayuga beyond: it would have been 'like a Magritte painting of the landscape where the building has disappeared, which was the view which existed before the building was built.' It is clear that the drawbacks of an overloaded site could not be cancelled out, and gave strictly limited room in which to manoeuvre. Behind the loggia, work spaces had to be stacked up in front of the proscenium's flytower (which could only go at the rear), resulting in too many corridors in the studio and classroom block. However, the architects have managed to negotiate their way successfully through the acknowledged difficulties, and the result is an accessible building which makes the most of its context between town and landscape, at once formally effective and linguistically stimulating.

The symmetrical gable end of the Center (with the bell-tower behind) is juxtaposed with the east end of the loggia, an octagonal pavilion and a small, front-facing plaza. Along the steel-framed colonnade runs an internal ramped entrance for use in bad weather.

CULTURAL & PUBLIC AMENITY BUILDINGS

The main entrance hall also functions as a foyer during intervals, with long wooden benches and the freedom for visitors to spill out on to the terraces overlooking the gorge: grandeur is mixed with informality. The glazing bars are made of enamel-finished aluminium.

The upper balconies of the mezzanine foyer of the proscenium theatre and other performance spaces overlook the triple-height main entrance hall. The central lift shaft rises through these areas to the external campanile above the building.

The warm ambience of the public lobby with access to performance spaces.

CULTURAL & PUBLIC AMENITY BUILDINGS

4.5
Cité de la Musique (west side)

CHRISTIAN DE PORTZAMPARC
La Villette, Paris, France

The Cité de la Musique is a pair of buildings at La Villette to which the mighty French Conservatoire Nationale has recently been relocated, providing the north-eastern cultural/commercial site of the Parc de la Villette with yet another cultural focus. It also strengthens further the dynamic redefinition of the suburb of La Villette from its former identity as a desolate outer zone occupied by slaughterhouses to a site of invention and new possibilities.

Christian de Portzamparc has designed two large and varied wings, which dramatically contrast in tempo with the centrally positioned Grand Halle, revived and reopened in 1990 as a trade fair venue. The west section, devoted to teaching and classes, and due for completion in December 1991, exerts a powerful presence at the vast main

approach to La Villette, with its 125-acre park of post-industrial museums, exhibition spaces and follies. Its eastern counterpart, due to open in 1992, will contain a concert hall, a museum of musical instruments and rehearsal spaces. The two wings will eventually complement each other dramatically: the west wing is situated along avenue Jean Jaurès, with a large white street-orientated façade defined by transparent areas, while the east wing, with the truncated cone of its concert hall, opens up towards the park in a more free-form geometry.

The asymmetry of the two parts of the programme reflects the carefully composed interior scheme. In terms of the site, it serves to realign the emphasis of the entrance to the park of La Villette, breaking the old, static axis of the Grand Halle to take away some of its dominance, and creating a new, dynamic axis positioned towards the park and the distant Gèode of Adrian Fainsilber's Museum of Science. From the avenue, one is presented with a rich vista of the city opening into the expanse of a large park, a wholly new 'window' which forms the focus of a landscape which is a coherent entity, but one no longer concerned to keep within traditional urban restraints.

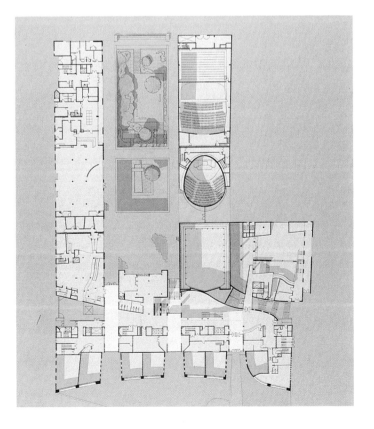

Low-hanging downlighters and a wood block floor add intimacy to this recording space.

Ground-floor plan of the complex, with west side on the left.

The west wing is an exceptional concentration of rooms, which could have been claustrophobic inner volumes juxtaposed without respite, particularly since most of them are needed to be acoustically correct spaces for playing music. However, the relationship between each room is an easy one, with a bright and open ambience. De Portzamparc creates a subtle 'disposif', which achieves a simultaneously compact and light resolution of groupings in isolated sections between corridors and reception areas. These are deliberately not soundproofed, giving them a lively resonance.

There are two large 'families' of spaces, the first made up of study areas, with many middle-sized or small rooms for studios, study rooms, listening booths, offices and a médiathèque. The second is a bundle of much larger rooms for communal activities, some open to the public: a mélange of interdisciplinary workspaces, rooms for organ music, orchestra and jazz – even a 'salle d'art lyrique'. De Portzamparc has given them a flat base at the heart of the plot, on the ground floor so that instruments can easily be brought in. Around them in a crown-shaped area are the study areas.

The whole building is divided into four bays: those on the north and south are separated by light-filled, transparent corridors. On the south side, classrooms are grouped into 'plots' on the building's four floors, giving a rhythm to the façades, which are protected acoustically from the lower floors. The west bay, by contrast, is a long, continuous volume with the médiathèque, students' accommodation and a gymnasium, crowned by a dramatically undulating roof punctuated by a large circular opening. Another refreshing slot of space is positioned between the dance rooms and classrooms of the east bay.

De Portzamparc's design of the interiors of the west wing has been motivated by the desire to contrast the plain, opaque volumes of varied sizes and dimensions which form the acoustical envelopes of the musical workspaces with the slots or even 'canyons' of natural light which lie in between them. In so doing, even deep in the heart of the building, the circulation and meeting spaces are filled with daylight, via glazing or spaces open to the sky. This 'webbing' of light and movement is the central theme of the interiors, and is reflected in the different materials used: concrete shells, wooden floors, ceramic tiles, stucco walls and

The organ hall.

wool carpets, in warm and cool tones. The outside world is never divorced from the building's intense internal activities. As such, the play of voids and volumes, density and lightness, is a metaphor for the cityscape, with its contrasting buildings and streets.

Between the calm white exteriors is an interior court with a patio and garden, with a view of the conical mass of the organ room and the flytower. The larger rooms open out on to the patio garden, which is seven metres under street level. By contrast, the east wing will contain a series of varied programmes to cater for those interested in music, united in a 'village' composition; once again, the guiding concept of distinct volumes bound together by a net of transparent intermediary spaces is of paramount importance. The concert hall will also create settings which 'challenge the usual relationships between audiences and musicians'.

De Portzamparc's architecture is impossible to 'seize in one sight'. Its dynamic spaces are not fixed, or static, but fluid and mobile. At the Cité de la Musique, he has successfully created an architectural analogy to music itself, with its diverse durations, sequences, breaks and discoveries – architecture 'made to be listened to'.

Multi-angled views of the Parc and surrounding areas can be obtained from the building's upper floors.

The beautiful contours of the music studios filter light through asymmetrical windows.

The slanting movement of the façade of the building's grand staircase.

CITÉ DE LA MUSIQUE (WEST SIDE)

The dynamic form of the stainless steel and opaque glass information desk.

The computer screens of the information centre on the ground floor. Curving benches in grey-tinted wood are placed on a grey, rubber-tiled floor with a grid of lighter grey squares echoing the larger grid in which the folly plays a major part.

CULTURAL & PUBLIC AMENITY BUILDINGS

4.6

Folie, Parc de la Villette

BERNARD TSCHUMI
La Villette, Paris, France

Bernard Tschumi's park of follies at La Villette represents for many people the first 'deconstructivist' project to be built — a theoretically defined site, as well as a series of small buildings set out in a 'twenty-first-century urban park', along a grid system with intersecting walkways creating two axes.

Tschumi established a series of systems of points, lines and surfaces within a grid; a major axis following the side of the Ourcq Canal is animated by bright red, porcelain-coated follies — all variations on a 36 × 36 × 36-foot cube, intersected by cylindrical or triangular volumes. Some have a communal or commercial *raison d'être* (including a semi-al fresco café); others concentrate on being just follies, potent compositions of form which justify their existence as symbols in the park.

At the point where the axes of the walkways meet is the most prominent folly. More than just a belvedere from which to survey the surrounding park, it is made up of two distinct programmes, each with contrasting colours applied: a 511-square-metre information centre for the Parc (red part, on three levels) and a 518-square-metre restaurant (grey part, on two levels above). The exterior of the folly gives it an aesthetic connection with others sited in a 'field' around the Parc: red enamelled steel intersected by a banded triangular mass of hung granite panels.

It is geometrically defined, and based on a 11.2-metre cube. Another geometrical relationship defines the triangular form of the restaurant: the angle formed by the Parc's Allée du Triangue and the Canal de l'Ourcq. A further consideration helped to define its character: the structure's foundation had to be superimposed on an existing nineteenth-century infrastructure still in use today. What Tschumi aimed to achieve was the design of 'a single architectural object which would express the two distinctly different programmes while still responding to the constraints of site and function.'

Between, and part of, the constructions created with the help of engineer Peter Rice — which rely largely upon the tension of angled supports and hung structures for their wind- and gravity-defying appearance — are walkways, canopies and internal spaces. Some of the follies feature familiar forms: giant mill wheels, a water cascade. The main one at the intersection of the main axes encompasses a computerized information centre on the ground floor — bold sculptural forms laid out in a curved floor area and encircled by a rubber-tiled ramp accentuated by the curve of blue neon tube lighting. Another open stairway enclosed by metal balustrades rises through the centre of the building.

Its hard-edged forms and strong counterpoint of grey, red and blue create a bold environment, deliberately avoiding a synthesis. In the Parc's theoretical programme, this particular folly explores and questions the notion of unity in architecture. A project which Tschumi sees as being 'comprised of repetitions, distortions, superpositions', it has its own 'internal logic', but is not 'aimlessly pluralistic'. It confronts many formal issues which have a bearing on how architecture and the city might be perceived: 'the idea of order is constantly questioned, challenged, pushed to the edge'.

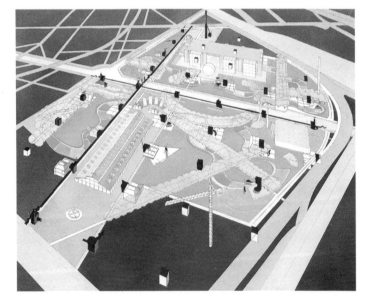

Bird's-eye view of Parc de la Villette, showing the follies laid out in a grid. The information centre/restaurant building is positioned at the intersection of the two main walkways.

The horseshoe-shaped concert hall rigorously adheres to optimum technical acoustic requirements. To establish visual order, it has been clad in a modular grid of African makore wood panels with brass and American cherry frames. Two monumental limestone columns support the seating tiers and frame the proscenium.

4.7

Morton H Meyerson Symphony Center

PEI COBB FREED & PARTNERS
Dallas, Texas, USA

The Morton H. Meyerson Symphony Center was designed to create a world-class concert hall which was both visually pleasurable and acoustically refined. A second aim was equally ambitious: to ensure that it became a focus of civic pride and a symbol of economic and urban revitalization, helping the city of Dallas and its Symphony Association to 'anchor a fledgling arts district in an under-utilizated downtown area'.

Aspirations on this level do not come cheaply. I.M. Pei's design was developed in the early 1980s and completed in 1989 at a cost of $81 million. The Center — an inward-looking concert hall surrounded by an outward-looking lobby — is set at an angle to the street to maximize the small 2.8-acre site. The building is based on a series of overlapping geometries that unfold from a square, with impressive, radial public spaces within a lobby that

wraps around the rectilinear concert hall on three sides; administration and musicians' wings are positioned along the fourth side, behind the hall's stage. The Center's angled position is harmonized by the introduction of a sculptural armature, a 60 × 90 foot frame, projecting from the front to focus its main entrance and align it with the main street.

The expansive wrap-around glazed lobby is a dynamic and elegant place in which to wander and congregate; from the exterior, its transparency day and night reveals the activity within to a wider audience. The complex shape of the Center is a clear volumetric expression of function, and the lobby, tapering from ground level to the less crowded areas of the upper seating tier, serves as an outer shell to the music chamber, cushioning the hall from street noise while at the same time celebrating activities in its public spaces through great expanses of transparent glass, with window walls up to 18 foot high on the building's vertical planes, consisting of over 200 individually computer-dimensioned panes. To support the glazed slope, an intricate system of bowstring trusses has been used, each curved to a different radius. The structural steel mullions holding the panes in place give the Center's exteriors a tension like a stringed instrument.

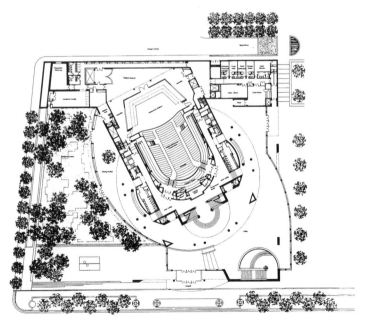

Ground-floor plan
(orchestra entry level).

Although the Center presents an inviting main entrance to the street, many of its car-bound visitors arrive via the drop-off area beneath the building. Everyone ends up in a glazed lower lobby housing the box office, shop and cloakrooms. This is a large and low-ceilinged space with an entrance area lit by rhythmic semi-circles of spotlights accentuating the curve of the side wall. Their starriness also anticipates circular sweeps of lighting in the main concert hall. From here, visitors ascend a monumental staircase walled with limestone – one of the most important circulation arteries and focal points in the building – up to the main lobby. Here, floods of sun-screened light, soaring curved ceiling planes and countless shifting vanishing points greet the view. The Center is certainly not a hermetic music box: Pei's radial geometries – the circular cut of the lobby spaces, curved walls, open balconies and sweeping skylights – are intended to express the vibrancy of the city's spirit.

The building gains it dynamism from the asymmetry of its public spaces. However, the central core of the concert hall itself is necessarily symmetrical for balanced sound. The transition takes place around the main staircase, where circulation systems adopt more orthodox patterns. A pair of imposing steel-and-onyx light standards at the foot of the staircase focuses the upward movement, while adding a free-standing sculptural element to the lobby's circular forms.

The music chamber of the concert hall is a towering narrow space, 85 feet high (making it one of the tallest concrete rooms in the world), seating an audience of 2,062. The architects nonetheless aimed to create a sense of intimacy, allowing each concert-goer to feel close to the stage regardless of position. The narrowness of the room helps this perception, but it is undoubtedly the treatment of the interior which achieves the desired effect. Detailed like a musical instrument in a modular grid of polished wood panels with brass and cherrywood frames, the hall's colour scheme employs more than two dozen different hues of brown which make the walls appear to recede.

Layered acoustical curtains emerge from hidden wall niches to 'tune' the hall for different performances. A huge acoustical canopy in four parts hovers over the performance area, and can be tilted and raised for maximum resonance for choral performances, or lowered by up to 37 feet to provide intimacy for soloists or string quartets.

Overhead, on the ceiling and on the scrims behind, a dark blue hue refers to the open air which was a part of performances in ancient amphitheatres. Monumental limestone columns support the seating tiers and frame the proscenium, reinforcing this allusion. Lighting subtly picks out details: backlit onyx panels and light strips on the balcony fascias, brass and onyx sconces on the upper boxes. Some 400 bulbs in the ceiling and acoustic canopy shine through diffusing glass: this concentrated, horseshoe-shaped field of lights helps to dematerialize the auditorium and lighten the appearance of the canopy.

In concert halls the upper levels are frequently relegated: they have less pleasing public spaces and cramped circulation. This has been avoided: each audience level has been accorded a high quality of finish and provides a rich spatial experience.

At the foot of the main lobby staircase, an 18-foot steel-and-onyx light standard focuses upward movement to the concert hall chamber.

The wrap-around public lobby spaces (occupying a total of 24,000 square feet) create an atmospheric circulation route with constantly changing views and light qualities; a sunny café terrace on the first floor has views out to the garden beyond.

The monumental staircase joining the spacious lower ground box office, shop and cloakroom areas is made of polished limestone; its side wall is scooped out to form a precise concave area following the ascending pattern of the stairs.

Projecting from the front of the broad glazed and limestone-clad surfaces of the Center is a sculptural armature, focusing its main entrance. In the foreground, the branch-like projections of Eduardo Chillida's forged Corte steel sculpture 'De Musica' reach out towards each other.

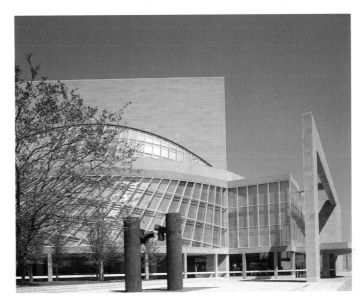

The interior space of the church (right), with its angled wall and powerful cross-shaped opening through which light penetrates to float in the darkness of the pristine space. Much later in the day (above), the light carves powerful shapes across the bare concrete.

Axonometric diagram.

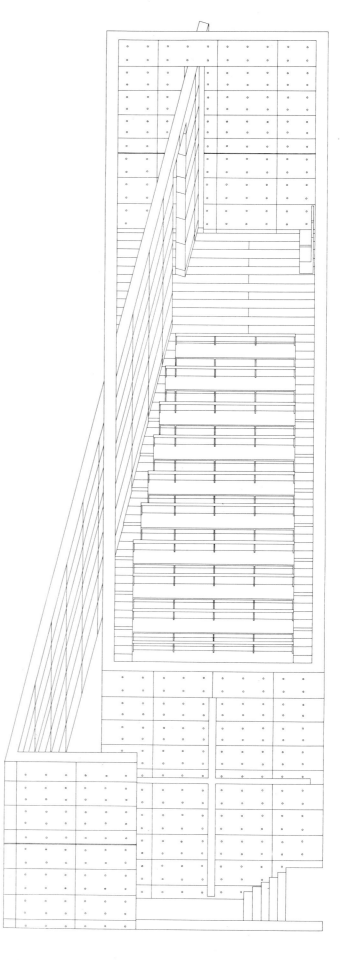

CULTURAL & PUBLIC AMENITY BUILDINGS

Church of the Light

TADAO ANDO
Ibaragi, Osaka, Japan

This, the simplest and least conspicuous of Ando's church buildings (others include the Church on Mount Rokko and the Church on the Water), is located in a quiet residential district of Ibaragi City, a suburb of Osaka. The church was planned as an addition to the chapel and minister's house, both wooden; proximity to these was important, but the church's solar orientation was the key to its design.

The building is essentially cuboid, a rigid frame of reinforced concrete, with a plan of 6.28 × 18 metres, penetrated by a free-standing wall placed at a 15-degree angle. This diagonal wall is 18cm lower than the building itself, and divides the space into an entrance area and a chapel.

To enter the inner sanctum of the chapel, one passes through an opening in the diagonal wall, turning sharply into the rear of what is a resolutely austere place of worship. The floor of rough scaffolding planks descends in stages towards the altar, with two rows of simple seating made of the same planks on either side. Behind the simple, box-like altar, a cruciform has been cut out of the exposed concrete wall. Morning sun entering through this embrasure creates a cross of light which forms a pattern on the floor, changing in character as the day develops.

There are no decorative effects or uplifting paintings here to gaze at but, says Ando, by studying the shifting cross 'one may come to recognise in a fundamental way the relationship of humanity to nature.'

Ando made as few openings as possible in the building because, like a magic lantern, the light of the cross becomes brilliant only against a very dark background. As it is such a bare, dark and enclosed space, one is immediately drawn into deep contemplation of the play of light with the ascetic, abstract forms of the church. The visitor's encounter with nature is dramatized, and nature rendered abstract. In turn, the architecture, adapting to this light, becomes 'purified'. The intention is that by paring down architectural form to the absolute minimum, the spirit of the visitor is uplifted. At the same time, the presence of natural elements in one single form gives greater significance to the increasingly fragmented relationship between nature and urban space. The church authorities

initially wanted the cut-out cross shape to be glazed over, fearing that the space would be cold, but Ando resisted any compromise of his original idea.

By using basic, unadorned materials, Ando has created an economical building and given the chapel a definite tactile dimension. This quality relates not to sensuality or self-indulgence, but to direct physical experience by the human body of natural materials such as wood and stone. The extended planes of Ando's walls are made of exposed concrete produced to his own scientifically researched requirements, so that the essential properties of this rather unpredictable material can be controlled, given a more refined expression, and thus adapted to the climate.

Ando initially had doubts that the church could be finished, because of the likely cost of the roof. So he conceived at first a roofless chapel, which would undergo gradual construction until, after about five years, sufficient contributions from the congregation had accumulated. Fortunately, their generosity permitted the roof to be completed with the rest of the building, thus permitting the cross of light to work to maximum effect. The church was completed in early 1989 at a cost of 25 million yen.

The irregular but inconspicuous external form of the church conceals its power from the suburban environment.

CULTURAL & PUBLIC AMENITY BUILDINGS

The second-floor exhibition space offers stunning views over the glazed void, and down through a glazed circular hole in the smooth wooden floor revealing a succession of cutaway storeys to the basement.

4.9

German Postal Museum

BEHNISCH AND PARTNERS
Frankfurt am Main, Germany

The new German Postal Museum has kept to its old site close to the Deutsches Architekturmuseum on Frankfurt's Schaumainkai, now referred to as the 'Museumsufer', or 'river bank of museums' on the south side of the River Main. This was designated some time ago as a cultural growth area, and currently a thriving industry is devoted to all manner of cultural histories. At first glance, the Postal Museum's compact composition of glass and aluminium planes suggests technology put at the service of a more flexible type of museology than some of its more traditional-looking neighbours.

Günter Behnisch, whose practice won an architectural competition held in 1982 to design the new museum, took on a range of problems. The river bank's many stately mansion buildings today house insurance companies and trade associations as well as museums, and all are subject to state preservation orders. The architects were therefore obliged to preserve the building which had housed the Museum since 1956, as well as the surrounding trees. The building occupied the best part of the plot, leaving a relatively narrow area along the edge of the site in which to shoehorn a new building. Any new exhibition space had to be modest; the location of storage rooms and workshops was unresolved; future annexes would be impossible.

The architects solved many of these problems by putting much of the exhibition space underground, beneath the garden behind the mansion. They linked it with the basements of the old building which was thoroughly restored, and which now houses the administrative offices and a library. Above ground, the five storeys of the new glass-and-aluminium building are closely interconnected by a strong central focus: a truncated glass cone within a patio area to which the cafeteria, auditorium and main stairway are adjacent, which pulls together the whole museum, and endows the interior with light from a huge lightwell.

The new building has two underground floors: the lower houses the car park, storage and technical installations; the upper, the exhibition space and seminar rooms. The entrance is on the ground floor which contains an information desk, shop, cafeteria and auditorium for film screenings and talks. Above ground, the first and second floors house permanent and temporary exhibition spaces and, up on the roof, an amateur radio station. The floors now display exhibits ranging from historical equipment, vehicles and artefacts to the latest electronic inventions. However, as the exhibition design was developed independently, the exact nature and layout of the displays were not imparted to Behnisch in great detail. He therefore designed voluminous exhibition spaces which were sufficiently fluid in character to incorporate a wide range of artefacts, illuminated – even underground – by more natural light than would be acceptable in a fine art museum, filtering through the lightwell and skylights.

In creating the expansive underground exhibition areas, a compromise with nature has paid off: these lower spaces are designed around the root bales of the site's most prominent trees, including a large plane tree. The resulting cylindrical forms enrich this subterranean environment, which is lit by halogen fittings at points where natural

View from the main entrance of the staircase running down through the building's upper floors. In the foreground is one of the many spiral staircases that twists a vertical tunnel through the building.

Inside the cone, the entrance leads to exhibition floors above and below ground.

light cannot spill down from the glass cone, the skylights or an articulated curve of clerestory windows set in the lawn. From the airy and satisfyingly resolved glass-covered centre, orientation through the Museum's spaces is carefully orchestrated, with a mix of layered planes and natural light filtering from innovative glazing forms held by pivoted steel arches.

While the old building's spaces dictated hierarchical forms, here there is a contemporary, decentralized layout, reflecting innovative communications systems. The Museum will not only impart information on the technical aspects of postal and telecommunications history, but will firmly link the history of communications to the development of individuals, societies and nations; instead of a chronological pattern, thematic 'islands' of objects supported by text and interactive technology are intended to develop a broader understanding of the subject within an inspiringly individual building.

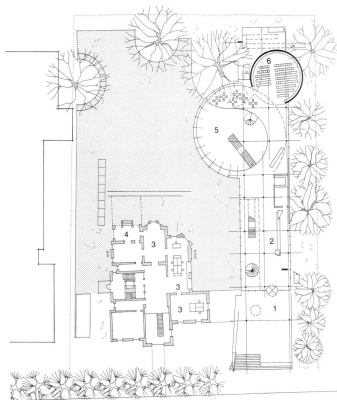

Seen from beneath the loggia of the Museum's restored administrative headquarters, a glowing cylindrical cone of braced glazing covers the central focus of the building.

Ground-floor plan.
1 Entrance area.
2 Information desk.
3 Library (mansion building).
4 Loggia.

5 Air space beneath glass shell, with staircase connecting exhibition areas.
6 Film theatre.
7 River Bank

Light pours through the high glazing on to the pale wood floors of the basement exhibition areas beneath the garden.

Second-floor plan with swimming pool and rear playing courts.

The flat urban façade is a symmetrical composition of forms and planes of artificial stone, and a row of small, alternately positioned, glass windows above the central porch.

Soft orange-brown walls and striped ceilings are juxtaposed with a polished wood floor and a grid of glass block windows divided by lighting columns.

Double-height walls of uncovered brickwork and tiles flank a marble staircase, which fans out into a semi-circular form in the entrance hall below, taking natural light with it through rhythmic rows of ceiling panels.

4.10

Polideportivo de Gracia

JAUME BACH/GABRIEL MORA, ARQUITECTOS
Barcelona, Spain

Callé Perill is situated in a highly populated district of Barcelona; the area's only open spaces are its public squares, making it in practical terms a far from ideal site for the creation of a new sports centre. But, like many other central districts of Barcelona, it lacks public buildings, especially for sports facilities. The Polideportivo de Gracia has therefore provided the area with a much-needed asset, one which will help to put residents in the right frame of mind for the 1992 Barcelona Olympic Games.

The issue of limited space was resolved without compromising the spaciousness of the interiors. Building underground was too expensive and complicated; instead, architects Jaume Bach and Gabriel Mora chose to slide their design for a multi-sports centre into a plot measuring 34 × 29.5 metres between two housing complexes. Permission to use the large patio roof of the neighbouring underground garage to the south was granted, and this has provided raised playing courts at the back. The architects felt the need to present a hard, urban façade to the street. Behind this, the task

of accommodating spacious and well-lit facilities at various levels could be accomplished. These had to be adapted to the height of the surrounding buildings, so that the public building could be shoehorned into their midst without visually disrupting an essentially residential environment.

The project provides a response to the challenge of positioning an urban service building in a residential area. On the north side, the building's height is in accordance with the other buildings surrounding it, setting back the bigger volume of the courtyard. The façade is symmetrical, its dominant form a play on fullness and emptiness, but still with a degree of classical *gravitas* which maintains its dignity among the varied buildings along the street. Divided into three sections, it has an idiosyncratic order: a plinth of bricks over the entrance porch; above this, a grid of artificial stone representing the wide space of the gymnasium on the second floor, and a blind top portion with a wide plane of artificial stone.

Because the positioning of interior levels was central to the project, it evolved through its section as an asymmetrical layout. From the hard, abstract geometry of the façade, a ground-floor entrance leads to basement squash courts and changing rooms through a central hallway and staircase linking all floors, which is the dominant element of the whole project. Soft-toned brick balconies cut across its grand, but fairly narrow, marble stairs, which lead to a semi-circular expanse on the ground floor. The building opens up on the south façade, filtering light into the grey-tiled swimming pool on the second floor, which is illuminated by uplighters around its perimeter. The soft hues of its pillars and walls are carried through to orange pillars above the

basement squash courts, and the blue-tiled walls of the café. The second floor is on a level with the communal patio, now appropriated to become outdoor courts by the south façade. This floor is the most widely used area, with a gymnasium as well as the swimming pool, and a café-restaurant.

The second and ground floor levels are synchronized with the raised patio at the back and the street at the front, which dictate the shape of the spaces on the first floor, occupied by the frame of the swimming pool and the changing rooms. The third floor contains a high multi-sports courtyard given even extra height by a tilted, light, metallic structure which provides an intriguing convex roof adjoined by windows, and a long raised balcony for spectators.

The public areas of the centre are sensitively proportioned, with simple forms and natural, soft-toned materials mixed with touches of more vivid orange and blue which are psychologically and sensually pleasing. Numerous wall and ceiling openings pull in natural light. The Polideportivo provides the perfect antidote to the shoddily built, badly planned and gimmick-laden multi-sports centres often found in the heart of the city, hemmed in but rarely rooted in place. The most visually arresting feature of the project is the main staircase which, with its elegant form, and white marble flanked by uncovered brick, has the aura of a cultural building. It is a statement about the potential for grand gestures, even within an unprepossessing infill space in bustling central Barcelona.

The central lightwell
and large wall apertures
allow the
interpenetration of
modulated light and
strong spatial forms of
plaster over masonry;
the calm ambience
permeates the varying
scales of all four gallery
spaces. In the corner are
Frank Gehry's 'Little
Beaver' armchair and
stool.

Vitra Museum

**FRANK O. GEHRY
& ASSOCIATES
Weil am Rhein, Germany**

The Vitra Museum is a double first: Gehry's first European building, and the world's first museum of furniture. Californian architect Frank O. Gehry was commissioned by Rolf Fehlbaum, managing director of the family firm of Vitra, one of Europe's most enlightened furniture manufacturers, to house his collection of over 1,200 chair designs. The Museum, an all-white gem in a verdant rural setting in the Rhine valley, clearly reflects the company's commitment to the embrace of industry and culture. It is situated on the edge of the Vitra complex, at 1 Charles Eames Strasse, a new street named after America's foremost furniture designer, whose pioneering work features prominently in the collection which includes a recreation of his office.

Initially, Fehlbaum planned to add a new production unit to the complex, with an adjacent private museum and conference space to house his original collection of 300 chairs and to create a focus for research. Two crucial encounters opened up new possibilities. After meeting the collector Alexander von Vegesack, who became the Museum's curator, Fehlbaum was helped to pursue his great passion and acquire further items. As the collection grew in size and stature, the scope of the proposed educational programme became

correspondingly more ambitious, encompassing the concept of a public facility. After fruitful dialogues with Gehry, the exhibition element of Fehlbaum's plan, originally peripheral, assumed centre stage in Vitra's new phase of activities.

Both from afar and close up, the Museum is a breathtaking construction, a sculpturally complex but harmonious succession of simple cubes on a trapezoid base. These are massed in a dynamic composition like the complex order of a crystal form; they twist and jostle, enclosing closely grouped inner volumes, with a swirling 'arm' containing a spiralling staircase, punctuated with skylights seemingly coming up for air, one dominantly positioned in an irregular tower form. The Museum's multi-angled façades, curved and flat, are rendered in gleaming white plaster, mixed with titanium zinc panels which shine like ribbed satin in the sun, and cover the areas most at the mercy of the elements.

The writhing forms of the building are dramatic in the valley's gentle rural setting, pure white and enigmatically ambivalent against the green grass. Do they represent a tense power struggle, or a

more tender tussle between orthogonal and organic forms? Is architecture redefining itself as sculpture, or sculpture possessing architecture? It certainly has the strong expressionist overtones acknowledged by Gehry, and the almost religious calm of its beautifully executed, light-filled spaces recollect for many Le Corbusier's Chapel of Notre Dame du Haut at Ronchamp in France. The strong dynamic which exists between exterior and interior is extraordinary: Gehry's fascination with process defies easy categories and definitions.

An area of 8000 square feet encompasses four galleries, including a central, double-height space, a library, an office and storage/support areas on two floors. Architecturally, the Museum's interiors are refreshing and uplifting: a series of connected spatially interpenetrating rooms, which allow ideas and themes to pass from one to another in an expressive continuity.

Fehlbaum aimed to create a non-élitist institution with accessible facilities which would encourage the wider dissemination of knowledge and exchange of ideas about the theory and practice of furniture design. The Museum galleries clearly reflect this openness of motivation. Selected pieces from the collection show the evolution of industrial furniture design, from Thonet's experimental and

'Balancing tools': Claes
Oldenburg and Coosje
van Bruggen's
sculptural assemblage
of work tools is set in
the grass in front of the
tilting and swirling
forms of the Museum,
evoking the powers of
creative construction.

mass-produced bentwood models from 1836–60 and 1860–90 through to the contemporary Vitra Editions, a series of experimental limited edition designs by luminaries such as Ron Arad, Philippe Starck and Gaetano Pesce. Changing thematic exhibitions highlight design theories, materials, techniques and product evolution, demonstrated by works from the permanent collection, which allow a greater understanding of the creative processes of design. Many reproductions which visitors can try out in turn distances the Museum from the incongruous 'entombment' of design artefacts practised by many design collections. Direct bodily contact is encouraged, to underline design's sensual as well as intellectual qualities, its hand-worked constructional values as well as its relationship with technology.

The galleries are bare and austere, with natural toplight from skylights which subtly connects the various rooms and walkways. Window wells and niches of a variety of scales and proportions refract the incoming light, creating a rich interplay of forms. The Museum's services and access routes (two staircases, one a winding spiral; lift and hydraulic ramp) are arranged around the periphery of the plan, with the four interlinked galleries in the central core around a lofty double-height light well crowned by a dramatic, cruciform skylight in the vaulted roof. The wall separating the double- and single-height spaces on the ground floor split the space, modulating the light around shadowed and illuminated forms.

The lower gallery is an open, fluid space with two galleries flanking the double-height space. Two staircases provide a curved or winding route to the upper floor. Here, the colliding walls meet the cross-shaped lightshaft. These interior spaces exert a serenity which belies the muscular contortions of the exterior, but the two are sculpturally linked. In spite of its unsettled spontaneity, the bold and original presence of Gehry's Museum is not arbitrarily defined. Gehry's facility with three-dimensional form creates an expressive architecture of rich irregularity which is conducive to the Museum's aspirations — open-ended spaces with a spiritual aura which does not confine the artefacts exhibited but encourages a limitless embrace of forms and ideas.

A short walk away, the façades of Gehry's 90,000-square-foot factory unit are a mix of equally dazzling white forms — a seating assembly plant with adjacent office, mezzanine and distribution area. It is intended to create a dialogue with the existing low-lying plant buildings designed by architect Nicholas Grimshaw, between which it takes up a position in front of the Museum. Essentially a rectilinear volume, it has skylights, large industrial windows and a bleached white stucco finish. The unit echoes the exposed high-tech elements of Grimshaw's sheds, but with a wholly contrasting interpretative stance towards technology based on sculptural forms, which gives it the impression of pre-dating Grimshaw's design without compromising its independent language.

The public face of the factory is on the north side, facing the road: the mezzanine offices here have spectacular

The curved staircase from the left side of the foyer to the upper exhibition space. The window over the stairwell, set in the sloping curve of the 'winged' forms flanking the entrance, draws in light and forms a contrast with the curving planes around it.

views of the mountains as well as of the Museum and a playful installation by Claes Oldenburg and Coosje van Bruggen nearby. On this façade, sculpturally shaped ramps and entrance canopies flank the factory's façade, creating witty 'bookends' to the Museum, forming an animated dialogue with its own flanking entrance 'wings'. Further afield on this extraordinary green-field site, other innovative and internationally acclaimed architects and designers have been commissioned to create a showroom and walkway (Antonio Citterio), entrance and parking area (Eva Jiricna), a fire house (Zaha Hadid) and a pavilion (Tadao Ando).

Ground-floor (far right) and upper-floor (right) plans.
1 Entrance. 2 Foyer.
3 Two-storey exhibition space. 4 Large exhibition space. 5 Exhibition/conference room.
6 Café. 7 Access to

upper storey.
8 Elevator. 9 Spiral staircase.
10 Storeroom.
11 Hydraulic ramp.
12 Office. 13 Kitchen.
14 Service facilities.
15 Bathroom.
16 Upper-storey exhibition space.
17 Air space.

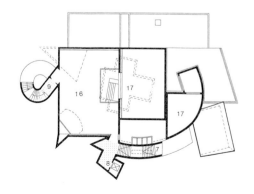

CULTURAL & PUBLIC AMENITY BUILDINGS

The glass cruciform skylight above the apertures of the central wall of the Museum makes an awe-inspiring play of light, space and volume.

A temporary exhibition in the larger, single-storey space on the ground floor shows models by Charles Eames and other pioneering bentwood designs 'floating' in space or positioned on wide platforms without cases.

The double-height gallery is entered from a timber-floored, high-level viewing bridge which runs the length of the room, screened on the street side by a large blue-green curtain wall. For a closer view, small staircases lead down to the stone-floored gallery.

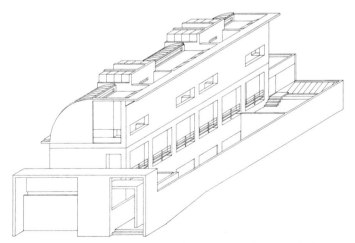

Axonometric diagram.

The curve of the lead-covered barrel-vaulted roof and the sand-coloured walls of the student block beneath add expression to the building's monolithic concrete forms.

CULTURAL & PUBLIC AMENITY BUILDINGS

4.12
Gotoh Museum

DAVID CHIPPERFIELD ARCHITECTS
Chiba Prefecture, Tokyo, Japan

The site of the privately owned Gotoh Museum is a narrow strip of land in a quiet, but densely built, residential area in the amorphous sprawl of Tokyo's northern suburbs. Mr Gotoh, the client (who also owns Marc Newson's miniscule Pod Bar in the heart of the city) wanted to house his collection of contemporary art in a small public building on the site of his former home. Because of the hemmed-in nature of the site, the Museum is a public gallery with an intensely private demeanour to its concrete façades: a retreat shielded from the cramped apartments flanking its narrow front, providing calm, double-height spaces set in a concrete structure and screened from the exterior world by tall, opaque glass windows.

Chipperfield faced numerous restrictions governing the density of interior spaces and height of the building. Gotoh proposed that the Museum become dual-function in order to subsidise its running costs, so student rooms rented by the local university occupy the top two floors. In such a crowded locale it was vital to maintain privacy, both from neighbouring apartment blocks and between the two components of the building, while coherently housing two very different scales — one domestic, one public — in the interior spaces.

Chipperfield decided to construct the galleries 5.5 metres below ground level; the student rooms, with their own cloister-like access, sit above. In a country which has perfected the use of concrete, this seemed a natural choice of material for the building, although the surface of the roof is sheet lead. On a site with very bad soil conditions, constructing a concrete building which would comply with earthquake resistance regulations meant introducing a degree of uniformity that gives the building a monolithic exterior appearance.

A complex relationship is established between internal and external spaces, based on semi-protective, interlocking volumes. The entrance leads to a wooden-floored bridge, running along one side of a double-height white-walled gallery and supported by intersecting structural girders. Large rectangular opaque glass windows cut into this wall allow diffused light into the gallery. Along the length of the bridge runs a blue-green curtain wall, overlapping with the balustrade, and concealing the gallery at ground level.

The rear opaque glass windows overlook a sunken patio garden, adjoining a small café area reached from ground level by a running stair. This is overlooked by the students' cloister on the floor above. In contrast, on the almost closed street side, close to the ceiling, are clerestory windows casting long shafts of light down through the double height. Above these, the student rooms with their small private courtyards fit neatly beneath the curved roof. This is the building's most idiosyncratic form, a half-curved barrel-vault structure of sheet lead intersected with protruding geometric skylights. The geometry of the windows is a smaller, inverted variation of the Museum's lower windows.

Chipperfield has endowed the roof with expressive potential not possible lower down the building. 'Modern architecture, in an attempt to become more abstract and geometric, has denied the powerful characteristic of the roof,' Chipperfield reasoned. The pitch roof, in particular, symbolizes traditional architecture, and so is often avoided in modern buildings. However, by not hiding the roof away behind the parapet but giving it a positive form, the architect is obliged, he explains, to show an engagement with its practical and physical problems. With the Gotoh Museum, Chipperfield's curved roof confronts the monolithic concrete building below and, at a level he and his client are happy to have highly visible, complements the building's other geometries.

The Museum's complex interlocking volumes above the lofty double-height gallery help to protect this space from the exterior, and ensure that its forms are kept separate from the smaller accommodation block above. Light filters in from high clerestory windows.

Section, with, from left to right: theatre, conference building and tower, galleries at the rear.

The conference hall is a mixture of draped sculptural effects, yellow carpet, curvaceous ceiling with recessed spots, and stern black furniture, intended for both meetings and banquets.

CULTURAL & PUBLIC AMENITY BUILDINGS

Art Tower, Mito

ARATA ISOZAKI & ASSOCIATES
Mito, Ibaragi Prefecture, Japan

Isozaki's aim was to create a new typology for a cultural complex appropriate for a regional city such as Mito. The Art Tower was commissioned as part of Mito's centenary celebrations, the long-term aim being to stimulate growth in the surrounding areas. Isozaki therefore looked back at historical architectural forms; not, he has said, to provide the

emphasise and encourage their interdependence. The intermediary role of new media facilities assists a further dissolution of perceived cultural boundaries. However, Isozaki has based each of the facilities on enduring building types developed in Western cities which, he felt, were best suited to the scale and intended longevity of the project.

The prototype for the theatre is the Swan Theatre of William Shakespeare, chosen because it was designed to allow close proximity between actors and audience. The stage certainly juts forward like the 'thrust stage apron' of the Swan, into a cylindrical space where the audience is arranged on three levels. This is not in fact a simple appropriation of another cultural form, since Isozaki's researches revealed that stages for Noh dramas in the sixteenth and seventeenth centuries had similar shapes to the Swan and the Globe theatres in London.

Isozaki sees this solution not as an attempt 'to run roughshod over current trends in theatrical production', but to return to 'primitive' forms, and thus escape from 'a modernity in a state of cliché' to a freer, and thus more productive, mentality for future architectural design.

The art gallery is based on Sir John Soane's Art Gallery in Dulwich, London, completed in 1815 and a revolutionary design at the time in terms of its placement of rooms and overhead natural

View of the cultural centre from the south, with the Tower at the right, facing the theatre and conference building across an expanse of square areas of grass and bands of granite and porcelain tiles.

city's inhabitants with an instant dose of fake nostalgia, but to shake up the increasingly slavish 'forward circulation structure of the Modernists' which he perceived as underlying the design of a number of other contemporary Japanese cultural buildings.

A 100-metre-high tower symbolizing progress sits at the centre of an urban square. Around it, like a small-scale town, are arranged various cultural facilities occupying 22,432 square metres — a theatre, concert hall and contemporary art gallery — positioned close together and linked by communal spaces in order to

The entrance hall has a double colannade and in the rear is a pipe organ. Limestone and concrete pillars are mounted on the balcony, which is supported by stouter columns below. Rows of concrete blocks along the ceiling, reinforced by aluminium, emulate wooden rafters.

lighting. Isozaki feels that this much-copied model still has more to offer than some modern Japanese art museums which 'fail to set up a rhythmical response between the works of art and the people viewing them. Ornamentation and the introduction of odd forms are not the ways to introduce such a response.' Galleries of different sizes, proportions and lighting conditions are arranged to create 'an unbroken experience'.

Further historical references abound: the foyer is based on a Romanesque basilica; the banquet hall on Ledoux, with a Soane-inspired ceiling and 'draped' sculpture derived from Bernini. And yet the tower outside — based not on any historical edifice, but futuristically billed the 'Column of Infinity' — is an exercise in pure form, celebrating contemporary technology. Isozaki successfully accommodates such an improbable juxtaposition of styles precisely because the cultural models he has used are not slavishly imitated; rather, their geometric forms are studied and applied within a contemporary context, using modern building materials and technologies for what they can contribute in their own right. The interior is not without the occasional inappropriate detail: at Mito, Isozaki makes his quotations generally conspicuous. However, the architectural narrative maintains a healthy level of irony, and never collapses into cliché-ridden story-telling.

Arches and marble columns support the central domed shell which extends over the concert hall, a light space with white oak walls and floors and wooden seating.

The theatre, modelled on Shakespeare's Swan Theatre, is all monochromatic solemnity. The seats are arranged on three levels in a semi-circle of tiers of wood painted with cobalt to give a textured effect.

CULTURAL & PUBLIC AMENITY BUILDINGS

Kleihues establishes a quiet, provocative dialogue between the traditional and the modern. The spiritual calm is uninterrupted by the introduction of plain glass and aluminium cases and tall torchières which follow the tree forms of the arches.

A view of the Roman collection in the apse, with long pieces of I-beam grey steel sections cut from another context and placed here as low pedestals: the new supporting the old.

Museum for Pre- and Early History

JOSEF PAUL KLEIHUES
Frankfurt am Main, Germany

As an architect who has designed over sixteen museums (of which five have been built), Josef Paul Kleihues understands well the contrasting requirements that museums are increasingly expected to reconcile. The classic responsibilities of a museum – to collect, document, study, preserve, exhibit and educate – often do not leave much room for the observer's intellectual and sensual enjoyment. The socially defined expectations of a museum, he claims, are for the most part confusing. As a 'poetic rationalist', Kleihues is motivated in his designs by an awareness of history that is determined not only by the intellect but by the emotions. This has led him in his design for the Museum of Pre- and Early History to create an equilibrium between functionalism and the atmospheric qualities of its spaces, where exhibits are not 'holy' mute objects, but artefacts which say something about their secrets.

Through a rich dialogue with the Museum's own historical context, Kleihues' architectural forms explore the contradictory and subjective nature of remembrance.

The Museum has taken a decade to come to fruition: Kleihues won an open competition for its design in 1980; construction began on the DM34 million project in 1986, and it opened in May 1989. The task involved the rehabilitation of a late Gothic Carmelite church and the addition of new wings to create a 40,840-square-foot archaeological museum. This Kleihues aimed to establish as 'a simple place of perception and recollection', where intellectual and sensual enjoyment could be experienced. In order to maximize the amount of valuable display space above ground, he put conservation workshops and archives below ground in basement levels under the new building.

Kleihues' restoration of the church achieves a balance between traditional and modern forms: the new plan draws on the structure of the old church, a dialogue articulated in the patterns of the floor tiles, lighting torchières and toothed pattern of the stone brick arches. His treatment of the mediaeval context of the site is best defined by the architect John Hedjuk, who likened the relationship between the old church and the new building to 'some kind of phantom ship carrying a sacred cargo'. It is a quiet but also a provocative dialogue. The new wings are aligned with the street and abut the transept of the old church without an intermediary reveal, demonstrating a dramatic change of texture from old gable to rhythmic coloured bands. By contrast,

Ground-floor plan, with the wings of the new building shown in red.

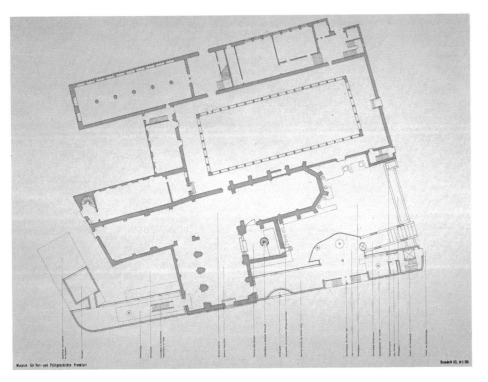

the interiors of both buildings are closely related in their materials and language, without becoming at all interchangeable, and display a sensitive treatment of exhibits.

The church and adjoining chapel building were crying out for restoration, but the chapel could not be structurally altered. Kleihues adjusted the traditional architectural emphasis of the old buildings by introducing along the Alte Mainzer Gasse a parallel building echoing their length. By enclosing the side wing of the old church, he made the whole building complex more introverted. The exhibition areas were opened out to the north, facing courtyard lawns with views of the church. This emphasis on north-facing windows made it unnecessary to provide much protection against the sun, and instead draws attention to the interplay of light and shadow on the old buildings.

Sandstone and stucco were applied to repair the walls of the church. The new roof over the nave is a good example of the use of traditional forms interpreted in perfectly integrated modern materials. In place of the original stone vaults destroyed during the Second World War, he has introduced new torch-cut steel rib trusses which evoke a Gothic style. It is this which leads Hedjuk to make interesting and evocative analogies with medicine, comparing the architect to a physician, carrying out a healing process by replacing worn or missing structure.

The Museum's interiors within both old and new buildings show a distinct sobriety of materials: the glass-and-aluminium display cases are light and modern, but not without a distinctive personality. They establish a subtle

dialogue with the old church building which can continue without disturbing the visitor's attention to the exhibits.

The red sandstone tiled floor is laid out in a grid pattern which underlines the conjunction of historical and modern forms. It also dictates the geometry of the plain aluminium display cases and the steel plinths for the Museum's statues. By reducing the display areas to three materials, set within calm, white-painted walls offset by the soft tones of the brick arches, Kleihues allows the wide variety of exhibits maximum emphasis.

The display cases are not arranged in one single, regimented format — this would create awkwardly shaped residual space in the tall, H-shaped exhibition space in the old church, intermediary transept area and new exhibition wings alongside. Instead, although there are series of single rows of cases, there are also 'street', 'courtyard' and more free-form configurations. These geometrically patterned compositions allow the objects on display their own space in which to communicate their unique qualities.

The same solid steel doors are employed for both interior and exterior, with two smaller versions joining the new building with the central nave of the church. Underlining the transition, Kleihues places an identical pair on a viewing balcony above.

The new wing initially looks as if it is raised up from the old building, but in fact it has deeper roots which house subterranean conservation studios, storage space and workshops. Above ground, the new wing on either side of the transept stretches out parallel with the old church, containing the main entrance, exhibition space and administration offices.

While the inner wall of the new building is expressive, with a curved and glazed façade looking out on the church courtyard and the restored tracery of its walls, the outer wall is a solid, enclosed structure, an enigmatic sweep of sandstone interlocked in a grid of steel

bolts which dominates the length of a small street, its wings closely juxtaposed with the gable end of the church. The wall is Kleihues' own newly constructed 'archaeological' artefact, with its own layers and contradictions. Its wide, horizontal, two-toned banding is inspired by the work of late eighteenth- and early nineteenth-century architects influenced by Italian striped façades, and by Schinkel. It directly refers to the red and green striped Frankfurt Stock Exchange, a mid-nineteenth-century building by Stüler, a student of Schinkel, which was destroyed in the Second World War. On Kleihues' façade, each rectangle of stone has two evenly placed bolts punctuating its surface, demonstrating that the stone is cladding, and not part of the structure. Here, the model is Otto Wagner's practice of leaving visible the means by which his 'cladding' was fixed in place, as a mark of confidence in the craftsman's skill; by some, however, this was seen as an example of purely wilful creativity.

Kleihues prefers plain materials; his understanding of their properties and their history lets him reveal the richness of their longevity, and judge best how to apply them in order to highlight their contrast with the original Gothic church architecture. It is Hedjuk who points to the main principle underlying the Museum's design: it is the responsibility of the new to take care of the old, and to carry forward its fruits for posterity. And just as the old church has been given new life, the Museum's plain materials articulate its guiding concept of recollection as an uncovering process which embraces both the emotional and the rational aspects of perception.

View of the new roof of the church's main nave: the cut steel structure forms a counterpoint with the restoration of the stone vaults elsewhere.

The austere galleries of the new building have a contemplative air underpinned by subtly applied geometries which maintain a dialogue of diction and contradiction with the traditional church adjoining.

The symmetry of the main entrance, set to the left of the old church gable, opens up a balanced aperture in the almost uninterrupted run of wall which dominates the street with its rhythmic horizontality.

The west elevation includes vast spheres for meetings and performances, and a metal gauze tree 'clock'. Along the yellow concrete wall, perforated aluminium teardrop shapes screen windows, and help to diffuse light in the interior spaces.

Basement plan.
1 Dressing rooms below Citizens' Theatre.
2 Rehearsal room.
3 Ramp. 4 Office.
5 Exhibition hall.
6 Gymnasium above plaza (civic centre).
7 Lounge. 8 Sunken garden. 9 Meeting hall.
10 Kitchen.

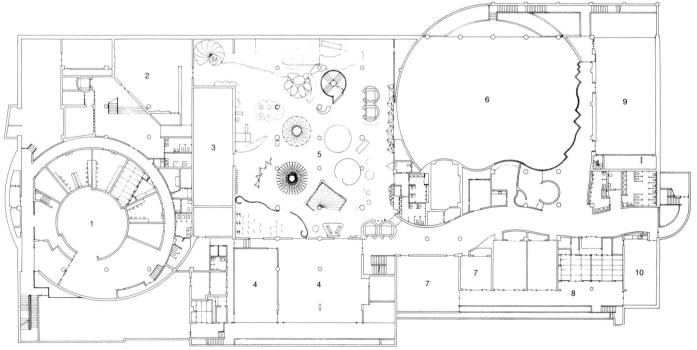

ITSUKO HASEGAWA
ARCHITECTURAL DESIGN STUDIO
Fujisawa, Kanagawa
Prefecture, Japan

The result of a competition for a cultural centre combining children's pavilion, civic centre and public theatre, Hasegawa's winning entry was a design that could 'bring together and adapt to many different classes of people: children and the elderly, women and men, the handicapped and those without handicaps.' To meet such needs, the project was designed as multiple, informal structures that form a complex which nevertheless has a single identity. 'This special place should have many different faces and be in constant flux: it should be able to accommodate multiple events,' explained Hasegawa.

The rectangular, landscaped site has a futuristic aesthetic which is not quite what it seems at first glance. A series of spectacular, metallic domes gathered at its west end house a theatre, meeting spaces and a children's museum, each connected by bridges and walkways from which visitors view the various activities. A miniature geodesic dome surrounds a radio station; behind it is a planetarium; further on, devices activated

by light, wind and sound, as well as mechanical devices within natural forms, such as a tall metal 'tree-clock'. Viewed from above, this space-age landscape is a glittering family of spheres and forest-like clusters of triangular sheets of semi-transparent punched aluminium sheet. The sinuous curves of a small waterway break up the ground area, and the surrounding plantation breaks down the initial sense of artifice in the building.

In design terms, the Center is a total environment and an intoxicating mixture of forms; and, thanks to Hasegawa's rational planning and clear signage, it is not a place in which you can easily get lost. Along with her desire to provide sensible orientation, Hasegawa believes that architectural forms should have a closer relationship both with nature and human psychology. This is manifested in a spirited architectural language that is applied to every aspect of the Center, from the spheres to the windows and the furniture within.

The globes are 'natural structural forms', not meant to be 'physically assertive', but arenas where the rational and the irrational can coexist. Their interiors are extremely spacious and flexible, allowing large numbers of people and equipment to come together for a variety of projects.

In the theatre gallery, coloured discs like portholes emblazoned on exterior 'flags' of aluminium provide a transitional zone for the visitor emerging from the Piranesian gloom of the theatre.

In keeping with the original aim to create playful, user-friendly architecture, the rooms and corridors are full of decorative forms played upon by light. Punched aluminium sheet is used to screen different areas, using light for decorative effects without reducing visibility. One challenge was to ensure that modern materials of this kind were blended in with those that are more traditional, such as Japanese slate for roofing and white plaster for walls. The basement rooms and corridors face a sunken garden, which provides a means to admit light and air, as well as a clear evacuation route in case of emergency.

The facilities for children within a purpose-built space are an unusual feature of a cultural centre. In addition to a children's museum, a spacious hall is laid out with activity tents and other interactive displays set against a backdrop of mosaic murals. Whimsical plastic trees and mushrooms on the periphery of the space relate it to the Center's playful vegetation of metallic trees outside.

Inside the global theatre, instead of a fixed proscenium arch separating performers from audience, there is a half-circle of seating, as in early outdoor theatres, which allows a better dialogue to be established. The soaring heights of the dome are painted black and filled with lighting equipment. The architect describes the atmosphere as redolent of Piranesi's 'prison' etchings, but the effect is intriguing rather than intimidating. Equipped with technological wizardry, the archetypal theatre form presents a new face.

An unusual but stimulating feature of this project was intensive local consultation. The design and development of the Center — built within a tight two-year schedule — involved Hasegawa in nearly fifty meetings consulting the citizens of Shonandai. The building therefore had to be sufficiently complex to accommodate a wide variety of views, and this led to Hasegawa's strong competition entry taking on a softened, group image, but without any diminution of its quality.

The consultations brought forward requests for plants to cover the site so that it would 'be like a giant ikebana reflecting the changing seasons', as well as the airing of major issues such as maximum ease of use, efficiency and comfort. From these talks the Center developed an identity as a landmark promoting the improvement of the environment. Incorporating the wishes of the community meant simplifying some of the detailed design work, but Hasegawa was still able to keep the costs to a budget of just under 6½ billion yen. Since the Center's grand opening, the citizens of Shonandai have voted with their feet for its undoubted success.

The generous occasional seating is variegated in its forms. Undulating glass brick walls echo the curving lines etched on the ceiling and walls.

A corridor gallery space has a stepped ceiling and jauntily decorative window forms.

The main auditorium is a theatre housed within the largest sphere, with walls of concrete and steel panels. Filled with equipment up to its 24-metre ceiling and painted black, it is a visually arresting spectacle. The global form engenders a greater intimacy between performers and audience.

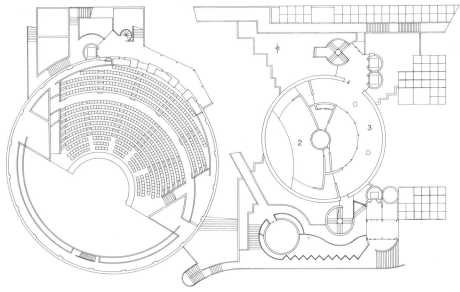

Second-floor plan.
1 Citizens' Theatre stage. 2 Cosmic theatre. 3 Lobby.

CULTURAL & PUBLIC AMENITY BUILDINGS

Visitors descend Pei's corkscrew helicoidal stone staircase to the light-filled limestone-clad Hall Napoleon, the museum's new reception area. A skylit public square, it can be visited without admission to the exhibition galleries, functioning as a cultural space with plenty of amenities: information desk, orientation centre, restaurants, cafés, bookshop and access to a concourse of shops.

4.16
Grand Louvre

The Grand Louvre, the 'jewel in the ground' monument which forms part of President Mitterrand's intended legacy for the next generation, has a glass pyramid of relatively modest size — which has been variously described as the eighth wonder, a scandal, an iceberg and an icon — in a courtyard one and a half times the size of the Piazza San Marco. Since it was opened as the Louvre's main entrance in 1989 it has invited probably almost as many definitions as it has glass panels, but it undoubtedly has a multiplicity of ascribed functions: as a facelift to the 7.2-acre Cour Napoleon, a stunning backdrop for modelling sessions, a twentieth-century shrine with an accessible identity and a powerful magnet for tourists.

However, it is the space created below ground which gives the Louvre a new

A restrained repertoire of materials was used to create simple and effective display cases.

lease of life. The beauty of the Grand Louvre lies in its simplicity of function, orientation and materials, combined in an underground building and bridge between the Louvre's three wings which extend in an elegant series of interconnected

spaces half a mile long. These provide what architect I.M. Pei describes as 'a vital connective tissue with new pedestrian links to the surrounding city', as well as a much-needed support space.

A recessed glass entrance leads to a projecting triangular balcony with a wide view on to the main entrance hall, which rotates the plan of the pyramid by 45 degrees, creating well-defined access routes to the three adjoining pavilions. On one side double escalators and on the other a spiralling helicoidal staircase provide suitably dramatic modes of entry. In the middle, a cylindrical elevator platform for the disabled has been added to 'transform vertical circulation into an exhilarating experience'.

The subterranean building is light and beautifully scaled, with an accessible central arena for meeting and relaxation with facilities which can be used without penetrating the Museum's inner spaces. Many visitors will reach the new underground galleries from within the Louvre, but this arrival from the central focus of the pyramid is the most popular choice. Its welcoming ambience markets the Museum to those who might not otherwise go. It could, however, become a deeply compromised reflection of the Louvre, and degenerate into a banal shopping mall on the original site of Philippe Auguste's fortified castle and Louis XIV's entrance moat.

The architectural impulse has been realised in an exemplary way in the Grand Louvre's entrance hall, with its matte, honey-coloured limestone walls, polished floors and white concrete ceilings. Designer Jean-Michel Wilmotte and lighting consultant Claude Engle have worked on specialist aspects here with great success.

Unlike the well-trodden, labyrinthine galleries of the Louvre, which evolved awkwardly from its royal residences, the Grand Louvre is much easier to negotiate. Within easy reach is an array of facilities: a 420-seat auditorium, exhibition galleries, shop, a Louvre history exhibition, eight escalators, two cafés, one restaurant and access routes punctuated by light from two smaller pyramid skylights – all contained in nearly 190,000 square feet of public underground space. Eventually there will be a new subterranean parking system, service tunnels and a conservation centre.

Jean-Michel Wilmotte who, with job designer Massimo Quendolo, designed the Grand Louvre shop, exhibition display cabinets and fittings, as well as a children's library, worked quite independently of architects I.M. Pei and Partners, but their separate design solutions complement each other very well. Wilmotte's aesthetic language is refined, and manifested in durable, well-made and visually strong architectural forms: maple desks, shelving units, print troughs and display plinths which blend well with wood flooring, supported by elegantly turned grey steel structures and glass façades. Both Pei and Wilmotte designed display cases. Wilmotte's are designed for versatility, in grey aluminium, with adjustable panels concealing switchboards, lamp housing and retractable wheels to allow the creation of various layouts for the display of three-dimensional objects.

This first phase cost an estimated 2000 million francs. Over the next eight years, the entire Museum will be reorganized, creating a new 22-acre 'operational infrastructure'. Already, with the departure of the Ministry of Finance from the northern Aile Richelieu, a whole first floor of the main Louvre buildings is being planned as exhibition space scheduled for completion in 1993. From this point on, the Louvre will function exclusively as a museum for the first time in its history. In the newly available north wing, Wilmotte has embarked on designs to create vast new spaces for displays within the historic fabric of the Louvre: another redefinition of a facet of France's cultural heritage which is certain to be much debated.

The generous proportions and beautiful materials of the Grand Louvre's underground passages.

CULTURAL & PUBLIC AMENITY BUILDINGS

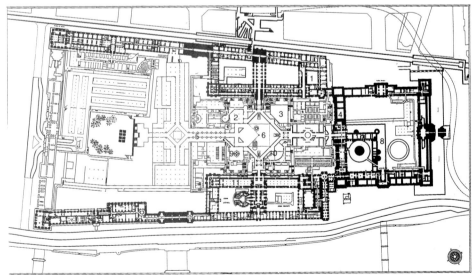

Wilmotte's dual-level book/gift shop, well lit by lighting consultant Claude Engle, within one of four different programmatic quadrants at the side of the Hall Napoleon, diagonally rotated in the centre of the U-shaped Louvre.

Mezzanine-level plan.
1 Richelieu pavilion.
2 Café/restaurant.
3 Auditorium. 4 Sully pavilion. 5 Passage to Place du Carrousel.
6 Lobby. 7 Temporary exhibitions. 8 Crypt of Philippe Auguste.
9 Bookstore/shops.
10 Conference rooms.
11 Denon pavilion.

Detail of the edge of the metal-and-glass balustrade, its elegant, unadorned forms complementing the fabric of the cathedral.

Almost full-height, and fronted with quarter plate glass, this row of cases is dramatically scaled. Lighting is kept within recommended levels for conservation, but manages to dramatise the form, colour and texture of the stone exhibits.

CULTURAL & PUBLIC AMENITY BUILDINGS

Triforium Gallery, Winchester Cathedral

STANTON WILLIAMS
Winchester, UK

The Triforium Gallery is a magnificent space in the south transept of Winchester Cathedral, containing a wealth of ecclesiastical treasures. These have been put on show in a new exhibition area designed without a trace of compromise or conceit, and avoiding the ill-conceived, merchandise-led approach sadly adopted by many historical or religious institutions strapped for cash to pay mounting repair bills. Instead the cathedral, with grants from many sources, has bestowed on its public an asset of a high order: a dramatic and effective setting for its rare fragments has been achieved with a design of great subtlety and balance.

Stanton Williams, renowned for their intelligent restraint and specialist exhibition and museum design skills, carried out the design of the Gallery over a six-month period. Their intention was to 'retain the architectural integrity of the space, and where necessary clarify and reinforce the original structure', and to heighten visitors' perceptions by giving visual priority to the unique collection of medieval and post-medieval objects: this had to be done without compromising the stringent conservation requirements. Stanton Williams' sensitive resolution of the commission was voted Best Fine and Applied Arts Museum of the Year by National Heritage in the UK in 1990.

Materials were chosen to blend in with the existing stone fabric of the gallery. A series of vertical showcases and a low desk case were clad in Whitbed Portland stone, with glazing held together by minimal fixings and opening

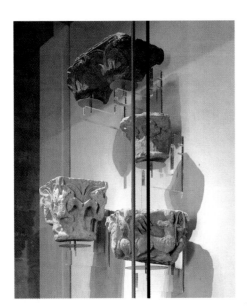

Special fittings of L-shaped Perspex support objects as weighty as these corbels, positioned on stainless steel rods and discs.

mechanisms hidden in the top and the base. The tall cases, made of stone slabs based on traditional paviours, back on to one another, separated by a pair of vertical stone blades. The smaller, inset glass cabinets allow the stone structure to act as a backdrop for objects on display.

The lightness of the cases' structure is achieved by the juxtaposition of double plate glass and layered planes of stone; the simplicity of their fittings helps to create the appearance of objects floating in space. Set into a carefully orchestrated display area, the cases are well integrated into the high volume of the west arcade.

The design highlights the scale, value and variety of the objects displayed, without jarring elements which would diminish their austere integrity. Cases, plinths and graphic panels are clearly seen as secondary elements, but complementary to the exquisite sculptured heads, Romanesque capitals and other conserved architectural fragments, retrieved from the cathedral over many centuries.

The amount of daylight allowed to enter the Triforium had to be limited for conservation reasons. Within the showcases, optical fibre display lighting dramatises the form, colour and texture of the objects, creating maximum focus and impact. To create the correct mood for the surrounding spaces, indirect lighting is used. The designers carried out tests to ensure that a balance could be achieved between the dramatic impact of object presentation and the architectural strength of the Triforium. Such a subtle equilibrium is reflected in every aspect of the resulting space.

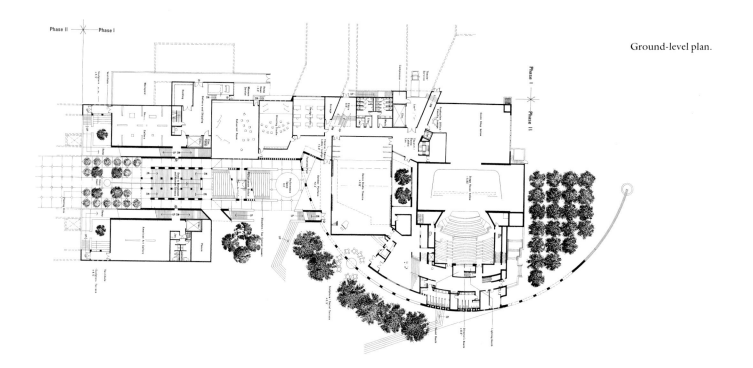

Ground-level plan.

The second-floor American art gallery is illuminated by suspended rows of solar-activated clerestory monitors that filter the ultraviolet rays from the fierce daylight sun. Predock's understanding of light-filtering structures has helped to create a careful balance between the need to display and conserve works of art. Incandescent spotlights installed on tracks on the underside of the louvres add extra task lighting.

4.18

Fine Arts Center, Arizona State University

ANTOINE PREDOCK
Tempe, Arizona, USA

The Fine Arts Center at Arizona State University is at once a 'naked desert building' and an 'intimate oasis' within a campus in suburbia — a particularly challenging combination of nature and culture which architect Antoine Predock manages to harmonize with great skill. The site borders the urban sprawl of the southwestern city of Phoenix, Arizona. Looking at the anonymity of the built-up area beyond its boundaries, the Center could be almost anywhere in the country, but climatically the area is rooted in the desert, with summer temperatures often exceeding 48°C/120°F.

The project began as an invited competition funded by the National Endowment for the Arts. Predock's successful response to the brief was to reaffirm a sense of the original place through a sophisticated aesthetic language which anchors the 'man-made ephemera' in and around the sprawl of the city, and emphasises the experiental aspect of the Center's architectural forms. Adopting an anthropological approach,

Predock took his inspiration from the structure of the natural and cultural environment of the desert, and from an understanding of the art forms the Center is intended to engender.

Within the larger context of the University campus, the Center presents a low, unifying silhouette highlighted by towers and loft projections reflecting the forms of surrounding mountains and buttes. There are no fixed circulation routes; instead, orientation relies heavily on image and experience, woven into a highly articulated layout — it is an expressive landscape, operating above and below ground, which reveals itself bit by bit. The main buildings are conceived on a large scale, manifesting a simplicity in their massing around a central plaza with an open performance space. Tangential routes lead to adjoining buildings housing numerous workshops, offices, seminar rooms, archives, rehearsal and relaxation spaces. Linking staircases, courts, terraces and arcades manifest an almost choreographed processional richness that challenges the senses of arts students and members of

the public wooed to exhibitions, plays and performances. Throughout the 122,000-square-foot Center, Predock presents an exploratory journey, following contemplative cave-like spaces of deep dark shade with expanses filled with light, used for a continuous pattern of creative practice, from research, direction and rehearsal to performance.

The sun glare potential is very fierce, and the need to balance southern and northern light rays necessitated strict control of apertures. Essential climatic controls have been transformed into applied aesthetic elements within Predock's overall design, exerting considerable sensory power. Non-reflective wall and paving surfaces, self-shading, deep-set windows, 'bleachers' or sun-controlling louvres, and trellis grilles — all these lend abstract expression to their individual buildings. Respite from the heat is obtained from the many shade structures, including low, labyrinthine passages with delicate trellis structures that filter light into intricate shadows.

The public edge of the Fine Arts Center on Mill Street borders Frank Lloyd Wright's Gammage Auditorium, and presents a ceremonial entrance. Moving from the periphery into the museum galleries represents an almost seamless transition from exterior to interior; in part, there is a playful ambiguity between the

The spread of building forms, many with punctuated groups of small, recessed, glass block windows. From left to right: a tower bridge with anodized aluminium trellis; the louvred, sun-shading concrete roof to the nymphaeum; the red brick arcade-cum-acqueduct, and the stucco-finished concrete structure of the dance studio theatre and playhouse behind; between, images are projected on to the fly-tower wall.

Shady passages covered
in anodized aluminium
trellis grilles lead from
climate-controlled
galleries to outdoor
performance areas.

two in what strives to be one organic unit.
Soft desert colours are used, in places
with a raw stucco finish commonly applied
in Phoenix to reinforced concrete façades.

Visitors entering here can either
plunge down to the sunken museum
entrance, or perambulate around the
plaza. In either direction, exterior
materials invade the interiors: the grand
stucco stairways leading down to the
nymphaeum (water court) and entrance to
the museum below ground pull the
aesthetic strength of this material in from
the baking sun outside and down through a
series of progressively cooler and shaded
areas. Once down in the underbelly of the
gallery the sound of water prepares the
visitor for the actual sight of evaporative
pools further along in the nymphaeum.
The cool atmosphere of this subterranean
forecourt is brought about by the
introduction of water and air which, in this
context, become 'soft' design elements.
Its pitched roof of sun-controlling louvres
combines aesthetics and practicality by
capturing breezes and acting as a hot air
exhaust. Conceptually, it is based on an
old Indian method of excavating water
channels to extract water from the desert;
its ambience prepares visitors for another,
more demanding type of perceptual
experience – looking at art.

The museum is the largest
component of the complex, housing the
University's $15 million art collection in a
symmetrically laid out series of galleries,
many with concrete pillared borders
emphasising their proximity to exterior
terraces. Central to Predock's display
strategy is the natural lighting scheme
which, within conservation requirements,
is consistent with his lighting elsewhere.
This eliminates the infiltration of
ultraviolet light, but achieves a
compromise with a controlled level of
diffusion so that the gallery's environment
does not become overly uniform or static.

Long terraces
encourage a relaxed
ambulatory pace, so
that visitors can take in
an array of stimuli. Art
is seen in both a
museum and a garden
context.

The main dance studio and 500-seat
proscenium theatre are linked by shared
lounge spaces, which reinforce their
shared identity as performing arts. The
Center offers numerous studios equipped
for rehearsals, and the atmosphere of
these back-stage spaces is transferred to
the main theatre itself, via an array of
exposed acoustic media suspended over
the audience. The theatre feels like a
workshop where plays are crafted – itself a
spectacle where methods and means are
clearly visible.

The theatre is given a ceremonial
access route through a palm court
culminating in an open patio café with
fountains. Both spaces are bounded by a
curved red brick 'arcade cum aqueduct'
which recirculates water for the fountains
of the Arts Plaza. Its moon-shaped form
also links the Arts Plaza with the central
campus. Within its bounds, raked outdoor
seating next to a grid of shading trees and
a sculpture garden encourages informal
performances and events – a
demonstration of Predock's emphasis on
externalizing interior-based activities
within carefully screened parts of the
campus. As well as light, water and other
forms of aesthetically implemented
atmospheric controls, the Center's

sensory 'programme' extends to its
planting. Aromatic herb borders enhance
groves and arbours of orange, olive and
African Sumac. Predock has used local or
widely available plants and shrubs rather
than imported exotica, siting in strategic
positions cacti and palm trees,
bougainvillea, and urns with Spanish
broom.

The entire Center has a spectacular
presence, both above and below ground.
Predock makes a dramatic
superimposition of light to draw further
attention to the activities of its creative
community: at night, the fly tower on one
side of the theatre, a huge vertical blade
of reinforced concrete, becomes a
projection wall with a movable screen of
drive-in movie proportions – an American
pop culture institution, and another of
Predock's eclectic influences. In the
darkness, animated with the light of
projected images, it appears almost as a
talisman within the broad sweep of the
Center's landscape.

CULTURAL & PUBLIC AMENITY BUILDINGS

Designers' Biographies

MORRIS ADJMI was born in 1959 in New Orleans, Louisiana, and studied architecture at Tulane University and the Institute for Architecture and Urban Studies, New York. In 1981 he began working with ALDO ROSSI in Milan. After three years, he returned to the USA and directed the practice's projects in North America and Japan. Major works include the Carlo Felice Theatre, Venice; the Viadana House; housing on Friedrichstrasse, Berlin; Lighthouse Theatre, Lake Ontario; houses in the Poconos, Pennsylvania; School of Architecture, University of Miami (1989); and Hotel Il Palazzo, Fukuoka (1989).

TADAO ANDO was born in 1941 in Osaka, Japan. He is a self-taught architect who established his own office in 1969. In 1989 he was awarded the Medaille d'Or de L'Academie d' Architecture. He became well-known in the 1970s for residences such as the Horiuchi Residence, Osaka (1979) and the Row House in Sumiyoshi (1975–6). The Rokko housing projects of 1983 and 1985 won international acclaim, as did the Kidosaki Residence of 1988. Ando has lectured and exhibited widely (e.g. "Intercepting Light & Nature" in New York, 1985; "Breathing Geometry" at the 9H Gallery in 1986, and at European venues). His larger scale recent work, the OXY Unagidani, Osaka (1987), Galleria Akka, Osaka (1988) and the Collezione building (1989), as well as smaller projects, e.g. the Church on the Water, and of the Light (both 1989), show continued use of simplified concrete forms to create "poetic urban dwellings".

APICELLA ASSOCIATES was founded in 1988 by Lorenzo and Fereshteh Apicella. Lorenzo studied architecture at Nottingham University and the Royal College of Art before working for SOM, and on commissions such as the interior design of the Diplomatic Club, Riyadh. From 1986 to 1988 he was Associate Director at IMAGINATION where he designed exhibitions and interiors. Fereshteh studied at the American College, London and worked for BRANSON COATES ARCHITECTURE. Recent projects include offices for Wickens Tutt Southgate (1989–90).

ARCHITECTURE RESEARCH UNIT is a combined teaching, practice and research unit founded at the Polytechnic of North London in 1978. Directed by FLORIAN BEIGEL, with staff members Philip Christou, Julian Lewis, Suresh A'Raj and Jonathan Freeman, ARU works on architectural projects for specific communities which require a high degree of research input, including the Half Moon Theatre, London (1979); the PNL Theatre bar (1989), and restoration of the adjacent Great Hall; and the refurbishment of a housing estate in Harlow, UK.

ARMSTRONG ASSOCIATES was founded in 1986 by Kenneth Armstrong, and is based in London. Jenifer Smith joined in 1986 after training at the Bartlett School, University College, London and became a partner in 1989. Armstrong trained at the Mackintosh School in Glasgow and the Royal College of Art. He worked for Foster Associates (1982–84), DEGW, and in 1984 set up Armstrong Chipperfield with DAVID CHIPPERFIELD. Armstrong Associates have completed offices, shops, private residences, a school and masterplanning studies. In 1990 they won a major competition for the Maison du Japon, Paris, the last of the current Grands Projets, and were runners-up in the Banco de Portugal competition. Their recent projects include a consultancy for FOSTER ASSOCIATES on the masterplan for King's Cross, London; the Imperial War Museum shop with Arup Associates; and offices and showrooms for Elementer.

ARQUITECTONICA was founded in 1977 by Bernardo Fort-Brescia (born in Lima, Peru, in 1951) and Laurinda Spear, and now has offices in Miami, New York, San Francisco and Chicago. The partners studied architecture at Harvard and Columbia Universities respectively. Their work in Miami is extensive, including housing, offices, the Kitsos Medical Building and the North Dade Justice Center. Other major projects include a Center for Innovative Technology, Virginia; the Banco de Credito del Peru, Lima; and the Banque de Luxembourg (1990). The practice has received several Progressive Architecture and AIA Honor Awards.

ALFREDO ARRIBAS was born in Barcelona in 1954, and studied at the Escuela Tecnica Superior Architectura where he is currently Professor. In 1982 he became President of the Spanish interior design organization INFAD. Notable projects in Barcelona include the Elisava School of Design (1986) and L'Hort des Monges restaurant (1987). In 1986 he designed Network Café and the Francisco Valiente shop with Eduard Samso. In 1987 Miguel Morte (born in 1957) joined Arribas' practice, and they designed Velvet Bar and the discothèque Louis Vega (Tarragona). The restaurant Gambrinus, the Clik dels Nens hall at the Science Museum in Barcelona and Torres de Avila (1990) were designed with JAVIER MARISCAL. Barna Crossing (1989) was his first major project in Japan. Apart from Spanish commissions, Arribas also works in Italy and Frankfurt.

BACH AND MORA is a Barcelona-based architectural practice formed in 1979 by Jaume Bach (born in 1943), and Gabriel Mora (born in 1941). Both studied at Barcelona School of Architecture in the late 1960s, and are currently senior design tutors there. Bach worked for Dols, Millet and Paez, and Mora for Hello Pinon and Albert Viaplana before collaborating on projects such as the State School of Barcelona (1984–1988); a winery/school for Raventos I Blanc; Jujol school (1988); Polideportivo de Gracia (1989); and the Palacio Macaya Cultural Centre. They are currently working on projects in Spain, France and the Netherlands.

STÉPHANE BEEL was born in 1955 in Kortrijk, Belgium. He studied at the St Lucas Institute, and the Architectural Institute, both in Ghent, graduating in 1980. Projects include residences, offices, showrooms, studios, an old people's home and a school (in Djibuti, Africa); the Spaarkrediet Bank, Bruges (1988); BAC office, Bruges, with Luc Morel (1989); and the Museum Roger Raveel, Zulte (1990). In 1989 Beel won the Eugène Baye Award, and in 1990 first prize for his design for a residence/doctor's practice, Mortsel. In 1990 his work was exhibited in Moscow.

BEHNISCH AND PARTNERS is a Stuttgart-based practice established in 1958. Günter Behnisch (born in 1922 in Dresden), Winfried Buxel, Manfred Sabatke and Erhard Trankner have designed a great variety of projects, many resulting from competitions. The bias is towards large-scale public projects such as the award-winning development designed for the Olympic Games in Munich; the Solar Institute at the University of Stuttgart; and the library of the University of Eichstätt (which won the BDA-Preis Bayern in 1987). In 1982 the practice won a major competition for their design for a new German Postal Museum, Frankfurt (1982–90). Recent projects include a research and development building for Leybold AG (1987); a kindergarten and station square in Stuttgart (1990); a school and sports hall at Bad Rappenau (1991); and parliament buildings in Bonn (due for 1992 completion).

FLORIAN BEIGEL was born in 1941 in Konstanz, Germany and trained as an architect at the University of Stuttgart, and at the Bartlett School of Architecture, University College, London. He worked as an assistant to GÜNTER BEHNISCH and Frei Otto, Stuttgart, principally on the Munich Olympic structures. In 1979 he formed Architecture Bureau (with Peter Rich and Jon Broome), with whom he designed the Half Moon Theatre, London. In 1973 he became a tutor at the Polytechnic of North London (PNL), and in 1990 Head of the Diploma School. He is currently Director of the ARCHITECTURE RESEARCH UNIT. His own practice designed the furniture for the ARU's PNL Theatre Bar (1989).

MARIO BELLINI was born in Milan in 1935 and graduated in architecture from Milan Polytechnic in 1959. Since 1963 he has been Olivetti's head consultant on office equipment design, and has also produced industrial design for firms such as Cassina, Vitra, Brionvega, Artemide, Poltrona Frau, Flos and Fiat. Architectural work includes the Italian Science and Technology pavilion interiors at Expo'85, Tsukuba; office and industrial developments in Italy; exhibitions including "Treasure from St. Mark's Venice" (1984); a showroom for Cassina in TADAO ANDO's Collezione building, Tokyo (1989), Yokohama Business Park (1991) and Tokyo Design Centre (1991–2). He has taught extensively, won numerous awards including the Compasso d'Oro, and has edited the architectural and design magazine *Domus* since 1986.

BRANSON COATES ARCHITECTURE was formed in 1985 by Nigel Coates and Doug Branson. Nigel Coates was born in 1949 in Malvern, UK, and studied at Nottingham University and the Architectural Association (AA), where he has taught since 1976, becoming Unit Master in 1979. In 1983 he founded NATO (Narrative Architecture Today) with eight unit members, publishing a magazine and exhibiting work. Doug Branson graduated from the AA in 1975 and worked for DEGW and in practice as the Branson Helsel Partnership (until 1984). Branson Coates' first built project was a house for Jasper Conran in 1985, followed by a shop (1986); Silver jewellery shop, London (1987); shops for Katharine Hamnett and Jigsaw. A growing repertoire of projects in Japan includes the Metropole restaurant, Tokyo (1985); the Bohemia jazz club (1986); Caffe Bongo, Tokyo (1987); Noah's Ark restaurant, Sapporo (1988); the Hotel Otaru Marittimo (1989); the Nishi-Azabu building, Tokyo (1990); Taxim restaurant/bar/club, Istanbul (1991). Current projects include another shop in London for Jigsaw; a tower at Nishi Azabu; and a restaurant and cardroom at the Mayflower Golf Club, Tokyo. Coates also designs his own ranges of furniture, e.g. "Tongue" (marketed by Rockstone in Japan and SCP in the UK/Europe). In 1990–91 he designed furniture for Poltranova, Cavaliere, the Dolphin hide-all wardrobe/shelving system for Andaesse, and a range of vases for Amphoreau.

BUILDING is a Los Angeles-based practice established in 1985 by Michele Saee, who was born in Iran in 1956. He studied architecture at the University of Florence and urban planning at Milan Polytechnic. After working for Adolfo Natalini at Superstudio in Florence for two years he moved to Los Angeles in 1983 to work for MORPHOSIS on local projects such as the Venice III House; Angeli Cafe (1984); and Kate Mantilini (1985), which won AIA and Progressive Architecture Awards. Building's projects include Trattoria Angeli (1988); Ecru (1988) plus branches at Marina del Rey (1989); and residences. In 1990 Saee designed a gateway to Venice for the Biennale. He currently teaches at SCIARC, Los Angeles.

DAVID CHIPPERFIELD ARCHITECTS was founded in 1984 and opened a Tokyo office in 1987. The practice is currently constructing a number of buildings in the UK and Japan. David Chipperfield was born in London in 1953 and trained at the Architectural Association (1974–77). He worked with major practices including Richard Rogers and FOSTER ASSOCIATES and is a founder member and director of the 9H Gallery, London. He is currently Visiting Professor at the University of Naples. An initial series of award-winning retail interior and residential projects guided the transition to larger-scale work. The practice has recently been involved with urban planning projects in London with SOM, Stanley Tigerman and Frank Gehry, masterplanning sites at the King's Cross and Paternoster Square developments. Recent projects include Studios, Camden (1980); Kenzo; a house in Richmond; and the Gotoh Museum, Tokyo (1990). Current projects include a rowing museum, a city office development and a new multi-use building in Kyoto.

STUDIO CITTERIO DWAN is a Milan-based architectural practice run by Antonio Citterio and Terry Dwan who became a partner in 1987. Citterio was born in Meda, Italy in 1950. He studied architecture at Milan Polytechnic until 1980 and worked primarily on industrial and furniture design projects. In 1981 he set up his own studio, working with manufacturers such as B & B Italia. In 1983 he began to work on architectural design projects including a showroom for Santini & Dominici, and a collaboration with Gregotti Associati on the renovation of the Pinacoteca di Brera (1983). Terry Dwan (born in California in 1957) studied architecture at Yale. Recent projects include Esprit headquarters in Milan and shops in Europe; showrooms in Paris and Weil for Vitra; a commercial complex near Milan; World's Creative Fashion Dome (1989) and other building projects in Japan with TOSHIYUKI KITA.

COOP HIMMELBLAU was founded in Vienna in 1968 by architects Wolf Prix (born in 1942, in Vienna) and Helmut Swiczinsky (born in 1944, in Poland) and the practice now has offices in Vienna and Los Angeles. Their earlier work consisted of installations, speculative projects and conversions in Vienna such as the Baumann Studio (1985); the Iso-Holding offices (1986); Passage Wahliss (1986) and Rooftop Remodelling (1988); and the Funder Factory 1 & 3 (1988). They have recently graduated to larger-scale industrial projects in Austria, France, Germany, California and Japan. In 1987 they won two major competitions: the Ronacher Theatre, Vienna, and the Melun-Sénart city planning project near Paris. Both partners lecture and exhibit internationally; Prix is currently Adjunct Professor at SCIARC, Los Angeles.

DENTON CORKER MARSHALL PTY LTD was founded in Melbourne in 1972 by John Denton (born in 1945), William Corker (born in 1945) and Barrington Charles Marshall (born in 1946), all graduates in architecture from the University of Melbourne (1968). From offices in Melbourne, Sydney, Canberra and Hong Kong (and more recently from Singapore, Jakarta, Tokyo, Beijing and London), the practice has designed 1 Collins Street, Melbourne's first multi-storey offices (1980); the Powerhouse Museum of Applied Arts and Sciences, Sydney (1989); offices for Emery Vincent & Associates, Melbourne (1989–90); and the Australian Embassy in Tokyo (1990).

CHRISTIAN DE PORTZAMPARC was born in 1944, and studied at the Ecole Nationale des Beaux Arts, and with Beaudoin and Gandilis. After research in New York and for CORDA, he worked with Antoine Grumbach on Marne la Vallée (1970–4, including La Tour Verte). Major projects include La rue des Hautes Formes, Paris (1975–9); the planning of Les Halles, and in 1980 the Conservatoire de Musique Erik Satie, Paris, with Frederic Borel; housing in Lognes and in Paris; the award-winning Ecole de Danse, L'Opera de Paris, Nanterre (1983–7); Café Beaubourg (1985–6); Boutique Emanuel Ungaro (1989); Cité de la Musique, La Villette (west side 1986–90; east side due for 1992 completion); housing in Japan (1989); and an extension to Musée Bourdelle (1990).

D4 DESIGN PTY was formed in 1987 by Bill MacMahon (born in 1959), Stephen Roberts (born in 1959) and Michael Scott-Mitchell (born in 1960). Their expertise combines architecture (MacMahon, who trained at the University of New South Wales), interior, furniture, exhibition and graphic design (Roberts), and theatre and film design (Scott-Mitchell). Major projects in Australia include the Rockpool (1989) and The Third Man restaurants; Regents Court Apartments; a members' bar for the Powerhouse Museum; as well as private residences; theatre, retail, furniture and product design.

DIN ASSOCIATES was founded in 1986 by Rasshied Ali Din (born in 1956) who trained in interior design at Birmingham Polytechnic. Din Associates' expertise encompasses office, retail, leisure and exhibition sectors, as well as graphic design and packaging. Major projects include Next, Next Jewellery, a Next department store and Department X; French Connection showrooms (1988); showrooms, offices for Nicole Farhi (1989, and winner of a D & A D Silver Award in 1990); a designer room for Fenwicks; and a Covent Garden shop (1990). He has also worked on shops for Asda/George Davis; and Polo Ralph Lauren Paris (1990). Exhibition and TV clients include the Victoria and Albert Museum, the BBC and London Weekend Television.

MARIE-CHRISTINE DORNER was born in Strasbourg in 1960. After graduating from the Ecole Camondo she spent a year working in JEAN-MICHEL WILMOTTE's office before going to Tokyo where she was commissioned by Idée to design a range of furniture, and worked on interior design projects. In 1987 she returned to Paris and established her own practice, designing furniture for Cassina and items for Scarabat, Baccarat, Elisée Editions, Artelano and Snecma. Interiors include La Villa Hotel (1988); and La Comédie Française restaurant, Palais Royal, Paris (1989). Dorner continues to work on furniture design (for Idée, and in Paris a presidential stand for military parades); product design (Bernardaud); and interior design (Yamagiwa lighting showroom, Tokyo).

ÉCART was founded in 1978 by Andrée Putman who was born in Paris. She studied piano at the Paris Conservatoire with François Poulenc. After a few years as a journalist she moved into industrial design, and in the 1970s co-founded Createurs et Industriels, teaming up designers such as Issey Miyake and Castelbajac. In the mid–1970s her interest in Eileen Gray led to the reproduction of twentieth-century furniture which came to be regarded as innovative classics. From 1989 Écart specialized in re-editions, and interior design projects. These include Bordeaux Museum of Contemporary Art (1984, and furniture in 1990); Morgan's Hotel, New York; St James's Club Hotel, Paris (1987); headquarters, boutiques and a public relations centre in Switzerland for Ebel (1987); Carita beauty salon, Paris (1989); Wasserturm Hotel, Cologne (1980); a boutique for Balenciaga (1989); and headquarters for the Foundation for the Rights of Man, La Défense, Paris (1989), and for Channel 7 in Paris (1990).

FERN GREEN PARTNERSHIP was formed in London in 1987 by designers Nigel Green and David Fern, who together have 16 years' experience working for international design groups. Prior to setting up the firm, which specializes in interiors, furniture and exhibitions, the partners worked for clients such as British Airports Authority, the Arts Council and Virgin Records. Major

projects include an estate agent's office (1988); shops for Red or Dead (1988 & 1990) and Michiko Koshino (1990); fashion and graphic design studios and exhibitions. The practice is currently designing a studio and workshop in London, and jewellery display units in Tokyo, for Michiko Koshino.

NORMAN FOSTER was born in Manchester in 1935, and studied architecture and city planning at the University of Manchester and at Yale University. He established Team 4 in 1963 with his late wife Wendy, and Su and Richard Rogers, and in 1967 founded Foster Associates. Foster has a world-wide reputation for his refined, high-tech approach. Many of his projects are the outcome of competitions, such as the Sainsbury Centre for the Visual Arts at the University of East Anglia (1978, currently being extended); the Hong Kong and Shanghai Bank (1979–86); the Barcelona Tower and Bilbao Metro; Stansted Airport, East Anglia; and since 1988 the practice has been masterplanning the 120-acre King's Cross site. Current projects include new headquarters for Independent Television News; galleries for the Royal Academy; the Century Tower in Tokyo; a Médiathèque in Nîmes (1990); and new offices and apartments at Chelsea Reach (1990). The practice has also designed the award-winning Nomos range of furniture as well as London shops for Katharine Hamnett and Esprit (1988), and has won numerous international awards.

DANIEL FREIXES AND VICENTE MIRANDA are architects who have worked together since 1972. Freixes was born in 1946 in Barcelona, studied at the University there, and since 1975 has taught design in the city, and sat on numerous juries. Miranda was born in Logroño in 1940, and studied at the Barcelona School of Technical Architecture. The duo have won many awards. Projects include an apartment building in Horta (1976); Bar 33 (1983); Bar Zsa Zsa (1989); exhibition designs at Barcelona City Hall and the Berlin IBA (1990). Recent projects include designs for a hotel and shopping mall in the Ramblas (1987); the Parque Central, Viladecans; extension of the Big Ben discotheque, Lleida (1989); exhibitions on Mies van der Rohe, Bunuel. "A Hundred Years in Barcelona", and from 1990 exhibition projects for Expo '92 in Seville.

SPENCER TAK-SHING FUNG studied architecture at Churchill College, Cambridge University and at the Architectural Association before joining DAVID CHIPPERFIELD ARCHITECTS. He has worked on projects such as the Wilson & Gough Gallery, London; the Gotoh Museum, Tokyo; and the National Rowing Museum, Henley-on-Thames. Projects in the Far East include workers' housing in Borneo; the National Bank of Indonesia, Singapore; and the Admiralty Commercial Centre, Hong Kong. In 1987 he won first prize at the fifth RIBA International Student Competition, and in 1990 first prize for his entry to the Fukuoka apartment building competition, Japan. In 1990 he left Chipperfield and Partners to start his own practice. Individual projects include the Isometrix showroom and offices; residences in London and Barcelona; and Zoo hairdressers, London. Fung currently teaches at the University of Bath.

FRANK O. GEHRY AND ASSOCIATES was established by Frank Gehry in California in 1962. Gehry was born in Toronto in 1929. After studying urban planning at Harvard and architecture at the University of Southern California, he worked for practices in the US and France. He has won more than 25 AIA awards, the 1989 Pritzker Prize, and his work has been exhibited internationally. Major projects include substantial work in California: residences, the Loyola Law School (1981–4); Aerospace Museum (1982–4); Rebecca's (1984–6); the Temporary Contemporary for MOCA Los Angeles (1983); international competitions e.g. Médiathèque, Nîmes (1984); as well as cardboard furniture, lights, art happenings and exhibitions. Two major European projects signal a new international phase: the Vitra manufacturing facility and museum (1989), and the American Center in Paris (due for completion in 1992).

GRINSTEIN/DANIELS, INC is based in Culver City, California, and was formed in 1980 by architects Elyse Grinstein and Jeffrey Daniels, both former associates in FRANK O. GEHRY's practice. Grinstein studied at the University of Southern California before working in the visual arts. She took a Masters degree in architecture at the University of California, Los Angeles in 1978. Daniels studied at Princeton University, Massachusetts Institute of Technology, worked for Michael Graves and Ricardo Bofill, and studied with artists Richard Serra and Barry Le Va. Both partners maintain strong links with the visual arts/education. Grinstein was a founding member of the Museum of Contemporary Art in Los Angeles. Daniels teaches at Santa Monica College of Design, Art and Architecture. Recent projects include Chaya Venice

restaurant (1990) and Kentucky Fried Chicken, Los Angeles (1990).

ZAHA M. HADID was born in Baghdad, Iraq, in 1950. She trained in architecture at the Architectural Association, London, where she won the Diploma Prize in 1977. Unit Master of her Diploma school (1977–87), she is now involved with the AA Council, runs her London-based practice, and lectures internationally. In 1982–3 she won awards for her schemes for Eaton Place, London and the Peak Club, Hong Kong, and took part in the 1985 Grand Buildings competition, London. She designed for the IBA in Berlin. Recent projects include urban regeneration in Germany (including a media park in docklands); a folly for the Osaka Garden Festival; Moonsoon restaurant in Sapporo (1990); a music video pavilion in Groningen; and a fire station for Vitra in Weil-am-Rhein. Since the 1983 AA show "Planetary Architecture" her work has been widely exhibited and published.

ISUKO HASEGAWA established her architectural design studio in Tokyo in 1976. She graduated in architecture from the Kanto Gakuin University in 1964, and from 1964–9 worked for Kiyonori Kikutake. After two years' architectural research at the Tokyo Institute of Technology, she became a lecturer at the Women's College of Art. In 1986 her design scheme for the Shonandai Cultural Center won first prize (1990). Other awards include the Japan Cultural Design Award (1986) and the Avon Award to Women (1990). Key projects include houses in Yaizu, Kuwabara, and in 1990 at Shimorenjaku; Tokumaru children's clinic (1979); the AONO building (1982); Sugai clinic (1986); and Cona Village (1990).

HERRON ASSOCIATES was founded in 1982 by architect Ron Herron, now a director of Imagination Ltd, with which the practice merged in 1989. In the early 1960s Herron was one of a team of architects who designed part of London's South Bank. A founder-member of the seminal Archigram group (1960), he designed the Walking (1964) and Instant Cities (1968) with Peter Cook and Dennis Crompton, becoming Visiting Professor at the University of Southern California in the 1970s, and teaching at the Architectural Association from 1965 onwards. In 1977–80 he was a partner at Pentagram. Recent projects include exhibitions; an urban project for Hamburg docks; L'Oreal's Karlsruhe headquarters (1988); Imagination headquarters (1989); "water experience" for GTM in Barcelona; estates office at Waddeston Manor (1990); and the new Canada Water Station for London Underground.

IMAGINATION is a London-based multi-media design/events company founded by designer Gary Withers, and joined by architects HERRON ASSOCIATES and designers Virgile & Stone in 1989. Interior designer Shirley Walker (born 1961), who designed Gary's, the in-house restaurant and office plan at the company's new headquarters, studied at Leeds Polytechnic. She has worked on numerous exhibitions for Ford, Iveco Ford, British Telecom and Zanussi, and is currently involved with the Natural History Museum's new Dinosaur Gallery, due for 1992 completion.

ARATA ISOZAKI was born in Kyushu in 1931 and studied at the University of Tokyo. He founded his own studio in 1963 and continued to collaborate with other architects and studios as well. Among his projects are the Gunma Prefectural Museum of Modern Art at Takasaki (1971–2), the Kitakyshu City Museum of Art (1972–4), the Shukosha Building at Fukoka (1975), the Fujimi Country Clubhouse at Oita (1972–4), the City Hall in Tokyo and the Museum of Contemporary Art in Los Angeles (both 1986). He completed Art Tower, Mito, and the Barcelona Olympic Sports Hall in 1990. He has been awarded major prizes in Japan and the RIBA gold medal in 1986.

CARLOS JIMÉNEZ (born in 1959 in Costa Rica) studied architecture at the Universities of Tennessee and Houston. In 1983 he established his own practice in Houston, and has now completed over 20 works, including housing and public/cultural buildings, notably the Houston Fine Art Press (1989). His designs have been exhibited in New York, Los Angeles, Houston, Moscow and Helsinki, and he is a visiting lecturer at the University of Texas and many other universities in the US.

EVA JIRICNA ARCHITECTS is an 11-strong, London-based practice headed by Eva Jiricna. Born in 1938 in Prague, Czechoslovakia, she qualified as an engineer and architect at the University of Prague in 1963. After arriving in London in 1968 she worked at the GLC before joining the Louis de Soissons Partnership in 1969. Eva set up in partnership with David Hodges in 1980 and then formed Jiricna Kerr Associates in 1985, which reformed as Eva Jiricna Architects in 1987. Major projects include Le Caprice (1981); Joe's Café (1985); Legends (1985);

interiors of Lloyd's headquarters (with Richard Rogers, 1985–86); and many stores for Joseph, including Kenzo (1982), Pour La Maison (1985), Joseph at Brompton Cross (1988) and Sloane Street (1989). Recent projects include new headquarters for Vitra; interiors for Jardine Insurance (with Michael Hopkins); a salon for Neville Daniel Hairdressing; two residences; a church conversion and a mixed development in London; new US shops for Joan and David; and hotel interiors in Monte Carlo.

BEN KELLY DESIGN was established in London in 1976 by designer Ben Kelly (born in 1949), who studied at the Royal College of Art, graduating in 1974. Sandra Douglas (born in 1958) joined in 1982, and Elena Massucco (born in 1958) and Peter Mance (born in 1963) in 1987; all are graduates of Kingston Polytechnic's interior design course. Kelly's best known projects include Howie (1977); work for Malcolm McLaren/the Sex Pistols; Lynn Franks' office (1981–6). BKD's major projects include The Haçienda, Manchester (1982); Smile hairdressers (1983); and a shop and office for Quincy (1987–8); the Dry bar, Manchester (1989); and Factory Communications' headquarters, Manchester (1990). Kelly has won a D & AD Silver Award for his record sleeve designs.

TOSHIYUKI KITA was born in Osaka, Japan, in 1942. After training as an industrial designer in his home town, he established his practice there, dividing his time between Japan and Italy, and producing furniture and accessories for manufacturers such as Cassina, as well as designing interiors. His Wink armchair and Kick table are part of the permanent collection of the Museum of Modern Art, New York. Kita has won many awards and exhibited work internationally. In 1989 he designed Sony's multi-purpose hall in Tokyo, and collaborated with STUDIO CITTERIO DWAN on World's Creative Fashion Dome, Japan.
In 1990 he published *Movement as Concept*, which expounds ideas explored in his design work.

JOSEF PAUL KLEIHUES was born in Rheine, Germany in 1933, and studied architecture at the Technical University in West Berlin and with Hans Scharoun before establishing his Berlin practice in 1982. In 1979 he became director of planning for Berlin's IBA (1945–7), and directed subsequent IBA exhibitions in 1987–8. Since 1972 he has produced designs for 19 museums in Germany, over a quarter of which are now completed, including the Museum for Pre- and Early History, Frankfurt am Main (1980–9), and the award-winning Museum Henninger, Kornwestheim (1987–9). In 1989 he won a competition to design an art museum in Berlin (1991). He has held chairs in architectural/urban design at the University of Dortmund since 1973, and was appointed International Professor at the Cooper Union, New York in 1986.

GARY KNIBBS (born in 1960) studied interior design at the London College of Furniture, and played the field before working for X.1 Design, where he specialized in music industry projects. In 1986 he formed Three Associates with Mark Farrow, designing private residences for pop stars Neil Tennant (Pet Shop Boys) and Bros, and offices and exhibitions. In 1989 he quit to establish Gary Knibbs Interiors, and designed offices for Vivid (1989). In 1990 he established King Knibbs Design with Caryl King.

SHIRO KURAMATA was born in 1934 in Tokyo, trained in woodwork at Tokyo College of Art and graduated from the Kuwasawa Design Institute in 1956. Since establishing his own practice in 1965 he gained wide renown for his interior and furniture design projects for Issey Miyake, Esprit, Tokio Kumagai and others (Bar Lucchino, Combré and Oblomova at Hotel Il Palazzo). His furniture (including collaborations with Idée, Vitra and Memphis) has been exhibited widely, and works such as the "How High the Moon" chair are represented in permanent collections of museums throughout the world. In 1990 he was awarded the Chevalier by the French Ministry of Culture. His untimely death in 1991 robs the design world of an internationally respected figure renowned for his poetic and prolific output.

CHRISTOPH LANGHOF was born in Linz, Austria. He studied at the Technische Hochschule, Vienna, and the Düsseldorf Art Academy. After postgraduate studies at the Hochschule der Bildenden Künste in Berlin he set up Christoph Langhof Architekten with Thomas Hanni and Herbert Meerstein. In 1982 he helped to found the Wilde Akademie in Berlin; from 1987–9 he was Diploma Unit master at the Architectural Association, London. Major projects in Berlin include housing; a day-care centre at the International Building Exhibition; swimming baths; and the Horst-Korber Sportzentrum. Langhof is currently working on a new International Trade Centre in Berlin; a basic strategy for the city's development; and a new urban area on its waterfront, to house 50,000 people.

JOSE ANTONIO MARTINEZ LAPEÑA (born in 1941 in Tarragona) and **Elias Torres Tur** (born in 1944 in Ibiza) established their architectural practice in Barcelona in 1968, after studying at the Escuela Tecnica (ESTAB) there. Lapeña now teaches at the Escuela Tecnica at Valles (ESTAV); Torres has taught at ESTAB, and has also been visiting professor at Harvard and UCLA. Major projects include housing in Barcelona and Ibiza; the Villa Cecilia gardens, Barcelona; bookshop at Centro de Arte Reina Sofia, Madrid (1985–6); the monastery of Sant Pere de Roda, Girona (1980–8); Barcelona Activa headquarters (1987–8); and a hospital at Móra d'Ebre, Tarragona (1982–88), for which they won a FAD Award.

JEAN LEONARD and **Xavier Gonzalez** are architects based in Paris who collaborated on the design of offices for Gallimard Jeunesse (1989), and in 1988 for Editions Denöel. Leonard (born in 1955 in Morocco) graduated from UP8 in 1978, the University of Columbia, New York, in 1981, and since 1983 has been in partnership with Martine Weissmann. Gonzalez (born in 1955 in Spain) graduated from UP8 in 1981, and worked with Andrée Putman of ÉCART and TADAO ANDO in 1985–6, and has been in partnership with architect Olivier Brenac since 1978. Public architecture commissions include Leonard/Weissmann's sheltered housing/hospital at Ivry (1992 completion), and a museum (1991). Gonzalez/Brenac's projects include hospitals, schools, housing in Paris and Val-de-Marne.

PETER LEONARD ASSOCIATES was established in London in 1981 by Peter Leonard (born in 1954 in Suffolk). He studied interior design at Kingston Polytechnic and theatre design at Chicago's Northwestern University. The practice specializes in interiors and graphic design; clients include TV-am, Jasper Conran, Robinson Lambie-Nairn, The Scotch House, Virgin UK and France (Megastore, Paris), Petrus (Atlanta), 3i, Welsh Channel 4, WH Smith, Review and the Science Museum. In 1986 a subsidiary firm, SOHO Design, was set up, selling furniture and accessories, and in 1991 Leonard launched a "Cubist"-inspired collection.

FUMIHIKO MAKI was born in Tokyo in 1928. He studied at the University of Tokyo, Cranbrook Academy and Harvard, and worked for SOM and Josep Lluis Sert in the US before returning to Japan to establish his own practice. Involved with the 1960 Metabolist manifesto, his early projects include the Kumagaya campus at Risho University (1968), and Tokyo Kuragaike Memorial Centre (1974). The practice has since designed the award-winning Fujisawa Gymnasium (1985); the SPIRAL Building, Tokyo (1985); the National Museum of Modern Art, Kyoto (1986), the Tsuda Hall, and Tepia (1988), and in 1990 won a competition to design Buropark Hallbergmoos, Munich. Maki has exhibited and lectured internationally.

P. MICHAEL MARINO was born in 1948 in New York and studied architecture at the Universities of California, Berkeley, and New Mexico before establishing his firm in 1983. A member of the AIA, he has won awards for his New York store for Norma Kamali (1982–3), and for the Architects & Designers Building renovation (1988–9). Other major projects include showrooms for Norma Kamali (1984–5), Jessica McClintock (1988), and shops for Pilar Rossi (1988) and Pet Bowl Retail (1989–90); residences in the US and Europe; offices in New York; the renovation of the New York City Center Dance Theater (1986–90); and a 42-acre ranch in California (1990).

JAVIER MARISCAL was born in 1950 in Valencia, Spain, trained as an artist and in 1971 studied graphic design at Escuela Elisava. In 1972 his first comic-strip, El Senor del Caballito, was published in El Ciervo; a host of others followed, before Mariscal took refuge in Ibiza from Franco's censorship, until his first show in 1977 at Barcelona's Galeria Mec-Mec. He began to design clothes, carpets, furniture, interior design, ceramics, and other artefacts, as well as drawing, producing comics, and painting, exhibiting and publishing regularly. An anthology of his work was shown in 1988 in Valencia; the same year he created Cobi, the Barcelona '92 Olympics mascot. His furniture has been produced by Akaba, BD Ediciones de diseño, Memphis; his artefacts by Vincon; his textiles by Bures etc. Collaborations with ALFREDO ARRIBAS include Torres de Avila, Barcelona (1990).

RICK MATHER was born in 1937 in Portland, Oregon, and studied architecture in the US and urban design at the Architectural Association (AA). In 1973 he started his own practice designing institutional, residential and commercial projects including the masterplan, and renovation of the AA (1978–83); buildings at the University of East Anglia, Norwich (UEA,1982–3); the Zen restaurants, London (1985–6), Hong Kong (1988) and Montreal (1990); and remodelling of Waddington Galleries (1988). Recent work includes the masterplan for the expansion of UEA (including new low-energy residences, social facilities and a conference centre, due for initial completion in 1992); an office development, another Zen restaurant and apartments in London; the Latif residential compound in Khartoum; and the winning scheme for a new restaurant complex in London Docklands.

MASAMI MATSUI was born in Tokyo in 1950, and studied art and architecture at Kuwasawa Design School, during which time he also imported racing cars. After working in the fashion business he founded Axe Company in 1976, and in 1981 designed Red Shoes in Tokyo, one of Japan's first café-bars. Matsui's creative involvement extends from interior design to uniforms, lighting, menus and business strategies. His projects include the Inkstick Shibaura Factory and Tango clubs (1986), both at Tokyo Bay; Paradiso; Strathisla; a disco and bar at the Kita Club (1989), as well as fashion show production. A New York-based company, AXE Venture Inc., develops commercial ventures in the US.

SOICHE MIZUTANI was born in Fukui, Japan, in 1955, and studied at Kyoto Junior Art College. After graduating in 1975, he joined Plastic Studio in 1979, and established his own practice in Tokyo in 1986. Major projects include restaurants Sakura (1984), Setsu, Getsu, Ka (1985), AOI (1986), Tambaya (1989) and D/A (1990), all in Tokyo; bars (Pranzo Ambiente in Kobe, 1987, and Hana, in Kyoto, in 1988); and shops such as Shizuka, Paris (1985), Kansai Yamamoto (1988), Katharine Hamnett, Hiromichi Nakano, and Renaud Pellegrino (1990) in Tokyo.

MORPHOSIS is a Los Angeles-based architectural practice founded by Thom Mayne and Michael Rotundi in 1977. A Tokyo office opened in 1990. Mayne studied at the University of Southern California and at Harvard; Rotundi at the Southern California Institute of Architecture, where he is now Director. The award-winning projects include numerous residences, offices, shops and restaurants in California, including 72 Market Street (1984), Kate Mantilini, the Leon Max showroom and branches of Politix (1990), as well as larger projects such as the Comprehensive Cancer Center at Cedars Sinai Hospital (1988), and the Higashi Azabu Tower, Tokyo. Current activities include numerous competitions, exhibitions and X-Tech, a new manufacturing company.

ERIC OWEN MOSS (born in 1943) established his architectural practice in 1976. Now based in Culver City, California, he studied architecture at the University of California's Berkeley College of Environmental Design, and at Harvard Graduate School. He is currently Professor of Design and on the board at the Southern California Institute of Architecture, and Visiting Professor at Yale University. Major award-winning projects include the Petal House, and the Fun House (1983), as well as industrial conversions in Los Angeles and Culver City, such as 8522 National (1988), the Lindblade Tower Office building, and Paramount Laundry building (1990). Moss has lectured throughout the US, and his work has been shown in exhibition there and in Europe.

STUDIO NAÇO was founded in 1986 by Marcelo Joulia Lagares (born in 1958 in Argentina) and Alain Renk (born in 1962 in France). Based in Paris, it has an energetic output of architecture, interior, industrial and graphic design, spurred by early successes in design competitions such as "Objet 2000" (1986); the Council Chambers of the Territories of Belfort (1988–9); and exposure via ID Magazine's Annual Design Review 1989 (for the radio Bianca M), and at Gallery Neotu (1987), "40 Architects under 40" at the Institut Français d'Architecture, Paris, as well as a commendation for their entry for the Red Zone at La Défense. Their interiors include shops (Tacoma records, Nantes, 1990), offices and exhibitions; industrial design includes lights for Lumiance, and car interiors for Matra. Lagares has designed houses in Mexico, and the duo have exhibited in France, the US and Japan.

JEAN NOUVEL (born in 1945 in Lot et Garonne) is an architect based in Paris. He graduated in 1971, and has since won many awards, including the Chevalier des Arts et Lettres. Merged with Emmanuel Cattani & Associes, Nouvel is best known for his Institut du Monde Arabe, Paris (1987); his projects also include the Hotel-Restaurant St. James, Bordeaux (1989); cultural centre at Melun-Sénart (1986); housing and school in Nîmes; renovation of l'Opéra de Lyon (1990, competition award), as well as work in Rotterdam, Strasbourg and Switzerland, and many international competitions.

PEI COBB FREED & PARTNERS (formerly I.M. Pei & Partners) was founded by Ieoh Ming Pei, who was born in Canton, China, in 1917 and studied at the Massachusetts Institute of Technology and at Harvard. He established his practice in New York in 1955; it has completed over 150 major projects in more than 100 cities across the US and around the world, and won over 100 design awards. Projects range from the National Center for Atmospheric Research in the Rocky Mountains, to the 4-million-square-foot Place Ville Marie, Montreal. Best known for buildings such as the East Wing of the National Gallery of Art, Washington D.C., the firm's recent projects include the 70-storey Bank of China and the Morton H. Meyerson Symphony Center. Works in progress include the US Holocaust Museum, Washington D.C., the Trade Center, Barcelona; and the expansion and renovation of the Grand Louvre, Paris.

GAETANO PESCE was born in 1939 in Spezia, Italy, and studied architecture at the University of Venice, graduating in 1963. Pesce works as an architect and an artist: his projects encompass architectural, interior and furniture design, sculpture, painting, product design, music and performance art. Major works include furniture design for C & B (1969), and Cassina (1980); Tribune Tower, Chicago (1980); project design for the Fiat plant, Turin (1983); museum designs in Switzerland (1986) and for the Municipal Art Museum, Aosta, Italy; exhibition design for Moda Italia, New York (1988), and Bar El Liston, Hotel Il Palazzo, Fukuoka (1989).

POWELL-TUCK CONNOR OREFELT (PTCO) was established in London in 1976 by Julian Powell-Tuck and David Connor, who studied at the Royal College of Art, and Gunnar Orefelt, a graduate of the Royal Institute of Technology and Architecture, Stockholm. Mark Lintott, based in Taipei, became a director in 1987. Major projects include housing (Villa Zapu, 1988); shops (World's End, 1979); recording studios (Research Recordings 1983, Metropolis, 1989–90); offices (St. Dionis Rd development, 1989); showrooms (Concord, 1990); exhibitions (Sport '90, Design Museum); and furniture/product design (Concord Lighting). Projects in Taiwan include a department store and cinemas. In 1990 the partnership was dissolved, and Powell-Tuck (assessor at Glasgow School of Art, and interior design tutor at UK colleges since 1977) established Powell-Tuck Associates.

ANTOINE PREDOCK is an architect based in New Mexico and California. He studied at Columbia University, and established his practice in 1967. A visiting critic at UCLA, he has also taught at a number of other US universities. His major projects, many of them award-winning, include extensive architectural and landscape design in New Mexico, Arizona and California; masterplanning in Albuquerque (1967–74); the expansion of the Museum of New Mexico with Edward Barnes (1980); masterplans for Rio Grande Nature Preserve (1982) and Tejon Ranch, California (1984); museums and cultural centres at the Universities of New Mexico (1977–8), Wyoming (1987), California (1987) and Arizona (1989); Thousand Oaks government center, California (1989); and many residences on the West Coast. Current projects include a science museum in Phoenix, Arizona, and museum of American Indian Arts, Santa Fe.

ALDO ROSSI was born in Milan in 1931, and studied architecture at Milan Polytechnic. In 1960 he was appointed editor of Casabella, a year after establishing his own practice. In 1965 he was appointed Professor at Milan Polytechnic, and later at the University of Venice, teaching at Zurich, Harvard and Yale. In 1988 he won first prize in the competition to design the German National History Museum in Berlin, and in 1990 the Pritzker Prize. Major works include Modena Cemetery; Gallaratese housing; the Teatro del Mondo; the Lighthouse Theatre, Lake Ontario; School of Architecture, University of Miami (1989); Hotel Il Palazzo, Fukuoka (1989); furniture for Molteni and Unifor, and product design for Alessi.

STANLEY SAITOWICZ is an architect based in San Francisco. Currently Associate Professor at the University of California, Berkeley, he gained his masters in architecture there in 1977, and his first degree at university in Johannesburg. His work has been exhibited throughout the US, including "Geological Architecture" at the Walker Art Center. His projects include many residences in California; the auditorium at UC's Architecture School, Berkeley; the Quady winery; and the California Museum of Photography (1990). Current work includes structures in the Mill Race Park, Columbus, Indiana; a loft building in San Francisco for the practice; and residences.

DENIS SANTACHIARA was born in 1950 in Campagnola, Italy. From 1966 he worked as a stylist for a motor firm in Modena, and as an artist. Since 1975 he has explored the soft potentialities of technology, creating images and objects situated between art and design. These include light stereo headphones (selected for the Compasso d'Ora in 1979); furniture for Vitra ("The Sisters" chair); lighting for Yamagiwa. He has lectured, and taken part in the

Milan Triennale; "La Casa Telematica", Milan (1983); "L'estetica dell'uso", Reggio Emilia (1990); and other events in Europe, Japan and the US. Recent projects include exhibitions for Montedison, Aquatech showrooms, Aquylone restaurant and Epsylon discothèque, Reggio Emilia. Studio Santachiara is based in Milan.

SCHWARTZ/SILVER ARCHITECTS was founded in 1980, in Boston, Massachusetts, by Warren Schwartz and Robert Silver (who studied architecture at Cambridge University, UK, and at Harvard). Associate Nancy Hackett studied interior design at the Universities of Colorado and Connecticut before joining the practice in 1986. Recent projects include Domain showrooms; shops for Maud Frizon and Hackett; a beauty salon and spa at The Heritage, Boston; the Coffee Connection; their own offices; and headquarters for Ajax International. Recent awards include a 1990 National Honor Award for Excellence.

SCHWEITZER BIM was established in 1988 in California by Josh Dawson Schweitzer. Prior to this he studied economics, and architecture at the University of Kansas, worked for practices including FRANK O. GEHRY AND ASSOCIATES, and set up Schweitzer-Kellen (1984–7). Recent projects include CITY restaurant/offices, Border Grill 1 & 2, Campanile restaurant; offices for Batey & Chan Advertising, Johns & Gorman Films, Eyework 3, and the Hard Rock Café; numerous residences in California; and furniture for many of his projects and private clients. He is currently developing a new range of furniture, lighting and accessories.

ETTORE SOTTSASS was born in 1917 in Innsbruck, Austria, and graduated in architecture from the University of Turin in 1939. In 1947 he founded his studio in Milan, and from 1958 was chief design consultant at Olivetti, also working for Alessi, Knoll, Zanotta and Venini. In 1979 he became associated with Studio Alchymia; in 1980 he set up Sottsass Associati with Marco Zanini and Aldo Cibic, and a year later initiated Memphis with various friends and young architects. Sottsass's work includes the "Valentine" typewriter (1969) for Olivetti; experimental furniture, ceramics, glasswork and "utopian" architecture, and art. The practice's architectural and design work includes shops in Italy for Alessi and Marisa Lombardi (1987); Bar Zibibbo at Hotel Il Palazzo, Fukuoka (1989); and a house in the Colorado Rockies for Daniel Wolf (1990). Sottsass has received the Compasso d'Oro on many occasions, and has also lectured and exhibited internationally.

STANTON WILLIAMS was established in 1986 by Alan Stanton (born in 1944) and Paul Williams (born in 1949). Stanton trained at the Architectural Association and the University of California. He worked with Piano and Rogers on the Pompidou Centre, Paris (1970–77), and with Mike Dowd designed a major exhibition space at the Museum of Science and Industry, La Villette, Paris (1985). Paul Williams trained at Birmingham College of Art and at the Yale Arts Center. The practice is renowned for exhibition and museum design. Major projects include: Hayward Gallery (English Romanesque Art, Leonardo); Royal Academy of Arts (The Age of Chivalry); the Japanese Gallery at the Victoria and Albert Museum (1986); three shops and an apartment for Issey Miyake (1987–90) which won a D & AD Gold Award in 1988; exhibition galleries for the Design Museum (1989); museums at Westminster Abbey (1987) and Winchester Cathedral (1989), awarded the Fine/Applied Art Museum of the Year award, 1990. Current projects include the extension of Birmingham City Museum and Art Gallery; new wings at the RIBA, and for the National Portrait Gallery's twentieth-century collection; Clearings III, a new office/retail development and a masterplan for St George-in-the-East church.

PHILIPPE STARCK was born in Paris in 1949 and is a prolific product, furniture and interior designer, increasingly working on larger-scale projects in France, the US, Japan, Spain and the Netherlands. His major projects include apartments at the Elysée Palace for President Mitterrand (1982); Café Costes, Paris (1984); Manin, Tokyo (1986); La Cigale Theatre, Paris (1987); the Royalton Hotel, New York (1988); La Flamme d'Or for Asahi, Tokyo (1989); Teatriz, Madrid; and the Paramount Hotel, New York (1990). Current projects include the MOMA Groningen; the Banco de Santander headquarters in Madrid; residences in Los Angeles; and buildings for "Starck Street", Paris. Starck's flow of new furniture designs for clients such as Baleri, Disform, Driade, Idée, Flos, Vitra and Kartell, and product design for Alessi, Beneteau and Vuitton, continues unabated.

JAMES STIRLING, MICHAEL WILFORD & ASSOCIATES was established in 1971. James Stirling was born in Glasgow in 1926, and studied architecture at the University of Liverpool, and town planning in London. He has been in

private practice since 1956 (with James Gowan until 1963). Michael Wilford was born in 1938 in Surbiton, Surrey, and studied at the Northern Polytechnic School of Architecture. In 1977 Stirling and Wilford won a major limited competition for the State Gallery and Chamber Theater, Stuttgart, Germany (1977–84). This led to many more cultural buildings: Wissenschaftszentrum, Berlin (1979–87); the Clore Gallery extension at the Tate Gallery, London (1980–86); the Tate Gallery, Albert Dock, Liverpool (1984–1988); the Performing Arts Center, Cornell University (1983–1988). Among projects in production are the Music and Theatre Academies, Stuttgart; the Science Library, University of California at Irvine, LA; Palazzo Citterio Gallery, Brera Museum, Milan; London housing; and a stadium in Seville.

TAKASHI SUGIMOTO was born in Tokyo in 1945. He graduated from Tokyo University of Art in 1968 and founded Super Potato Co. in 1973. He is a consultant to Seibu department store, Matsushita Inc. and Daiko Lighting, and has won a number of awards. Apart from interiors and store planning for Seibu, Sugimoto has designed projects such as Radio bar (1981–2); Brasserie Ex (1984); Ex Jun boutique (1985); No Brand Shop (1987); and Libre Space (1988). In 1988 he established Super Planning Co., a team of "producers".

SHIN TAKAMATSU was born in 1948 in the Shimane Prefecture of Japan. In 1971 he graduated from the Architectural Faculty of Kyoto University, and gained his doctorate from there in 1980. He established his own office in Kyoto in the same year. He is currently Assistant Professor at Seika University and lecturer at Kyoto University. Takamatsu has lectured widely on his work; many of his ideas about architecture are explained in *The Kyoto Origins of Non-Conceptual Form*. To date the office has won many awards and completed 50 buildings, including houses, stores and commercial buildings in Kyoto (such as the Origin I, II & III projects), but also in Osaka (Kirin Plaza), Migoto (1990), Syntax (1990).

KIYOSHI SEY TAKEYAMA is the Principal of Amorphe Architects & Associates, established in 1979. He was born in Osaka, Japan, in 1954, and studied architecture at the Universities of Kyoto and Tokyo, completing his doctorate in Tokyo in 1984. His dental clinics and residences in Takao (1982) and Koga (1983) led to projects such as the OXY building in Nogizaka (1987), an award-winning villa in Karuizawa (1988), and the D-Hotel, Osaka (1989). In 1986 he won second prize for his Shonandai Civic Center proposal and commendations for his new National Theatre (1986) and Aichi Prefectural Centre competition schemes.

BERNARD TSCHUMI was born in 1944 of French-Swiss parentage, and now lives in the US, with offices in New York and in Paris. He studied architecture at the Federal Institute of Technology, Zurich, and from 1970–80 he was Unit Master at the Architectural Association. From 1980–3 he was Visiting Professor at the Cooper Union, when he won the international competition for the $200 million Parc de la Villette project, Paris (masterplan, numerous facilities, 33 *folies* and a two-mile promenade of gardens). In 1989 he won first prize for his bridge scheme, Lausanne, Switzerland (under development). Other schemes include National Theatre/Opera House, Tokyo (1986), Flushing Meadows Park, New York (1987–9). Tschumi's work has been widely exhibited, and his deconstructivist theories much discussed.

SHIGERU UCHIDA was born in Yokohama in 1943 and graduated from the Kuwazawa Design School in 1966. In 1981 he founded Studio 80 with Ikuyo Mitsuhashi and Toru Nishioka. The practice has undertaken interior design projects for Issey Miyake and Yohji Yamamoto as well as residences, restaurants, furniture and products. Uchida organized Tokyo Designers' Week (1988–9), Japanese design exhibition at Europalia 1989, directed projects at Design Expo '89 (Nagoya), and lectures and exhibits internationally. Uchida was art director of the Hotel Il Palazzo and with Ikuyo Mitsuhashi designed the interiors.

JEAN-MICHEL WILMOTTE was born in 1948, and studied at Ecole Camondo before establishing Governor, his practice, in Paris in 1975, to design architecture, interiors, furniture and lighting, adding offices in Nîmes and Tokyo in 1986. Major projects include the renovation of Nîmes' town hall and museum, and design of a new opera house; galleries and bookshop at the Grand Louvre; offices for Canal +; Technal showroom, Toulouse; Grenier à Sel salerooms, Avignon; Espace Kronenbourg, Paris; and in Tokyo the Bunkamura cultural centre. Wilmotte is currently working on galleries in the Richelieu wing at the Louvre, and on the Museum of Art in Lyons; many other urban projects in France, and a golf club near Osaka. He has received many design awards, as well as the Chevalier des Arts et Lettres.

Credits

1.1 ARCHITECTS & DESIGNERS BUILDING LOBBY (& FAÇADE), New York, USA.
Architects: P. Michael Marino Architects. Project Team: P. Michael Marino, Margaret Newman; with: Vinod Devgan, Michael Dobbs. Client: afa Asset Services, Inc. Main Contractor: Clark Construction Corp. Mechanical Engineers: Kim Associates. Structural Engineers: Harwood Weisenfeld. Lighting Consultants: Steven Hefferan. Custom Lighting Fixtures and Design: Magnan Payne. Other Lighting Fixtures: Edison Price, IPI Lighting, National Cathode Corp. Natural Stonework: Marble Technics. Bronze Entrance Assembly: Ellison Bronze Co. Coloured Cement Plaster: Mares Manufacturing. Colour Consultant: Donald Kaufmann. Custom Cherrywood Panelling: William Sommerville. Custom Metal Work: Metal Forms Inc. Display System: DSA Phototech. Plastic Laminate: Formica, Inc. Paints: Glidden, Inc. Signage: ASI Sign Systems. Graphics: Salestrom & Zingg.

1.2 RIVERSIDE, London, UK.
Architects: Foster Associates. Project Team: Norman Foster, Ken Shuttleworth, Howard Gilby (Project director), Cordula Nies-Friedlander; with: Chris Abdell, Chubby Chhabra, Barry Cooke, Wendy Foster, Nigel Greenhill, Spencer De Grey, Karon Grant-Hanlon, Pauline Hanna, Katy Harris, Edward Hutchinson, David Langston Jones, Valerie Lark, Heiko Lukas, Michael Mak, David Nelson, Michael Ng, Graham Phillips, Chris Windsor. Client: Petmoor Developments. Main Contractor: O & H Construction. Structural Engineers: Ove Arup & Partners. Mechanical Engineers: JRP. Quantity Surveyor & project manager: Schumann Smith. Lighting Consultant: Claude Engle. Lighting: Erco. Curtain Walling Consultant: Emmer Hass Pfenniger. Acoustics: Tim Smith. Graphics: Otl Aicher. Flooring: Goldbach/Systemline, Zanetti & Bailey (marble). Carpet: Vorwerk. Electrical: Woodhouse Electrical. Steelwork: Tubeworkers Ltd, Amco. Fabric Ceiling: Landrell. Spiral Stair: Weland. Library Structure: Rareunit. Kitchen Fitters: T & Q. Furniture: Brent Metals (working tables and large round table), Vitra (small round tables and chairs), Tecno (reception desk), Rare Units (bar stools), Design Workshop (white furniture), Abodia (slide viewing units). Totems/Floor outlets: Ackermann Ltd. Glazing: T. W. Ide Ltd. Ironmongery: Elementer. Signage: Bull Signs.

1.3 ISOMETRIX, London, UK.
Architect: Spencer Fung. Client: Isometrix. Main Contractor: AFCO Services. Furniture and Joinery Fittings: David Archer, Jasper Morrison (sofa), Danny Lane (kitchen table). Adjustable Ceilings: Matthew Wells. Fish Tanks: Seabrey Aquariums. Steel Sculpture: Antony Donaldson. Installation: Jules des Près.

1.4 FUNDER FACTORY 1 (office) & 3 (factory), St Veit/Glan, Carinthia, Austria.
Architect: Coop Himmelblau. Project Team: Wolf D. Prix, Helmut Swiczinsky, D. Helml (Project architect (1)), Markus Pillhofer (Project architect (3)). General Planner: Achammer-Tritthart (3). Landscape Architect: Janos Koppandy (3). Steel Construction: Ing. W. Haslinger Stahlbau GmbH (3). Prefabricated Concrete Elements: Febau-Röhrs Fertigtoilwerk (3). Trapezoidal Sheet: Domico F. Krempelmeier KG (3). Glazed Roof: Ferro Glas GmbH & Co. KG (3). Glass Façade: Baumann Glas GmbH & Co. KG (3). Electrics: Mayerhofer ARGE (3). Roof: E. Dolenz, Alfred Laas. Flooring: Hohenberger (3). Electrics: Fa. Dietzel (1), Fa. Dujak (1), Fa. Selma (1). Steelwork: Fa. Treiber (1), Fa. Matzenberger (1). Marble: Fa. Lauster (1). Sliding Door: Fa. Treiber (1).

1.5 PARAMOUNT LAUNDRY Culver City, California, USA.
Architects: Eric Owen Moss. Project Team: Jay Vanos (Project associate), Dennis Igeand, Scott Nakeo (Project architects), Greg Baker (tenant improvements); with: Todd Conversano, Jerry Sullivan, Allen Binn, Dana Swinsky. Main Contractor: Scott Gates Construction Co. Client: Frederick Norton Smith. Structural Engineer: Joe Kurily. Mechanical Engineer: Paul Antieri. Electrical Engineer: Michael Cullen. Vitrified Clay Pipe: Pacific Clay Products. Lighting Consultant: Saul Goldin. Suppliers: Prudential Lighting, California Associated Power. Landscape Designer: Steve Ormenyi and Associates. Galvanized Sheet Metal: Marina Sheet Metal. Glazing: A to Z Glass & Mirror. Flooring: L & J Flores (concrete), C & L Coatings (concrete coating), Fabulon (birch floors). Carpet: Emser International. Furniture: Eric Owen Moss.

1.6 GALLIMARD JEUNESSE, Paris, France.
Architects: Jean Léonard and Xavier Gonzalez. Client: Éditions Gallimard. Structure and Concrete Engineer: Paul Vives. Metal Furniture, Frames and Stairs: Trouvelot. Furniture and Woodwork: De Sol. Wooden Flooring: Parquets Briatte. Glass Walls: Miroiterie Bret. Lighting: Espèce Lumière, Prisma Zizioli (Cosmo CL), Artemide (tables – Tolomeo Tavolo).

1.7 FACTORY COMMUNICATIONS HEADQUARTERS, Manchester, UK.
Designers: Ben Kelly Design. Project Team: Denis Byrne, Sandra Douglas, Ben Kelly, Louise King, Peter Mance, Elena Massucco, Nick Toft. Client: Factory Communications Ltd. Main Contractor: Tysons Contractors PLC. Quantity Surveyors: Speakes Hollingworth Associates. Structural Engineers: Bailey, Johnson, Hayes. Heating and Services Consultants: Pearce Associates.

1.8 WORLD: CREATIVE FASHION DOME, Kobe, Japan.
Architects: Studio Citterio/Dwan. Project Team: Antonio Citterio, Terry Dwan, Toshiyuki Kita, Thomas McKay. Collaborating Architects: IDK. Client: World Co. Ltd. Main Contractor: Takenaka Corporation. Electricity: Kinden Corporation. Furniture: Tendo Co. Ltd. Lighting: Matsushita Electric Works Ltd, Yamagiwa Co. Ltd. Wooden Staircase: Datmaru Design and Engineering.

1.9 VIVID PRODUCTIONS, London, UK.
Designer: Gary Knibbs. Client: Vivid Productions. Main Contractor: Three Associates. Lighting: Shiu-Kay Kan. Furniture: Cassina (chair by Le Corbusier, from Marcatre), Pallucco ("Salta Martina" chair), Philippe Starck ("Dr Glob" chair, from Maison). Glazing: Profilit. Carpets: Artelier Interiors.

1.10 TEPIA, Tokyo, Japan.
Architects: Maki & Associates. Principal-in-charge: Fumihiko Maki. Project Team: Tomoyoshi Fukunaga, Yukitoshi Wakatsuki, Eiji Watanabe, Hiroshi Miyazaki, Kei Mizui, Reiko Tomuro, Shuji Oki. Collaborating Designers: Kazuko Fujie (furniture), Kijuro Yahagi (graphics), Kei Miyazaki (carpets). Client: Machinery and Information Industries Promotion Foundation. General Contractors: Kajima Corporation, Shimizu Construction Co. Ltd., Hazama-Gumi Ltd. Structural Engineers: Toshihiko Kimura Structural Engineers. Mechanical Engineers: Sogo Consultants. Lighting: Flos, Arteluce, Yamagiwa.

1.11 IMAGINATION HEADQUARTERS, London, UK.
Architects: Herron Associates. Project Team: Ron Herron, Andrew Herron, John Randle (Project architect). Project Team: Kanal Latiff, Ralph Buschow, A. A. Nik, Terence Tang, Michael Kim, Anthony Leung. Interior Design: Shirley Walker, Imagination. Client: Imagination Ltd. Main Contractor: R. M. Douglas Construction Ltd. Structural Engineers: Buro Happold. Mechanical Steelwork: Buro Happold. Quantity Surveyor: Boydon & Co. Electrical Consultants: Electrical Engineering Contracts. Sound Studios: Acoustical Construction Service. Roof: Landrell (PVC-coated fabric), Sheetfabs. PVC Coated Fabric Roof: Landrell Fabric Engineering. Purpose-made Furniture: D. Ellwood Ltd. Other Furniture: Hille (desk chairs), Marcatre (desk systems), Xerkon Ltd. (Eileen Grey table), Marcel Breuer, Corbusier (black and chrome seating), Matthews (plan chests). Wall Panels: Phoenix Display Ltd.

1.12 EMERY VINCENT & ASSOCIATES, Melbourne, Australia.
Architects: Denton Corker Marshall Pty Ltd. Project Team: John Denton, Barrie Marshall. Client: Emery Vincent & Associates. Main Contractor: Conarc Projects Pty Ltd. Structural Engineer: W. L. Meinhardt & Partners. Steel Stairs: Eastern Suburbs Wrought Iron. Galvanized Steel Panels: Charles Marshall Pty Ltd. Furniture: North Eastern Welding Co. (reception desk), Zaha Hadid for EDRA, from Artes (reception seating). Sculpture: Akio Makigawa.

1.13 SPAARKREDIET BANK, Bruges, Belgium.
Architects: Stéphane Beel. Project Team: Stéphane Beel, Pieter Broucke, Paul Van Eygen. Client: Spaarkrediet Bank. Main Contractor: Van Tornhaut. Roof: Bral. Electrical: Leenknegt. Heating: Vergotte. Floors: Devos. Metal Constructions: Blomme. Furniture: Lust.

1.14 CENTER FOR INNOVATIVE TECHNOLOGY, Herndon, Virginia, USA.
Architects: Arquitectonica in conjunction with Ward/Hall Associates. Project Teams: Arquitectonica: Bernardo Fort-Brescia and Laurinda Spear (Principals in charge), Martin J. Wander (Project architect), Jennifer Briley, Tom Bittner, Toby Engelberg, Jennifer Luce, Derek Sanders. Ward/Hall Associates: G. T. Ward (Partner in charge), Charles Hall, Leo Sagasti (Project director), John Anderson, Andrew Pittman. Client: Center For Innovative Technology. Landscape Architects: Peter Walker/Martha Schwartz. Civil Engineering Consultant: Patton Harris Rust & Associates. Engineering Consultant: Silver Associates PA. Structural Engineering Consultant: Spiegel and Zamecnic, Inc. Electrical Consultant: Mona Electric, Inc. Structural Steel Contractor: Montague Betts. Miscellaneous Metals: Criss Brothers, Inc. Stainless Steel Windows: Columbia Architectural Products. Entrance Stone: Georgia Marble. Glass and Glazing: Regal Glass, Inc. Insulation: Richfield Group. Flooring: Roman Mosaic & Tile (terrazzo), Avon Tile (stonework/ceramic tile). Carpet: Bode Floor. Blinds: Sun Control Systems and Lavolor Lorentzen JV. Neon Lighting: Jack Stone.

1.15 WICKENS TUTT SOUTHGATE, London, UK.
Architects: Apicella Associates. Project Team: Lorenzo Apicella, James Robson. Client: Wickens Tutt Southgate. Main Contractor: RHS Interiors Ltd. Lighting: PAF (reception floor and desk lights), Erco (metal halide, low voltage downlights). Screens: RHS Interiors Ltd. Flooring: Tarkett. Fine Blinds: Hunter Douglas Ltd., Luxaflex (conference room). Ironmongery: RHS to design by Apicella Associates. Reception Seating: Conran Shop.

1.16 STUDIOS, Camden Town, London, UK.
Architects: David Chipperfield and Partners. Project Team: David Chipperfield, Michael Cullinan (Project architect). Client: Derwent Valley Property Developments. Main Contractor: E. C. Sames & Co., Ltd. Engineers: Price and Myers. Steelwork: HLC Engineering. Metalwork: Architectural Fabrication Systems, T. Nevill & Co. Electrical Engineers: Lumenglow Ltd. Lighting: Concord Lighting Ltd, Erco, Light Projects. Windows: HLC Engineering. Rooflight: T. W. Ide Ltd, Mellowes PPG. Flooring: Great Metropolitan Flooring Co. (wood), Millbank Floors Ltd (precast). Ironmongery: Elementer. Glass blocks: Pittsburgh Corning Corp., GBI, Ltd.

1.17 HOUSTON FINE ART PRESS, Houston, Texas, USA.
Architects: Carlos Jiménez Architectural Design Studio. Project Designer: Carlos Jiménez. Client: Richard Newlin/ Houston Fine Art Press. Structural Engineer: K. C. Shah. Flooring: Stratton Tiles (carpet), Benjamin Moore Paints (concrete stained floors), American Ocean Products (tiles). Hardware: Forms and Surfaces. Lighting: Lightolier, Artemide from M & M Lighting, Patina Metals (floating lighting fixtures, steel gates & fixture frames). Custom Steel Frame: Trio Metal Products. Furniture: Steelcase & Biaffe (office cabinetry and filing systems), Thonet (office chairs).

1.18 METROPOLIS RECORDING STUDIOS, London, UK.
Designers: Powell-Tuck Connor & Orefelt Ltd. Project Team: Julian Powell-Tuck (Partner in charge), Andrew Gollifer, Peter Murray, Angus Shepherd. Client: Metropolis Recording Studios Ltd. Main contractor: Kier Wallis. Studio fit-out contractor: Newman Shopfitters Ltd. Structural services: Whitby & Bird. Quantity surveyor: Harry Trinick & Partners. Acoustics: Acoustics Design Group. Technical installation: Greenwich Audio Services. Mechanical & electrical: Airflow Systems. Staircases: Kier Wallis. Lighting design: PTCO Ltd. Fabrication/supply of lighting fittings: Concord, Erco, Thorn, Isometrix (specials). Furniture: Maison (cane chairs).

1.19 CHAMBERS FOR THE CONSEIL GÉNÉRAL, HÔTEL DU DÉPARTEMENT, Belfort, France.
Architects: Studio Naço. Project Team: Marcelo Joulia, Alain Renk, Denise Conrady (interior design). Client: Département des Territoires de Belfort. Colour Consultants: Patricia Blaufoux. Lighting Consultant: Pierre Cabu. Prototypes: Alexis Bory. Glazing: St Gobain. Lighting: Studio Naço (design), Kobis Lorence (fabrication), Jumo Concorde GTE (ceiling spot lights). Signage: Studio Naço (design), Kobis Lorence (fabrication). Furniture: Studio Naço (design), Gouget (supplied councillors' chairs and audience chairs), Atelier (made conference table, reception desk, press table, bar tables), Mobilier National (public chair). Accessories: Studio Naço. Marble Work: Bugna. Carpets: Chauvier S. A. Door: Studio Naço. Plaster Work: Curti. Ceiling: Construction Rehabilitation Decoration Villeparisienne. Metal Work: Metal-est. Painters: Muratori. Blinds: La Storemania. Electrical Consultant: S. A. Zanelec.

2.1 HOTEL OTARU MARITTIMO, Otaru, Hokkaido, Japan.
Architects: Branson Coates Architecture Ltd. Project Designers: Nigel Coates, Doug Branson, Allan Bell.

Collaborators in Japan: Dan Sekkei Architecture (design), Shi Yu Chen, C. I. A. (creative producer/driving force), Jasmac Co. Ltd (developer and project management operation). Client: Tobishima Forms Inc. Furniture Design: Nigel Coates ("Tongue" chairs & sofas, "Chairs of the World", "Jazz chairs", coffee/console/bedside tables, dressers, desks, carpets, lights). Furniture Manufacture: Rockstone Co. Ltd Japan; SCP, London. Handmade Carpets: V'soske Joyce, Ireland. Purchase & Specification of furniture, fittings, furnishings, fine art & museum collection: Anne Brooks, Rebecca Du Pont, Omniate Ltd. Commissioned Artists: Beverly Beeland (sandblasted windows, main staircase; artwork to "flying fish" panels in restaurant lobby); Graca Coutinhou (painting in Napoli Ercolano; drawing in Bombay Market); Tom Dixon (solar chandelier, main staircase); Dirk Van Dooren ("Fish" video); Annabel Grey (fabric painting/hangings in restaurant etc.; friezes in guest rooms); Emma Harrison (wall paintings in Manhattan guest rooms, wall paintings in reception); Oriel Harwood (ceramic sconce, London Soane Museum room); Stuart Helm (wall paintings, main staircase); Steve Husband (wall paintings, guest room corridor lobbies); Andrew James (ceiling paintings/ installation, Star Bar); Wilma Johnson (paintings in Bombay Palace, Alexandria Napoli rooms); Kate Malone (ceramics: corals in restaurant fish tank; galleons for food trolleys, bowls); Simon Moore of Glassworks (icebergs in restaurant fish tanks); Tobit Roche (paintings in Bombay Jungle/Palace/Market); Karen Spurgin (embroidered bedspreads, Leningrad, Alexandria, Napoli, Hong Kong); James Hunting (embroidered bedspread, London); ZaZa Wentworth-Stanley (wall paintings, guest room corridor lobbies, Egyptian mummy, Alexandria suite); Why Not Associates (hotel graphic design).

2.2 KENTUCKY FRIED CHICKEN, Los Angeles, California, USA.
Architects: Grinstein/Daniels, Inc. Project Team: Jeffrey Daniels (Partner in charge), Elyse Grinstein, Iris Steinbeck, Larry Harris. Client: Jack Wilke. Main Contractor: Z. M. Construction. Structural Engineers: Erdelyi-Mezey & Associates. Mechanical Engineers: Comeau Engineers Inc. Kitchen Designer: Jack Wilke. Tables & Chairs: Jay Buchbinder.

2.3 BAR ZSA ZSA, Barcelona, Spain.
Architects: Dani Freixes & Vicente Miranda. Project Team: Dani Freixes, Vicente Miranda, Marta Bosch, Eulalia Gonzalez. Collaborating Graphic Designer: Peret (wall collage). Client: Bay S. A. Main Contractor: Edificacions Natura. Lighting: Erco. Acoustics: Aislamientos Jackson. Glass Panel Walls: Villesa. Showcases: Dani Freixes. Furniture: Dani Freixes & Vicente Miranda.

2.4 DRY 201, Manchester, UK.
Designers: Ben Kelly Design. Project Team: Denis Byrne, Sandra Douglas, Ben Kelly, Louise King, Peter Mance, Elena Massucco. Client: Factory Communication Ltd/ Gainwest, Ltd. Main Contractor: William Irwin & Co. (East) Ltd. Quantity Surveyors: Speakes Hollingworth Assoc. Structural Engineers: Bailey, Johnson, Hayes. Graphics: Peter Saville Associates/Johnson Panas.

2.5 ZEN, Hong Kong.
Architects: Rick Mather Architects. Project Team: Rick Mather, Pascal Madoc Jones, Douglas McIntosh. Consultants: Dewhurst MacFarlane (cascade), P. K. Ng Associates. Client: Blaidwood Ltd. Main Contractor: G. G. Dung. Stainless Steel work: M & M Contracts. Carpets: Texfield Services. Glass Moulding: John Bowden. Ironmongery: Elementer. Lighting: Isometrix.

2.6 HOTEL IL PALAZZO, Fukuoka, Kyushu, Japan.
Architects: Aldo Rossi/Morris Adjmi. Associate Architects: Mituru Kaneko, Dan Sekkei. Art Director: Shigeru Uchida. Client: Mitsuhiro Kuzuwa, Jasmac Co. Ltd. Project Manager: Shoki Daijoji, Studio 80. Main Contractors: Jasmac, Tatsumuragumi. Architectural Coordinator: Toyota Horiguchi, SDA Japan. Structural Engineer: Yoshitake Tsuboi/Hosei University. Mechanical Designer: Sumio Asaka, Jet Kikaku Sekkei. Hotel & Restaurant – Designers: Shigeru Uchida/Ikuyo Mitsuhashi, Studio 80. Furniture: Shigeru Uchida (chairs). Lighting: Harumi Fujimoto, Yamagiwa (floor lamps). Graphics/Logotype Design: Ikko Tanaka. Bar El Dorado – Designers: Aldo Rossi/Morris Adjmi. Furniture: Molteni (stools and chairs), Unifor (banquette seating and armchairs). Logotype Design: Erin Shilliday, Karen Adjmi. Bar Zibibbo – Designers: Ettore Sottsass, Mike Ryan, Marco Zanini. Logotype Design: Ettore Sottsass & Mario Milizia (Sottsass Associati Grafica). Lighting: Yamagiwa (wall bracket lamps). Furniture: Sottsass Associati ("Mandarin" chairs). Tables: Bieffeplast. Bar El Liston – Designer: Gaetano Pesce. Project Team: Patric Daumas, Parrish Puente, Tim Tait, Myriam Seckler. Logotype Design: Gaetano Pesce. Bar Oblomova – Designer: Shiro Kuramata. Logotype Design: Ryohei Kojima, Shiro Kuramata. Graphic Design in Bars: Kijuro Yahagi.

2.7 POLYTECHNIC OF NORTH LONDON THEATRE BAR, London, UK.
Architects of Bar and Great Hall: Architecture Research Unit, Polytechnic of North London. Project Team: Suresh A'Raj, Florian Beigel, Michael Casey, Philip Christou, Jonathan Freeman, Julian Lewis, Roeland-Jan Pijper, Peter St. John. Client: Polytechnic of North London. Main Contractor: CODAC (Common Ownership Design and Construct). Structural Glazing Installation: Sifran. Furniture: Florian Beigel Architects (Design), Architectural Research Unit, Polytechnic of North London (plywood chair seats and backs), Pearl Dot (free-standing benches), Lamina Concepts (built-in benches), Durcon Fabrications Int. Ltd (black bar top). Steelwork: The Holloway Sheet Metal Works Ltd, Jonso Furniture (bar frames and brackets), Argon ARC Welding Services (staircase). Bar Cooler Units: IMC. Neon Sign: Pearce Signs. Concrete Paving Slabs: North Enfield Precast Concrete Co. Ltd. Polyester powder coating to chairs and tables: D. P. Enamellers. Long Lamp Metal Reflector: Nor-Ray-Vac. Partitions & Panels: Architectural and Building Products Ltd.

2.8 LA FLAMME D'OR, ASAHI BUILDING, Tokyo, Japan.
Designer: Philippe Starck. Assistant: Dominique Voisin. Client: Asahi Breweries. Corresponding Architect in Japan: Gett. Main Contractor: Obayashi Gumi K. K. Representative in Japan: Philippe Terrien, KIC Corporation. Furniture: Maville, Marghieri (wood), Dacheville (aluminium). Wall Painting: Jean Michel Alberola.

2.9 BORDER GRILL, Santa Monica, Los Angeles, California, USA.
Architects: Schweitzer BIM. Project Team: Josh Dawson Schweitzer, Meriwether Felt, Patrick Ousey. Clients: Mary Sue Milliken, Susan Feniger, Gai Gherardi, Barbara McReynolds, Margo Willits/Border Grill. Murals: Donna Muir & Su Huntley. Main Contractor: Steve Winawer, Winawer Construction. Mechanical Engineers: Comeau Engineering. Kitchen Consultants: Abrams and Tanaka. Bar and Tortilla Station Counters: Cameron Aston. Furniture Design: Josh Dawson Schweitzer (yellow pine tables) made by Steve Winawer, Jasper Seating (chairs) refurbished by Cameron Aston. Refrigerated countertop display case: Simon Maltby (glass), Abrams & Tanaka (refrigerated base). Custom griddle: Abrams & Tanaka.

2.10 ANGELI MARE, Marina del Rey, Los Angeles, California, USA.
Architects: Building. Designers: Michele Saee; with Richard Lundquist, Sam Solhaug, David Lindberg. Design Team: John Scott, Max Massie, Florence Blecher. Consultants: Saul Goldin (lighting), Miquel Castillo (structural), Andrew Nasser. Client: Evan Kleiman, John Strobel. Main Contractors: John Rotondi/Rotondi Construction, Vince Naso (Supervisor). Lighting: Building. Furniture: Syavash Matjai (tables), L & B Contract Industries (chairs). Steel Fabricator: John McCoy. Glazing: L. O. S. Glass. Kitchen: Tony Singaus.

2.11 SET/OFF NOY, Tokyo, Japan.
Designers: Takashi Sugimoto/Super Potato Co. Ltd. Project Team: Takashi Sugimoto, Satomi Yuza; with: Shoji Kai. Client: Gabacho Planning Co. Ltd. Main Contractor/ Electrical: Stud Co. Ltd. Lighting: Ushio Spax Co. Ltd. Furniture: Ambiente International Co. Ltd., Sakura Manufacturing Co. Tableware: Super Potato Products Co. Ltd. Flooring: Koyano Sekizai Co. Ltd (stone), Inter Living Co. Ltd (wood), Walling: Izumi Sekizai (stone), Stud Co. Ltd (other).

2.12 ROCKPOOL, Sydney, Australia.
Designers: D4 Design Pty Ltd. Project Team: Michael Scott-Mitchell, Stephen Roberts, Bill MacMahon; with Jim Mullins, Margaret McKenna, Sarah Tooth, Caroline Diss. Client: Neil Perry/Mahla Holdings Pty Ltd. Structural Engineer: James Taylor and Associates Pty Ltd, McBean & Crisp Pty Ltd (restoration). Main Contractor: Stonehill Constructions. Furniture & Accessories: D4 Design Pty Ltd. Lighting: D4 with Mark Shelton, constructed by Wharrington International Pty Ltd. Painted Finishes: The Scumbling Team. Fabrics: Missoni. Steelwork: Copeland Engineering. Staircase: Petric Engineering.

2.13 MIGOTO, Kyoto, Japan.
Architect: Shin Takamatsu Architect & Associates. Project Team: Shin Takamatsu, Satoshi Seki. Client: Migoto. Main Contractor: Tanaka Futoshi (flooring/furniture). Structural Engineers: Yamamoto and Tachibana Architects. Mechanical/Electrical Engineers: Architectural Environment Design. Glazing: Nippon Sheet Glass. Wooden Structure: Kouji Karaushi. Steelwork: Tsukasa Shoten & Toji Technical. Paintwork: Megumi Toso. Environment: Nozaki Denki (electrical), Shinsei Kogyo (mechanical).

2.14 LA VILLA, Paris, France.
Interior design, furniture & graphics: Marie-Christine Dorner. Building Architect: Jean-André Dorel. Client: La Villa S. A. Tapestry Work: Atelier Mangau. Metalwork: L. C. S. D. Glazing: Guillaume Saalburg. Electrical: Bauthamy. Paintwork: Bechet. Woodwork: Chaput. Stonework: S2R. Carpets: Taiping. Lighting: L. C. S. D. Furniture: made by Mangau, Chaput (reception desk–wood), S2R (reception desk–stone). Bathroom Washbasins: Saalburg. Drapery: Placide Jolliet (Malaysian taffetas). Guestroom "clouds": O. T. S.

2.15 D-HOTEL, Osaka, Japan.
Architects: Kiyoshi Sey Takeyama/Amorphe Architects & Associates. Project Team: Kiyoshi Sey Takeyama, Ikuo Ogitsu, Kippei Katano, Hideji Matsumoto, Akiko Moriuchi. Client: Daitaki Co. Ltd. Main Contractors/Flooring: Makoto Construction Co. Ltd., Ishimaru Co. Ltd. Structural Engineers: Norihide Imagawa/T. I. S. & Partners. Mechanical Engineers: Masami Tanno/SOH Mechanical Engineers. Graphic Designer: Schuichi Yokoyama/ Diamond Heads. Lighting: Yamagiwa Co. Ltd, Yamada Shomei Lighting Co. Ltd. Furniture Design: Amorphe. Furniture Manufacture: Ishimaru Co. Ltd.

2.16 MOONSOON, KITA CLUB, Sapporo, Hokkaido, Japan.
Designer: Zaha Hadid. Project Team: Zaha Hadid; with Bill Goodwin, Dan Chadwick, Shin Egashira, Edgar Gonzalez, Kar Hwa Ho, Brian Langlands, Urit Luden, Yuko Moriyama, Satoshi Ohashi. Client: Mitsuhiro Kuzuwa/Jasmac Co. Ltd, Tokyo and Toronto. Coordinator: Axe Co. Ltd. Upstairs Seating and Objects: Zaha Hadid with Michael Wolfson. Supervision: Satoshi Ohashi, Zaha Hadid's Tokyo Office. Models: Dan Chadwick. Furniture: Minerva. Lighting: Ushio Spax Inc. Metalwork: Box Planning Product Ltd (stainless steel). Flooring: Textone (custom terrazzo). Glasswork: Central Glass Company Ltd.

2.17 MAELSTROM/AC ON CA GUA, KITA CLUB, Sapporo, Hokkaido, Japan.
Designers: Masami Matsui/Axe Co. Ltd. Project Team: Masami Matsui, Masakazu Ota, Kenji Suzuki, Shingo Yajima. Collaborator: Leopold Koukissa (painter). Client/ Main Contractor: Jasmac Co. Ltd. Furniture Design: Masami Matsui, made by Mineluba, Cassina. Furniture: Kawaragi Chair Inc. Imported Furniture: En Attendant Les Barbares. Interior Finishes: (Maelstrom) Box Planning, (Ac on ca gua) Kawaragi Chair Inc. Installation: Asahi-Kogyosha Inc. Electrical: Asahi Electric, Sanyu Denken Inc. Lighting Fixtures: Ushio Spax Inc. Lighting Consultant: Taiko Electric Inc. Disco Lighting: MGS Lighting Design.

2.18 BARNA CROSSING, Fukuoka, Japan.
Designers: Alfredo Arribas Arquitectos Asociados. Project Team: Alfredo Arribas, Miguel Morte. Creative Direction: Quim Larrea & Juli Capella. Driving Force: Shi Yu Chen, Creative Intelligence Associates. Client: Mitsuhiro Kuzuwa, Jasmac Co. Ltd. Collaborating Architect: Mitsuru Kaneko (Dan Architecture Construction). Operation Direction: Toshihiro Sato. Art Collaborator: Javier Mariscal. Graphic Designer: Alfonso Sostres. Uniform Design: Chu Uroz. Product Designer: Josep Puig. Lighting: Erco, Yamagiwa. Original Furnishings: Antonio Gaudí, Oscar Tusquets.

2.19 TAMBAYA, Tokyo, Japan.
Designer: Soiche Mizutani. Client: Sanny Days Co. Ltd. Main Contractor: Mitsukoshi Construction and Interior Co. Ltd. Furniture: Cassina Japan Inc. Lighting: Ushio Spax Inc. Flooring: Barcy. Walling: Epoca. Ceiling: Fine-Wall Deco. Artworks: Keiichi Tahara, Yoshiro Negishi, Takuji Azechi.

2.20 EPSYLON, Reggio Emilia, Italy.
Designer: Denis Santachiara. Assistant: Douglas Skene. Client: Opera SnL. Public Relations: Studio Immagine. Sound Equipment: Ortophono. Video Equipment: RCF. Lighting System: Clay Park. Metalwork & Furniture: Artioli Metal Furnishings.

2.21 TEATRIZ, Madrid, Spain.
Designer: Philippe Starck. Design collaborators: Christian Gavoille (Starck), Javier Calderon, Juan Fernandez (Sigla). Client: Placido Arango, Sigla S. A. Main Contractor: Pueyo & Martin. Furniture: Maville. Lighting: Arnold Chang/ Isometrix. Graphics: Javier Mariscal. Aluminium: OWO. Fabrics: Pepe Peñalver. Floors: Pavirroman. Lampshades: Maurin.

2.22 WASSERTURM HOTEL, Cologne, Germany.
Designers: Écart S. A. Project Team: Andrée Putman, Bruno Moinard, Georges Grenier; with Caroline Schmidt, Daniéla Fugger, Linda Andrieux, Pascal Teisseire. Collaborators: Bureau de Coordination, Bureau d'Études Techniques. Building Architects: Konrad Heinrich. Client: Hopft Company. Signage, furniture, wood panelling, decorative metalwork, wall sconce: Dennery. Rugs,

carpet: Tekima. Prefabricated bathroom shells tilework: Ahlmann MaschinenBau GmbH. Tilework: Dehnke. Upholstery: Soutumier. Carpentry: Idea GmbH.

2.23 TORRES DE AVILA, Barcelona, Spain.
Architect: Alfredo Arribas Arquitectos Asociados. Interior Design and Furniture: Alfredo Arribas, Miguel Morte & Javier Mariscal. Collaborators: Nelson Cabello, Xavier G. Franquesa, Marta Soriano, Laurent Duntze, Pedro Luis Rocha. Graphics: Javier Mariscal; with Cristina Rakosnik, Sergio Munoz, Yoya Mazorra, Carlos Errando. Artistic Collaborator: Jaume Casas. Client: Teatriz S. A./ Restaurants del Poble Espanyol S. A. Technical Architects: Albert Llorens & Jaume Muñoz. Musical Programme: Mingus B. Formentor. Coordination of music, lighting & special effects: Jordi Fernandez, Alfredo Arribas, Xavier G. Franquesa. Lighting Consultant: Jordi Espinosa. Video Consultant: Duque (FDG).

2.24 HOTEL-RESTAURANT SAINT JAMES, Bouliac, Bordeaux, France.
Architects: Jean Nouvel, Emmanuel Cattani & Associes. Designer: Jean Nouvel; with Emmanuel Combarel, Brigitte Pacaud, Eric Pouget. Client: Jean-Marie Amat, SCI "Les Jardins de Haute-Rive". Structural Consultant: Treffel, L. Fruitet. Consultant: Rauline Saul. Coordination: CEP. Contractor: Tilliet. Landscape Designer: Yves Brunier. Furniture: Jean Nouvel, Eric Pouget. Bathroom Hardware: Sopha Vola. Woodwork: Trad. Bois., Chabosseau. Painters: Mare (stucco). Plasterer: Musset – Eutrope.

3.1 ECRU, Marina del Rey, Los Angeles, California, USA.
Architects: Building. Designers: Michele Saee; with Richard Lundquist, San Solhaug. Design Team: Max Massie, David Lindberg, Florence Blecher. Client: Ecru. Main Contractor: John Rotondi/Rotondi Construction (Supervisor – Vince Naso). Mechanical Systems: Ward's Heating & Air Conditioning. Engineering Consultants: Andrew Nasser, Miquel Castillo. Furniture, fittings and custom light fixtures: Building. Lighting Consultant: Saul Goldin. Fabricators: Jeffers Machine Shop, Danny's Ornamental Iron Shop, Heritage Painting, Animal Fronts (glass).

3.2 ESPRIT, Paris, France.
Architects: Studio Citterio/Dwan. Project Team: Antonio Citterio, Terry Dwan; with Patricia Viel. Collaborating Architect: Agence Camus – Sandjan. Client: Esprit, S.A.R.L., France. Construction: Ometto Arredamenti Padova SrL, Florio SA. Lighting: Studio Citterio/Dwan (design), Ometto Arredamenti (fabrication). Other Lighting: Coemar SPA (spotlight). Furniture: Ometto Arredamenti.

3.3 MICHIKO KOSHINO, London, UK.
Designers: Fern Green Partnership (Partners in charge: David Fern, Nigel Green). Client: Michiko Koshino. Main Contractor: Design and Fittings Ltd. Lighting: B & T Associates. Neoprene covers for changing booths: Gul Wetsuits Ltd. Carpet: Decorin (UK) Ltd. Flooring: Crest Flooring Ltd (terrazzo). Furniture: Big Fish (upholstered stools), Design and Fittings (cash desk).

3.4 NICOLE FARHI SHOWROOM, London, UK.
Designers: Din Associates. Project Team: Rasshied Din, John Harvey (Directors), Lesley Batchelor (Senior designer), Kirstie Moon. Client: Nicole Farhi/French Connection Group plc. Main Contractor: Newhart Construction Ltd. Structural Engineers: Neil Thomas. Mechanical Engineer: Synergy. Quantity Surveyor: Christopher Smith Associates. Electrical Consultant: CMS Electrical. Heating & Ventilation Contractor: Glencool. Shopfitters: Charles Barrett. Lighting: Erco (T & M spotlight range), A. E. G. (industrial high bay light fittings). Double Glazing: Pilkington H. P. Insulight. Furniture Design: Din Associates (except for Havanna chairs, manufactured by Hitch & Co. for the Conran Shop, table in men's showroom: Matthew Hilton).

3.5 JASPER CONRAN, London, UK.
Designers: Peter Leonard Associates. Project Team: Peter Leonard, Gillian McLean, Simon Stacey. Client: Jasper Conran. Main Contractor: Quickwood. Furniture & Fittings: Peter Leonard. Lighting: Shiu-Kay Kan. Flooring: Hermitage Woodcraft. Electrical: LF Electrical.

3.6 JOSEPH, London, UK.
Architects: Eva Jiricna Architects. Project Team: Eva Jiricna, Jon Tollit (Project architect), Duncan Webster, Huw Turner. Consultant Engineers: Matthew Wells, Dewhurst MacFarlane & Partners. Client: Joseph Ltd. Main Contractor, Shopfitters: Quickwood Ltd. Lighting Consultant: Isometrix. Furniture & Fittings: Eva Jiricna Architects, Philippe Starck (café chairs and stools, from Ikon), Lacquerworks (oval tables), Durcon Fabrications Intl. Ltd. (bar tops). Staircase: Springboard Design, Wessex Guild. Electrical: Artel Electrical. Shopfitters/ Joinery: Quickwood Ltd. Oval Tables: Lacquerworks. Glass Doors: Design Workshop. Glass Shelves & Tables: Preedy Glass. Glass Cabinets: Click Systems. Flooring: Stoneage (supply), W. H. Frayleys Ltd (installation). Mirrors: Marcus Summers. Carpets: Waldorf Carpets. Stock Shelving: Quodeck. Plaster Work: Stratton Plastering. Shopfront: Acton Aluminium. Display Metalwork: Boswell Engineering. Bar Equipment: Hansens Kitchen.

3.7 BOUTIQUE EMANUEL UNGARO, Paris, France.
Architect: Christian de Portzamparc. Project Team: Christian de Portzamparc, Bruno Barbot, John Coyle, Marie-Elisabeth Nicoleau. Client: Emanuel Ungaro. Main Contractor: Bouygues. Painted Panelling: Danièle Fauvel. Stucco: Les 3 Matons. Plasterwork: Cabuy. Floor: Atecma (marble). Carpets: Tracé Intérieur. Furniture Design: Christian de Portzamparc (La Ligne). Furniture & Joinery: Legrand Fourniture. Carpentry: Millier. Metalwork: Boga (conque), LCSD (fittings). Resin Statues: Aligon. Lighting: Christian de Portzamparc (Le Soleil), Fey, Kobis – Lorenze.

3.8 ELEMENTER SHOWROOM, London, UK.
Architects: Armstrong Associates. Project Team: Kenneth Armstrong, Jenifer Smith (Principals), James McCosh. Client: Elementer Industrial Design Ltd. Main Contractor: David Humphreys. General Contracting Work: Stockbridge Services. Glazing: Solaglas. Steelwork: Fabricon Steelwork Ltd. Joinery/Cabinet Work: Woodcote Joinery Ltd. Electrics: Ray Lewington. D-line Ironmongery, toni taps: Elementer Industrial Design Ltd. Lighting: Elemsystems, Erco. Furniture: Dantrac. Kitchen: Baubilt. Stainless Steel Balustrades: Carl F. Petersen, Harrington Fabrication Ltd.

3.9 YOSHIKI HISHINUMA, Tokyo, Japan.
Designer: Shiro Kuramata, Kuramata Design Office; with Hisae Igarashi. Client: Yoshiki Hishinuma. Main Contractor: Ishimaru Co. Ltd.

3.10 LEON MAX, Los Angeles, California, USA.
Architects: Morphosis. Project Architects: Thom Mayne, Michael Rotondi (Principals in charge), Kiyakazu Arai, Will Sharp (Project architects). Project Team: Stephanie Adolf, Craig Burdick, Andrea Claire, Christopher Oakley. Client: Leon Max. Main Contractor: Al Russell. Furniture: Morphosis. Metal Fabrication: Metalmorphosis, B. & L. Fabricators. Aluminium Casting: Do-All Foundry. Structural Engineers: Gordon Polon Co. Electrical Engineers: Saul Goldin & Associates. Electrical: Marv Nixon.

3.11 DOMAIN AT BURLINGTON MALL, Burlington, Massachusetts, USA.
Architects: Schwartz/Silver Architects, Inc. Project Team: Nancy E. Hackett, Albert Ho, Mark Herman. Client: Domain Inc. Main Contractor/Casework: Herbert and Boghosian. Signage: Deirdre Tanton. Flooring: De Paoli Mosaic Co. (terrazzo). Paint Finishes: ARJ Associates. Lighting: Halo Lighting. Translucent Panels: Kalwall Corporation.

3.12 POLITIX, Cleveland, Ohio, & Portland, Oregon, USA.
Architects: Morphosis. Project Team: Thom Mayne & Michael Rotondi (Principals in charge), Kim Groves (Project architect, Cleveland), Scott Romses (Project architect, Portland); with Craig Burdick, Mauricio Gomez, Lauren Maccoll, James Meraz, Victor Hugo Salazar. Client: Moba Inc. Main Contractors: Fred Olivieri Construction (Cleveland), R & H Construction (Portland). Mechanical Engineer: I & N Consulting Engineers. Structural Engineer: Joseph Perazzelli. Metal Fabricator: Tom Farrage. Furniture & Woodwork: Morphosis/X-Tech. Lighting/Electrical: Saul Goldin. Steel and Aluminium Mannequins: Tom Farrage. Furniture: X-Tech.

3.13 ISSEY MIYAKE WOMEN, London, UK.
Architects: Stanton Williams. Project Team: Alan Stanton, Paul Williams, Robert Letts, Alan Farlie, Kulbir Chadha, Michael Langley. Client: Issey Miyake UK Ltd. Main Contractor/Joinery: Howard & Constable Contracts. Quantity Surveyor: Stockdale. Structural Engineer: Nickalls & Roche. Mechanical & Electrical: NE Inglis and Partners. Floors: Stone Age Ltd. (Pietra laro stone), Matthews Stone Ltd (granolithic floor). Lighting: Ace McCarron. Installations: Sally Greaves-Lord. Joinery: Howard & Constable Partnership. Metalwork: Coules Architectural Metalwork, Aeroment Ltd. Glazing: Solaglas Ltd, Colorminium. Blinds: Technical Blinds. Electrical: Geneva Electrics Ltd. Display Wall Structure: Unistrut Ltd. Furniture: Jeffrey James (tables), John Harwood. Specialist Paint Finishes: Peter Davis.

3.14 TECHNAL, Toulouse, France.
Architects: Jean-Michel Wilmotte, Governor Sarl. Project Team: Jean-Michel Wilmotte (Interior architect), Massimo Quendolo (Assistant architect). Client & Main Contractor: Technal, France. Masonry Consultant: Tecer. Electrical Consultant: Ege. Glasswork: Delord. Industrial Aluminium: Technal. Aluminium Fabrication/Installation: Entreprise Toulousaine de Tolerie. Lighting: Jumo Concord – GTE.

3.15 CASSINA, COLLEZIONE, Tokyo, Japan.
Designers: Studio Bellini. Project Team: Mario Bellini (Chief architect); with Giovanna Bonfanti, Marco Parravicini. Building Architect: Tadao Ando. Client: Cassina/Casatec Ltd. Main Contractor: Ohbayashi Co. Ltd (glasswork and concrete). Lighting: Matsushita Electric Works Ltd. Flooring: Board Co. Ltd. Furniture: Cassina, Hakusuisha Co. Ltd. Sculpture/Suspended Painting: Sandro Chia.

4.1 HORST-KORBER SPORTZENTRUM, Berlin, Germany.
Architects: Christoph Langhof Architekten. Project Team: Christoph Langhof, Thomas M. Hänni, Herbert Meerstein. Site Architects: Architektengemeinschaft Fehr & Partner. Client: Landessportbund Berlin E. V. Main Contractors: Hochtief AG, WTB Walter Thosti Boswau AG, Philipp Holzmann AG, Strabag AG. Structural Engineers: Arbeitsgemeinschaft Tragwerksplanung, LLZ. Structural & Environmental Consultant: Ove Arup and Partners. Electrical & Lighting Engineers: Dipl-Ing Joachim Schulz. Lighting: Lichtdesign Ingenieurgesellschaft mbH, Firma Colt International. Landscape Design: Dipl-Ing Hannelore Kossel. Surveyor: Dipl-Ing Gerhard Schiffer. Steelwork: Firma Maurer Söhne, Firma Gefatec mbH. Sports Hall Flooring: Firma Balsam Sportbau. Aluminium Supports: Firma Rheinhold & Mahla. Aluminium & Glass Work: Firma Kilimann. Doors & Gates: Firma Schoenwerk.

4.2 MÓRA D'EBRE HOSPITAL, Tarragona, Spain.
Architects: Jose Antonio Martinez Lapeña & Elias Torres Tur. Project Team: Oscar Canalis, Jordi Heinrich, Karin Hoffer, Inma Josemaria, Moises Martinez Lapeña, Benjamin Pleguezuelos, Marta Pujol, Marcos Viader. Site Managers: Alberto Ferrer Mayol, Josep Gilabert. Client: Generalitat de Catalunya. Main Contractor: Hispano Alemana S. A.

4.3 CALIFORNIA MUSEUM OF PHOTOGRAPHY, Riverside, California, USA.
Architects: Stanley Saitowicz Office. Project Team: Stanley Saitowicz, John Winder (Principal), Ulysses Lim, Daniel Luis, Dwight Long, Patrick Winters. Client: University of California, Riverside. Main Contractor: Magnum Development Companies. Structural Consultants: Vogel & Meyer Partnership. Electrical/ Mechanical Consultants: F. W. Associates. Steel Fabricator: W. C. Brown. Wire Cloth/Perforated Metal: McNichols Co. Lighting: Dan Malman. Skylight: Dur-Red Products. Doors/Frames: Security Metal Products Corporation. Heating & Ventilation: Triangle Mechanical Inc., Carrier Southern California, Perfect Air, Controls, Inc.

4.4 CENTER FOR THE PERFORMING ARTS, CORNELL UNIVERSITY, Ithaca, New York, USA.
Architects: James Stirling, Michael Wilford & Associates. Project Team: James Stirling, Michael Wilford, George Gianakopoulus (Partners in charge), Robert Dye, Steve Bono, Robert Kahn, Walter Naegeli, Ulricke Wilke, Joan Nix, Harry Spring, Leonard Franco, Val Antohi. Main collaborator: Wank, Adams, Slavin Associates. Client: Cornell University. General Contractor: McGuire & Bennett, Inc. (masonry/painting). Theatre Planning & Acoustics: Artec Consultants Inc. Theatre Seating: A. Jan Stalker Assocs. Inc. Theatre Wood Flooring: The Western N. Y. Floor Company. Carpentry & Fitted Furnishings: Roscoe Woodworking Inc. Stonework: Vermont Marble Co. Tiling: Syracuse Mosaic & Terrazzo. Structure: Severud Szegezdy. Plaster Work: Andrew R. Mancini Assocs. Inc. Mechanical & Electrical: Wank, Adams Slavin Associates. Electrical: Matco Electric Co. Inc. Signage: Works Inc. Exterior Lighting: Jerry Kugler Associates. Stage Lighting: Jennifer Tipton.

4.5 CITÉ DE LA MUSIQUE (WEST SIDE), La Villette, Paris, France.
Architects: Atelier d'Architecture Christian de Portzamparc. Project Team: Christian de Portzamparc (Principal architect), Bertrand Beau, François Chochon, Jean-François Limet (Assistant architects). Consultants – Technical & Construction: Sodeteg, Sogelorg. Acoustic: Commains BBM. Theatre: Dubreuil. Contractors & Suppliers (exteriors) – Structure: TPI. Floating Slabs: Robert. Dance School Roof: Brisard Nogues. Waterproofing: Soprema. Stone Cladding: Pradeau Morin. Exterior Wall Tiling: CMP. Rooflights/Glazed Walls etc.: Sotrame. Metalwork: Agedec. Contractors & Suppliers (interiors) – Suspended Ceilings: Ozilou. Floors: Eychamp (finishes), Briatte (parquet, floorboards), Steel (suspended). Interior Tiling: De Ca Mo. Acoustic Panels & Treatments: Stabi. Furniture: Tracé Intérieur, Quinette (auditorium seating).

4.6 FOLIE, PARC DE LA VILLETTE, Paris, France.
Architects: Bernard Tschumi Architects. Project Team: L.

Merlin, J. F. Erhel. Client: Établissement Public, Parc de la Villette. Main Contractor: CITRA.

4.7 MORTON H. MEYERSON SYMPHONY CENTER, Dallas, Texas, USA.
Architects: Pei Cobb Freed & Partners. Project Team: I. M. Pei (Partner in charge), Werner Wandelmaier (Partner, administration), George H. Miller (Partner, project management), Charles Young (Design architect, concert hall), Theodore A. Amberg (Architect in charge, Dallas office), Michael J. Flynn (Architect in charge, curtain wall); with Ralph Heisel, Ian Bader, Michael Vissichelli, Perry Chinn, Abby Suckle (interiors). Design Team: Kirk Conover, Chris Rand, Kyle Johnson, David Martin, Gordon Wallace, Tim Calligan, Walter Van Green. Client: The City of Dallas and the Dallas Symphony Association. Construction Manager: J. W. Bateson Company Inc. Aluminium/Glass/Glazing; Zimcor Co. Electrical: John Keys Associates. Mechanical: Brandt Engineering, Edwards & Zuck. Structural Consultants: Leslie E. Robertson Associates. Acoustics: Artec Consultants, Inc. Elevators: Calvin L. Kort, Inc. Lighting: Jules Fisher & Paul Marantz. Artists: Eduardo Chillida, Ellsworth Kelly. Major Subcontractors – Steel Truss: Austin Steel Co. Inc. Limestone/Masonry: Masonry Technology. Concrete: J. W. Bateson.

4.8 CHURCH OF THE LIGHT, Ibaragi, Osaka, Japan.
Architect: Tadao Ando, Tadao Ando Architect and Associates. Client: The United Church of Japan. Ibaraki Kasugaoka Church. Main Contractor/Lighting & Electrical Work: Tatsumi Construction Co. Ltd.

4.9 GERMAN POSTAL MUSEUM, Frankfurt am Main, Germany.
Architects: Behnisch & Partners. Project Team: Peter Schürmann (Project leader until 7/89), Gotthard Geiselmann (until 8/89), Felix Hessmert (until 10/89), Christian Kandzia (leader 89–90); with Martina Deiss/Eilers, Jochen Hauff, Margit Schosser/Ellensohn, On-site Supervision: Rudolf Lettner, Martin Hühn, Uwe Sachs, Sigrid Schäfer. Client & Project Coordinator: Bundesministerium für Post und Telekommunikation, Ministerialrat Prof. Joh. Möhrle, Oberpostdirektion Frankfurt Postmaster Bert Wichmann, Max-Werner Kahl. Landscape Consultants: Hans Luz & Partners. Structural Consultants: Schlaich, Bergermann & Partners. Lighting: Lichtplanung Bartenbach.

4.10 POLIDEPORTIVO DE GRACIA, Barcelona, Spain.
Architects: Jaume Bach/Gabriel Mora. Project Team: Jaume Bach, Gabriel Mora, Robert Brufau (Structural architect), Gerardo Garcia-Ventosa (Installations), Carlos Oliver. Collaborator: Josep Crivillers. Client: Barcelona Town Hall. Main Contractor: Agroman, S. A. Manager: Carlos Oliver.

4.11 VITRA INTERNATIONAL FURNITURE MANUFACTURING FACILITY AND DESIGN MUSEUM, Weil am Rhein, Germany.
Architects: Frank O. Gehry & Associates, Inc. Project Team: Frank O. Gehry, Robert Hale, Gregory Walsh, Berthold Penkhues, Liza Hansen, Edwin Chan, Christopher Joseph Bonura. Associate Architect: Gunter Pfeifer Associates.

4.12 GOTOH MUSEUM, Chiba Prefecture, Tokyo, Japan.
Architect: David Chipperfield Architects. Project Team: David Chipperfield, Andrew Bryce, Jamie Fobert, Spencer Fung, Michael Greville, Naoko Kawamura, Haruo Morishima. Client: Morio Gotoh. Collaborating Architect: Kamitani Space Planning Office (Yoshihlko Kamitani). Main Contractor: Kasahara Komuten. Lighting: Yamagiwa Corporation. Flooring: Dalken Trade and Industry Corporation Ltd. Display Cabinets: Amano Shoten.

4.13 ART TOWER, MITO, Mito, Ibaragi Prefecture, Japan.
Architects: Arata Isozaki & Associates. Project Team: Arata Isozaki (Prinicipal in charge), Toshihiko Kimura, Jun Aoki. Collaborator: Seiichi Mikami & Associates. Client: City of Mito. Main Contractors: Kajima Corporation, Taisei Corporation. Structural Engineers: Kimura. Lighting: Matsushita Electric Works Ltd. Furniture: Daimaru Inc., Kotobuki Co. Ltd. Flooring: Daimaru Inc. Walls: Takada Co. Ltd, Kunishiro Co. Ltd. Stainless Steel Windows: Tajima Junzo Ltd. Titanium: Sumitomo Metal Industries Ltd, Kikukawa Kogyo Co. Ltd.

4.14 MUSEUM FOR PRE- AND EARLY HISTORY, Frankfurt am Main, Germany.
Architect: Josef Paul Kleihues; with Mirko Baum, Thomas Bartels, Siobhán Ní Eanaigh, Günter Sunderhaus, Joachim Kleine Allekotte, Holger Rübsamen, Hermann Schnittmann, Christoph Wissmann. Client: City of Frankfurt am Main, Department of Culture and Recreation. Structural Engineer: Ing. Büro Rosenboom. Main Contractor: Frankfurter Aufbau AG (FAAG). Mechanical Engineers: Ing. Büro Hortechnic, Ing. Büro Matysik & Partner, Brendel Ingenieure GmbH, Ing. Büro ITA. Stonework: Zeidler & Wimmel (stone façade, new building), Waldemar & Gunther (stone flooring), Uhl Naturstein, Naturstein Jenschke GmbH (stonework restoration). Metalwork: Stahl und Metallbau Gebr Ernsthaus GmbH, Stahl und Metallbau (Lichtenthaler). Steelroof Construction, Nave of Old Church: Stahlbau. Aluminium Windows, New Building: Bietergemeinschaft, Konstruktionsbüro. Showcase Design: Josef Paul Kleihues, Schöninger Vitrinenbau GmbH (manufacture), Firma Suma. Furniture: Wesemann & Striepe (workshop), Kunz Söhne GmbH (office). Museum Didactics: Projektdesign. Lighting Design: Josef Paul Kleihues, Semperlux GmbH (manufacture).

4.15 SHONANDAI CULTURAL CENTER, Fujisawa, Kanagawa Prefecture, Japan.
Architects: Itsuko Hasegawa Architectural Design Studio. Project Designer: Itsuko Hasegawa. Client: Fujisawa City. Main Contractor: Obayashi Co. Ltd. Structural Engineers: Kimura Structural Engineers, Umezawa Structural Engineers. Mechanical Engineers: Inouye Uichi Research Corporation. Acoustics: Yamaha Acoustic Research Laboratories. Furniture, Children's Museum: Itsuko Hasegawa Architectural Design Studio.

4.16 GRAND LOUVRE, Paris, France.
Architects: I. M. Pei & Partners (exterior, interior corridors and public spaces). Associated Architect: Michel Macary. Interior designer of book and print shops, children's bookshop, temporary exhibition spaces, restaurants, furniture & fittings: Jean-Michel Wilmotte. Assistants: Massimo Quendolo, Jean-Luc Guigui, Zabeth Rapp. Lighting Consultant: Claude E. Engle. Project Direction: I. M. Pei (Partner in charge/design), Leonard Jacobson (Partner in charge/management), C. C. Pei (Partner in charge/design & administration), Yann Weymouth (Architect in charge/design). New York Office: Michael Flynn (Associate partner/Pyramid), Yvonne Szeto. Paris Office: Norman Jackson (Director), Arnaud Puvis de Chavannes (Director), Beatrice Lehman (Senior associate), Chris Rand (Associate), Andrzej Gorczynski (Senior associate); with Stephen Rustow, Masakazu Bokura. Head Architects at The Louvre: Georges Duval, Guy Nicot. Client: Établissement Public du Grand Louvre. Major Contractors – Civil Engineering: Dumez Travaux Publics. Pyramid: C. F. E. M. Industries, St Gobain (glass), Navitec (sub/rods/fittings), Nicolet Chartrand (structure/design concept), Rice Francis Ritchie (structure/construction phase site). Structural, Mechanical & Electrical: Sogelerg SA, Serrete SA; Fred Storksen, SEEE (for Dumez), structural engineer (concrete/steel). Architectural Concrete: Jean-Pierre Aury (for Dumez). Foundation perimeter, jet grouting, tieback wall: Quillery. Interior stone supply: Rocamat & Sogepierre, Pierreux de France (installation). Fountains: Entreprise Industrielle, SEPT & Jacques Labyt. Helicoidal Stair: Croiseau, Sitraba. Escalators: Otis. Glass Handrails: Croiseau. Cylindrical Elevator Platform: RCS – Schindler & Gerbauer. Lighting: Erco (majority of interior spaces), Guzzini (bookshop). Furniture: Knoll Ltd. Furniture/Fittings: CGCE, Métala fabrication. Graphics: Carbone Smolan Ass. (preliminary), ADSA (development and execution).

4.17 TRIFORIUM GALLERY, WINCHESTER CATHEDRAL, Winchester, UK.
Architects: Stanton Williams. Project Team: Alan Stanton, Paul Williams, Robert Letts. Client: Winchester Cathedral. Structural Engineer: Ove Arup & Partners. Lighting: Concord Lighting. Electrical: Dicks Electrical Installations Ltd. Object Installation: Plowden & Smith Ltd. Graphics: Crispin Rose-Innes. Joinery: Howard & Constable Partnership. Metalwork: Wessex Guild Ltd. Showcases: Glasbau Hahn GmbH & Co. KG. Cladding: Salisbury Cathedral Stonemasons.

4.18 FINE ARTS CENTER, ARIZONA STATE UNIVERSITY, Tempe, Arizona, USA.
Architect: Antoine Predock. Project Team: Antoine Predock (Principal), Geoffrey Beebe, Jon Anderson, Ronald Jacob, Tim Rohleder, John Fleming, Kevin Spence. Client: Arizona State University. Landscape Design: Antoine Predock. Landscape Consultant: James Abell. Structural Consultant: Robin E. Park Associates. Mechanical Consultant: Baltes/Valentino Associates Ltd. Security Consultant: E. B. Brown. Theatre Systems: John Von Szeliski. Acoustic/Sound Systems: Smith, Fause and Brarath Inc. Lighting: Richard C. Peters. General Contractor: P. C. L. Construction Services.

Suppliers' Addresses

A to Z Glass and Mirror, 5821 Beverley Boulevard, Los Angeles, CA 90022, USA. **Abrams and Tanaka**, 2908 Nebraska, Santa Monica, CA 90404, USA. **Ackermann Ltd.**, Michigan Drive, Tongwell, Milton Keynes MK15 8HQ, UK. **Acton Aluminium**, Unit 8, Graylaw Trading Estate, Whitby Avenue, London NW10, UK. **Afco Services**, 43 Cranley Gardens, Muswell Hill, London N10, UK. **Aislaminetos Jackson**, Gran Via de les Corts Catalanes, No. 658 ler la, 08010 Barcelona, Spain. **Ambiente International Co. Ltd.**, Sumitomo Seimei Bld, 1–30 Minami aoyama 3-chome, Minato-ku, Tokyo, Japan. **American Olean Products**, 5935–13, South Loop East, Houston, TX 77033, USA. **Architectural Woodworking**, PO Box 2045, Rockville, MD 20852, USA. **Argon Arc Welding Services**, 12 Lower Park Road, London N11, UK. **Artec Consultants Inc.**, 245 7th Avenue, 8th Floor, New York, NY 10001, USA. **Artel Electrical**, 114 Windermere Avenue, Wembley, Middlesex HA9 STP, UK. **Artemide GB**, 17–19 Neal Street, London WC2, UK. **Artes**, 620 Elizabeth Street, Melbourne, Victoria, Australia. **Artioli Metal Furnishings**, Via Contrada, 31, Prato di Correggio, Reggio Emilia, Italy. **Aston Cameron Design**, 7424 Beverley Boulevard, Los Angeles, CA 90036, USA. **Avon Tile**, 1151 Taft Street, Rockville, MD 20850, USA. **Takuki Azechi**, 1–17–6 Kamisoshigaya, Setagaya-ku, Tokyo, Japan.

B.L. Fabricators, 1661 West 226th Street, Torrance, CA 90501, USA. **B & T Associates**, 19 Oban Court, Hurricane Way, Wickford Business Park, Wickford, Essex SS11 8YB, UK. **Firma Balsam Sportbau**, Reichsstrasse 108, 1000 Berlin 19, Germany. **Barcy**, T.G.M. Inc., 2–21–8 Tomigaya, Shibuya-ku, Tokyo, Japan. **Baubilt**, Hennock Court, Hennock Road, Marsh Barton Trading Estate, Exeter, UK. **Beverly Beeland**, 401½ Workshops, 401½ Wandsworth Road, London SW8, UK. **Beta Construction**, 9010 Edgeworth Drive, Capitol Heights, MD 20791, USA. **Bietergemeinschaft**, Sassenscheidt-Seesle, Zur Helle 13, 5870 Iserlohn-Letmathe, Germany. **Big Fish**, Unit 16, Acklam Workshops, 10 Acklam Road, London W10, UK. **Board Co. Ltd.**, 5–4–1 Shinjuku, Shinjuku-ku, Tokyo, Japan. **Bode Floor**, 9035 Gerwig Lane, Suite Y, Columbia, MD 21046, USA. **Brent Metals Architectural Work Ltd.**, Alberton Lane, Wembley, Middlesex, UK. **W. C. Brown**, PO Box 2227, 9401 Eti Wanda, Fontant, CA 929335, USA. **Jay Buchbinder**, 2650 El Presidio, Long Beach, CA 90810, USA. **Enterprise Bugna**, 14 rue de Gris Pourceau, 90120 Morvillars, France. **Bulthaup**, 348 Kensington High Street, London W14, UK. **Buro Happold**, Camden Mill, Lower Bristol Road, Bath, Avon, BA2 3DQ.

California Associated Power, 404 West Chevy Chase Drive, Glendale, CA 91204, USA. **Cassina SpA**, PO Box 102, 120036 Meda, Italy. **Cassina Japan Inc.**, 2–9–6 Higashi, Shibuya-ku, Tokyo 150, Japan. **Chairs**, 5–17–1 Roppongi, Axis, Minato-ku, Tokyo, Japan. **Chauvier S.A.**, 12 Faubourg de Montbeliard, 90000 Belfort, France. **Chriss Brothers, Inc.**, PO Box 227, Bladensburg, MD 20710, USA. **Clark Construction Corp.**, 117 Hudson Street, New York, NY 10013, USA. **Clay Paky s.r.1.**, Via G. Pascoli 1, 24066 Pedrengo, Bergamo, Italy. **Click Systems**, 40 Blundells Road, Milton Keynes, UK. **Coemar SpA**, Via Inghilterra, 46042 Castelgoffredo, Mantova, Italy. **CODAC**, 99a Arnold Road, London N15 4JQ, UK. **Firma Colt-International**, Brienerstrasse 211, 4190 Kleve, Germany. **Concord Lighting**, 174 High Holborn, London WC1V 7AA, UK. **The Conran Shop**, Michelin Building, 81 Fulham Road, London SW3, UK. **Construction Rehabilitation Decoration Villeparisienne**, 24 rue des Martyres, 77270 Villeparisi, France. **Crest Flooring Ltd.**, Unit 13, 1/7 Garman Road, London N17, UK. **Dacheville**, 36 Avenue Leon Crete, 78490 Mere, France. **Daiichi Kougei Co. Ltd.**, 8–2–37 Shimoya matedouri Chuoku, Kobe, Japan. **Daiko Electric Co. Ltd.**, 15–16 Nakamichi 3-chome, Higashinari-ku, Osaka, Japan. **Daimaru Inc.**, Daimaru Core Bld, 2–18–11 Kiba, Koto-ku, Tokyo, Japan. **Dantrac**, Progress House, Whittle Parkway, Slough, Berkshire SL1 60G, UK. **Decorin U.K. Ltd.**, 116a Avenue Road, Acton, London N3, UK. **Delord**, Impasse de la Saudrune, 31140 Launaguet, France. **Dennery**, 1 Route Du Grand Pressigny, 37290 Preuilly/Glaise, France. **De Paoli Mosaic Co.**, 129 Magazine Street, Roxbury, MA 02119, USA. **Design Workshop**, 150 Penistone Road, Shelley, Huddersfield, Yorkshire, UK. **De Sul**, 27 rue du Clos, 91–130 Ris Orangis, France. **Dewhurst MacFarlane & Partners (Matthew Wells)**, 31 Corsica Street, London N5 1JT, UK. **Tom Dixon**, 28 All Saints Road, London W11, UK. **Do-All Foundry**, 1450 West 228th Street, No. 35, Torrance, CA 90501, USA. **Antony Donaldson**, 91a Pimlico Road, London SW1, UK. **D.P. Enamellers**, Imperial Works, Perren Street, London NW5, UK. **Driade SpA**, 29012 Fossadello di Caorso, Piacenza, Italy. **Arturo Duque**, Passeig Isabel II, 08003 Barcelona, Spain. **Durcon Fabrications Intl. Ltd.**, Bestworld House, Stirling Road, Slough, Berkshire, UK. **Dur-Red Products**, Cudahy, CA 90201, USA.

Eastern Suburbs Wrought Iron, 1 Clare Street, Bayswater, Victoria, Australia. **EGE**, 10 rue Alexandre Cabanal, 31000 Toulouse, France. **Elementer**, Progress House, Whittle Parkway, Slough, Berkshire, UK. **Elemsystems**, 7 Central Estate, Denmark Street, Maidenhead, Berkshire, UK. **Ellison Bronze Co.**, 125 West Main Street, Falconer, NY 14733, USA. **D. Ellwood**, Charlton Kings Industrial Estate, Cirencester Road, Cheltenham, Gloucestershire GL53 8DZ, UK. **Emser International**, 8431 Santa Monica Boulevard, Los Angeles, CA. **En Attendant les Barbares**, 50 rue Etienne Marcel, 75002 Paris, France. **Erco**, C/Tuset No. 1, 08006 Barcelona, Spain. **Erco Lighting Ltd.**, 38 Dover Street, London W1X 3RG, UK. **Espèce Lumière**, 17 rue des Lombards, 75004 Paris, France. **Jordi Espinosa**, C. Berlin n. 30–32 Local I-H, 08028 Barcelona, Spain.

Fabricon Steelwork Ltd., 9 Richmond Avenue, Benfleet, Essex SS7 5HE, UK. **Tom Farrage**, 1857 Berkeley Street, Santa Monica, CA 90404, USA. **Forms and Services**, 16479 Dallas Parkway STE 290, Dallas, TX 75248, USA. **W.H. Frayleys Ltd.**, Gas Street, Birmingham B1 2JY, UK.

Enterprise Galea Serge, Z.I. Les Planches, B.P. 10, 25870 Geneuille, France. **Glasbau Hahn Gm & Co. KG**, Hanauer Landstrasse 211, 6000 Frankfurt/Main 1, Germany. **Allen Glass**, 620a Gravel Avenue, Alexandria, VA 22310, USA. **Saul Goldin and Associates**, 1818 S. Robertson Boulevard, Los Angeles, CA 90039, USA. **Gouget**, Coulombs, 28210 Nogent-Le-Roi, France. **Great Metropolitan Flooring Co.**, 83 Kinnerton Street, London SW1, UK. **Sally Greaves Lord**, 2nd Floor, 55 Charlotte Road, London EC2 3QT, UK. **Gul Wetsuits Ltd.**, Walker Lines, Bodmin, Cornwall, UK. **i Guzzini Illuminazione U.K. Ltd.**, Unit 310–311, Business Design Centre, 52 Upper Street, London N1, UK.

Halo Lighting, 400 Busse Road, Elk Grove Village, IL 60007, USA. **Harrington Fabrication Ltd.**, Unit A, 51 The Spinney, Hoddesdon Road, St Margarets, Stanstead Abbots, Hertfordshire, UK. **Oriel Harwood**, 149 Camberwell Road, London SE5, UK. **Steven Hefferan**, 1000 12th Street No. 3, Boulder, CO 80302, USA. **Hermitage Woodcraft**, 14 Carylon Road, Atherstone Industrial Estate, Atherstone, Warwickshire CV9 1JE, UK. **High Technology**, Unit 5, Cardigan Trading Estate, Lennox Road, Leeds, Yorkshire, UK. **Hille Ergonom plc**, 365 Euston Road, London NW1 3AR, UK. **Matthew Hilton**, Unit D16, Metropolitan Works, Enfield Road, London N1, UK. **HLC Engineering**, Burnt Mills Industrial Estate, Basildon, Essex, UK. **Hochtief AG**, Bayerischer Platz 1, 1000 Berlin 30, Germany. **Holloway Sheet Metal Works Ltd.**, 30–34 Eden Grove, Holloway, London N7, UK. **Howard & Constable Contracts**, Canalside Studios, 2–4 Orsman Road, London N1, UK. **Hunter Douglas Ltd.**, Walsall Road, Norton Canes, Staffordshire, UK. **Su Huntley and Donna Muir**, 14 Percy Street (top floor), London W1, UK.

T.W. Ide Ltd., Glasshouse Fields, London E1, UK. **Idea GmbH**, Ebert Platz 19, 5000 Köln 1, Germany. **IDEA**, 5–4–44 Minami aoyama, Minato-ku, Tokyo, Japan. **The Ikon Corporation**, The Clove Building, 15 Shad Thames, London SE1, UK. **Inter Living Co. Ltd.**, 18–8 Yoyogi 4-chome, Shibuya-ku, Tokyo, Japan. **Ishimaru Co. Ltd.**, 7–3–24 Roppongi, Minato-ku, Tokyo, Japan. **Isometrix**, 2–4 Frederic Mews, Kinnerton Street, London SW1X 8EQ, UK.

Jonso Furniture Ltd., 2 Tavistock Terrace, London N19 4DB, UK. **Jumo Concord – GTE**, Tour Horizon, 52 Quai de Dion-Bouton, 92800 Puteaux, France. **Tajima Junzo Ltd.**, 2–14–3 Nagata-cho, Chiyoda-ku, Tokyo, Japan.

Kalwall Corporation, 1111 Candia Road, Manchester, NH 03105, USA. **Shiu-Kay Kan**, 34 Lexington Street, London W1, UK. **Donald Kaufmann Color**, 410 West 13th Street, New York, NY 10014, USA. **Kawaragi Chair Inc.**, 17 Oodori, Chuo-ku, Sapporo, Japan. **Kic Corporation**, Kobari Bldg. 5F, Nishi Azabu 41130, Minato-ku, Tokyo, Japan. **Firma Kilimann**, Friedrich-Seele-Strasse, 1b 3300 Braunschweig, Germany. **Kim Associates**, 110 West 34th Street, New York, NY 10001, USA. **Knoll International**, The Knoll Building, 655 Madison Avenue, New York, NY 10021, USA. **Kobis Lorence**, 67 rue de Reuilly, 75012 Paris, France. **Konstruktionsbüro**, Gerrits, Blumenallée 69, 4064 Nettetal 2, Germany.

Lacquerworks, 1 Station Road, Attleborough, Norfolk, NR17 2AS, UK. **Lamina Concepts**, Unit 16 Rosebery Industrial Park, Phase 2, Rosebery Avenue, London N17 9SR, UK. **Landrell Fabric Engineering Ltd., Station Road, Chepstow, Gwent NP6 5PF, UK. Danny Lane**, 19 Hythe Road, Scrubs Lane, London NW 10, UK. **L.C.S.D.**, 32 rue de Verdun, Le Pin, 77181 Courtry, France. **Light Projects Ltd.**, 23 Jacob Street, London SE1, UK. **Josep Llusca**, Larmella 4–6, 08023 Barcelona, Spain. **Lumenglow Ltd.**, 335 Underhill Road, London SE22, UK.

M & M Lighting, 5620 S. Rice Avenue, Houston, TX 77081, USA. **MGS Lighting Design**, No. 2 Tanisawa Building, 3–2–11 Nishi Azabu, Minato-ku, Tokyo, Japan. **Magnan Payne**, 208 West 85th Street, New York, NY 10024, USA. **Maison Ltd.**, 917–919 Fulham Road, London SW10, UK. **Makoto Construction Co. Ltd.**, 2–17–8 Kita Horie, Nishi-ku, Osaka, Japan. **Kate Malone**, 157 Balls Pond Road, London N14, UK. **Marble Technics**, 150 East 58th Street, New York, NY 10017, USA. **Marcatré**, 179–199 Shaftesbury Avenue, London WC2 8AR, UK. **Marghieri**, 10 Impasse Druinot, 75011 Paris, France. **Charles Marshall Pty Ltd.**, (Creative Metal Products), 451 Burnley Street, Richmond, Victoria, Australia. **Matsushita Electric Works Ltd.**, 2–1–3 Swhiromi Chuo-ku, Osaka, Japan. **Matthews**, 15–17 Hampstead Road, London NW1 3HY, UK. **Matthew Stone Ltd.**, 78 The Avenue, London NW6 7N5, UK. **Firma Maurer Söhne**, Frankfurter Ring 193, 8000 München 44, Germany. **Ingo Maurer GmbH**, Kaiserstrasse 47, 8000 München 40, Germany. **Maville**, 2.I. Le Ponteix, 87220 Feytiat, Limoges, France. **Ronald D. Mayhew, Inc.**, 10217 Piper Lane, Unit D, Bristow, VA 22013, USA. **McNichols Co.**, 4600 District Boulevard, Vernon, CA 90058, USA. **Mellowes PPG**, 14–18 High Street, Stratford, London E15, UK. **Metal-Est**, 8 rue de Buc, 70400 Chalonvillar, France. **Metal Forms Inc.**, 35 Walker Street, New York, NY 10013, USA. **Metalmorphosis**, 342 Sunset Avenue, Venice, CA 90291, USA. **Millar & Long**, 4824 Rugby Avenue, Bethesda, MD 20814, USA. **Mineluba Inc.**, 1–10–7 Hiratsuka, Shinagawa-ku, Tokyo, Japan. **Minerva Co. Ltd.**, 1–10–7 Hirasuka, Shinagawa-ku, Tokyo, Japan. **Miroiterie Bret**, 32 rue Gay Lussac, 71 94430 Chenevièvre-Sur-Maine, France. **Kei Miyazaki**, Plants Design Office, 1–23–3 Higashi-cho, Kichijoji, Musashino-shi, Tokyo, Japan. **Molteni Co. SpA**, Via Rossini 50, 20054 Giussano, Milan, Italy. **Montague Betts**, PO Box 11929, Lynchburg, VA 24506, USA. **Simon Moore**, Glassworks, 12 Victoria Terrace, London N4, UK. **Jasper Morrison**, 275 Kensal Road, London W10, UK. **Donna Muir and Su Huntley**, 14 Percy Street (top floor), London W1, UK.

Edificacions Natura, C/Tres Creus No. 219, 08202 Sabadell, Spain. **Naturstein**, Jenschke GmbH, Ausstrasse 98, 6057 Dietzenbach, Germany. **Yoshiro Negishi**, 489–1 Osachiku, Okaya-shi, Nag-no, Japan. **T. Nevill & Co.**, 2 Gourley Place, London N15, UK. **Nor-Ray-Vac**, Phoenix Burners Ltd., 8 Prince George's Road, London SW19, UK.

Ohbayashi Gumi K.K., Tsukasa-cho 2–3, Kanda, Chiyo, Tokyo 101, Japan. **Ometto Arredamenti SRL**, Via del Lavoro, 36040 Grisgnano di Zocco, Vicenza, Italy. **Steven Ormenyi and Associates**, 2014 Sepulveda Boulevard, Los Angeles, CA 90035, USA. **Orthofono s.n.c.**, (Sergio Caprara and Martino Rubeis), Via Michelino 95, 40127 Bologna, Italy.

Pallucco Italia s.a.s, Via Azzi 64, 31040 Castagnole di Paese, (TV) Italy. **Parquets Briatte**, Z. A. Villemer, RN 17 BP 20, 95500 Lethillay, France. **Patina Metals**, 9303 Clay Road, Houston, TX 77080, USA. **Pearl Dot**, 2 Roman Way, London N7, UK. **Peret Associados**, C/Guifre No. 11, 08001 Barcelona, Spain. **Richard C. Peters**, 1730 Franklin, No. 300, Oakland, CA 94612, USA. **Carl F. Peterson**, GL Koegevej 65, DK–2500, Valby, Denmark.

Phoenix Display Ltd., 453 London Road, North Cheam, Surrey SM3 8JP, UK. Pilkington Glass Ltd., Prescot Road, St. Helens, Merseyside, UK. Preedy Glass, Lamb Works, North Road, London N7, UK. Projektdesign, Taunusstrasse 19, 6000 Frankfurt 1, Germany. Prudential Lighting, 1774 East 21st Street, Los Angeles, CA 90058, USA.

Quickwood Ltd., Unit 10 McKay Trading Estate, Kensal Road, London W10, UK. Quodeck, 10 Richfield Avenue, Reading, Berkshire, UK.

RCF, Via G Notari 1/A, S. Maurizio, Reggio Emilia, Italy. RHS Interiors, Unit 8, The Fort Industrial Park, Chester Road, Castle Bromwich, West Midlands, UK. Enterprise Raichon, Z. 1. D'Argiesans, B.P. 15, 90800 Bavilliers, France. Regal Glass, Inc., PO Box 37, Chantilly, VA 22021, USA. Richfield Group, 14512b Lee Road, Chantilly, VA 22021 USA. Roman Mosaic & Tile, RD No. 3 Mountain Road, Manheim, PA 17545, USA.

Sakura Manufacturing Co., Ohmachi Nebutamachi, Kidagun, Kagawa, Japan. E.C. Sames & Co. Ltd., 417 New Cross Road, London SE14, UK. Schneider, Kunst & Bauschlosserel, Dülmenerstrasse 28, Germany. Schöninger, Vitrinenbau GmbH, Zamilastrasse 23, 8000 München 80, Germany. SCP Ltd, 135–9 Curtain Road, London EC2, UK. Koyano Sekizai Co. Ltd., 1–17 Sengawa-cho, Toshima-ku, Tokyo. Semperlux GmbH, Motzener Strasse 34, D–1000 Berlin 48, Germany. Sheetfabs, Nottingham Road, Attemborough, Beeston NG9 6DR, UK. Solaglas, 110 Great Suffolk Street, London SE1, UK. Soutumier, 23 rue de la Dhuis, 75020 Paris, France. Spring Design, Ninetree Studios, 5 Ninetree Hill, Bristol 1, UK. Karen Spurgin and James Hunting, 59 Lewisham Hill, London SE13, UK. Stahl und Metallbau, Gebr Ernsthaus GmbH, Kruppstrasse 116, 6000 Frankfurt 60, Germany. Stahl und Metallbau, Lichtenthaler, Wilhelm-Heinrich-Strasse 7, 6390 Usingen-Wilhelmsdorf, Germany. Stahlbau, Herdt, Messenhauser Strasse 42, 6074 Rodermark-Urberach, Germany. A. Jan Stalker Assocs. Inc., 1216 Maple Road, Williamsville, NY 14221, USA. Steelcase Inc., Grand Rapids, MI 49501, USA. Stockbridge Services, 45 Pilgrims Way West, Otford, Kent, UK. Stone Age, 67

Dendy Street, London SW12, UK. Stonehill Restorations Pty. Ltd., 9–11 Bromley Road, Emu Plains, N.S.W. 2750, Australia. La Storemania, 18 route de Monbeliard, 90400 Danjoutin, France. Stratton Tiles, Carpet Services Inc., 2303 Minimax, Houston, TX 77008, USA. Stud Co. Ltd., 8–14 Fujimicho 2-chome, Chiyoda-ku, Tokyo, Japan. Firma Suma, Martin-Zeller-Strasse 22, 8961 Sulzberg, Germany. Sumitomo Metal Industries Ltd., 1–1–3 Ohtemachi, Chiyoda-ku, Tokyo, Japan. Marcus Summers, Unit 2, Admiral Hyson Industrial Estate, Hyson Road, London SE16, UK. Sun Control Systems and Lavolor Lorentzen JV, 17 Darby Court, Bethesda, MD 20817, USA. John Von Szeliski, Performing Arts Facilities, Design and Planning (consultants), PO Box 11060, Costa Mesa, CA 92627, USA.

Keiichi Tahara, 4F 7–5–2 Minami Aoyama, Minato-ku, Tokyo, Japan. Taiko Electric Inc., 3–15–16 Nakamichi, Higashinari-ku, Osaka, Japan. Tai Ping, 30 rue des Saints-Pères, 75007 Paris, France. Takada Co. Ltd., 255 Asahi-cho, Tomobe-machi, Ibaragi-gun, Ibaragi, Japan. Tamaru Plant Co. Ltd., 1–4–4 Awaza, Nishi-ku, Osaka-shi, Osaka, Japan. Tanaka Futoshi Komuten, Ichijyo-cho, Taisho-gun, Kita-ku, Kyoto, Japan. Tarkett Wood Floor, PO Box 173, Blackthorne Road, Canbrook, Slough, Berkshire SL3 0AZ, UK. Tatsumi Construction Co. Ltd., 3–32 Uehonmachi 9-chome, Tennoji-ku, Osaka, Japan. Tecer, 10 rue Labat, Savignac, 31500 Toulouse, France. Technal, 3 rue des Arts, Toulouse, France. Technical Blinds, Old Town Lane, Woodburn Town, High Wycombe, Buckinghamshire, UK. Tekima, Atelier Für Teppichkunst, Herr Marks, Postfach 11 05 02, 5650 Solingen, Germany. Tendo Co., 2–13–28 Minamihorie Nishiku, Osaka, Japan. Thonet, Stendig International Inc., 410 East 62nd Street, New York, NY 10021, USA. Entreprise Toulousaine de Tolerie, 34bis rue Benjamin Constant, 31000 Toulouse, France. Trouvelot, 13 rue Carnot, 75012 Paris, France. Tsukasa Shoten & Toji Technical, Watase-cho 1, Shimotoba, Fushimi-ku, Kyoto, Japan. Tubeworkers Ltd., Kington Works, Craverdon, Warwick, UK.

Uhl Naturstein, Harheimer Weg 82, 6000 Frankfurt-Bonames, Germany. Unifor, Via Isonzo 1, 22078 Turate (Como), Italy. Ushio Spax Co. Ltd., Chisei Bld, 1–4–2 Motoakasaka 1-chome, Minato-ku, Tokyo 107, Japan.

Vermont Marble Co., 61 Main Street, Proctor, Vermont 05765, USA. Villesa, Avda. Tarradelles No. 55, 25001 Lleida, Spain. Virginia Food Equipment, 101 Timber Ridge Drive, Ashland, VA 23005, USA. Vitra International AG, 15 Henric Petristrasse, 4010 Basel, Switzerland. Vitra Ltd., 13 Grosvenor Street, London W1, UK. Vorwerk, Vorwerk House, Toutley Road, Wokingham, Berkshire RG11 5QN, UK.

WBH, Inc., 3016 Avenue East, Arlington, TX 76011, USA. Waldemar and Günther, Orberstrasse 9, 6000 Frankfurt 61, Germany. Waldorf Carpets, 278–280 Brompton Road, London SW3, UK. Harwood Weisenfeld, 1239 Broadway, New York, NY 10001, USA. Weland, Hardley Industrial Estate, Hythe, Southampton SO4 6NQ, UK. Zaza Wentworth-Stanley, 45 St Quintin Avenue, London W10, UK. Wesemann & Striepe, Max-Planck-Strasse 15/17, 2808 Syke, Germany. Wessex Guild, Unit 16, Stratton Road, Marshgate, Swindon, UK. The Western N.Y. Floor Company, 146 Halstead Street, PO Box 10247, Rochester, NY 14610, USA. Woodcote Joinery Ltd., Unit 44, Youngs Industrial Estate, Paices Hill, Aldermaston, Berkshire, UK. Wotan Lamps, Wotan House, 1 Gesham Way, Durnsford Road, London SW19, UK.

Xerkon Ltd., Ramsbottom, Bury, Lancashire, UK. X-Tech, 1718 22nd Street, Santa Monica, CA 90404, USA. XO, 3 Avenue Charles de Gaulle, 94470 Boissy-St-Leger, France.

Kijuro Yahagi, 1–37–1–202 Honmachi, Shibuya-ku, Tokyo, Japan. Yamada Shomei Lighting Co. Ltd., 3–16–12 Sotokanda, Chiyoda-ku, Tokyo, Japan. Yamagiwa Co. Ltd., 4–1–1 Sotokanda, Chiyoda-ku, Tokyo 101, Japan. Yamaha Acoustic Research Laboratories, 10–1 Nakazawa-cho, Hamamatsu, Shizuoka-ken 430, Japan.

S.A. Zanelec, Z.I. de la Justice, 90000 Belfort, France. Zanetti & Bailey, 110 Ashley Down Road, Bristol, UK.